Quotes and Endorsements

"Good Fat Bad Fat is the book I'd recommend to everyone who wants an easy way, based on simple principles, to set limits on bad fat and how to choose good-tasting foods to stay within that limit."

Stephen R. Covey
Author of *The Seven Habits of Highly Effective People* and *Principle Centered Leadership*

"Good Fat, Bad Fat is the best book there is to explain a simple diet plan to prevent coronary disease and its progression. I recommend it highly to my patients."

Carl J. Lavie, MD
Co-Director Cardiac Rehabilitation & Prevention
Ochsner Clinic

"This book makes it easy for our family to eat very well with very little fat."

Mollie and John Shaffer
Bountiful, Utah

"If I had this book years ago, I probably wouldn't have had the heart attack that almost killed me—and the bypass surgery that followed. Now we live by this book. *Good Fat Bad Fat* is helping me to keep this from happening again."

Henry W. Abts III
Author of the bestselling book *The Living Trust*

"The most comprehensive, yet understandable discussion of the topic I've seen. I recommend it to all my patients with cholesterol or heart disease problems."

Edward A. Smith, MD
Mesa, Arizona

"… a superb guide to lowering your blood cholesterol through diet, exercise and medication."

USA Today

GOOD FAT BAD FAT

How to lower your cholesterol & beat the odds of a heart attack

Glen C. Griffin, MD

Editor-in-Chief, Postgraduate Medicine and The Health Letter
Editorial Director, McGraw-Hill Healthcare Publications

William P. Castelli, MD

Medical Director, Framingham Heart Study

FISHER
BOOKS

Publishers   *Bill Fisher*
and   *Helen Fisher*
Editors: *Howard Fisher*
     J. McCrary

Associate
Editor: *Joyce Bush*
Art Director: *Josh Young*

Published by
Fisher Books
4239 W. Ina Road
Tucson, Arizona 85741
(602) 744-6110

Library of Congress Cataloging-in-Publication Data

Griffin, Glen C.
  Good fat, bad fat.

Includes index.
  1. Coronary heart disease—
Prevention—Popular works.
2. Low-fat diet—Recipes. 3. Low--
cholesterol diet— Recipes. I. Castelli,
William P. II. Title.
RC685.C6G75 1988 616.1'2305 88-24593
ISBN 1-55561-013-7

Printed in U.S.A.
Printing 20 19

Notice: The information in this book is true and complete to the best of our knowledge. This book is intended only as an informative guide for those wishing to know more about reducing the odds of a heart attack or stroke. In no way is this book intended to replace, countermand or conflict with the advice given to you by your own physician. The ultimate decision concerning diet or medications should be made between you and your doctor. We strongly recommend you follow his/her advice. Information in this book is general and is offered with no guarantees on the part of the authors or Fisher Books. The authors and publisher disclaim all liability in connection with use of this book.

Contents

About the authors

On his first day in medical school, Dr. Glen C. Griffin set a goal: take the gobbledygook out of medical writing.

Twenty-nine years later he became Editorial Director of McGraw-Hill Healthcare Publications. In the interim, his career has encompassed patient care, writing a syndicated newspaper column and several books, being a clinical professor and creating a drive-up-to-your-own-room medical office (front-page featured by the *Wall Street Journal*).

Griffin was almost killed by bad fat that plugged his coronary arteries before he knew he had a problem. The happy ending is a simple system of cutting down on bad fat that he and Dr. Castelli created to take the place of the usual complicated instructions about fat and cholesterol.

Crusader may be the best word to describe Dr. William P. Castelli. He constantly travels across the United States and internationally to educate his medical colleagues and the public about the dangers of saturated fat and cholesterol as related to heart attacks and strokes.

In 1979 he was appointed Medical Director of the Framingham Heart Study at The National Heart, Lung and Blood Institute. This is one of the National Institutes of Health.

In 1987 The U. S. Public Health Service awarded him a Meritorious Service Medal for his efforts. He is a commissioned officer in the Public Health Service Corps.

Castelli is also a lecturer at the Harvard Medical School and at the University of Massachusetts Medical School. He is an Adjunct Associate Professor of Medicine at Boston University.

I Would Have Been D.O.A.

Bad fat nearly killed me!

As we were finishing this book, I beat the odds of having a heart attack—but just barely! A few years ago, when I found out about my own problem with bad fat, I wanted to know how to enjoy eating without fat plaques forming in my coronary arteries. But the more I found out, the more mind-boggling things became. It seemed I would need a full-time personal mathematician and a gourmet dietician. It became obvious that I needed better answers and a simpler system than was available.

After documenting everything I ate for months, I was able to bring down my sky-high triglycerides which I monitored every day along with checking my cholesterol levels frequently. Then Bill Castelli and I got our heads together, and in the months that followed we came up with a simple way to limit saturated fat while eating enjoyably—and almost finished the book.

The problem was that all this didn't happen soon enough. Unknown to anyone, major obstructions had already formed in two of my coronary arteries. I was a massive heart attack waiting to happen!

The only clue was that after running a couple of minutes, my chest started feeling a little tight. I kept thinking I was just "out of shape." I should have known the tightness was really angina. But I put the problem out of mind by walking instead of running. Fortunately, my doctor wouldn't let me get away with this. He suggested

I should go through a typical day wired up to a Holter monitor. The report was bad news. The EKG tracing showed a marked depression of the ST segment every time I did a little running—proving part of my heart muscle wasn't getting enough oxygen-bearing arterial blood.

The next morning in the heart-catheterization lab, I felt the hot flush of dye rushing into my left anterior descending coronary artery. Looking up at the video monitor, I could see this vital coronary artery was almost completely blocked. My cardiologist confirmed a 98% obstruction, saying: "Even if the paramedics had been a block away when this shut off, they would've brought you in D.O.A."

Because there was also blockage in the right coronary, I was soon on my way to the operating room for open-heart coronary-bypass surgery. I was scared—especially as I vividly recalled watching bypass surgery being performed on each of my parents. I may be one of the few people in the world who has seen both parents' hearts stopped and started in the operating room.

My own eyes had seen the fat plaques blocking my parents' coronary arteries. I decided then that I didn't ever want to go through this myself. So I started eating more fish and less meat, thinking I was on a good program to prevent a heart attack. I wasn't! I was still eating lots of ice cream and cheese. And I loved to eat charcoal-broiled hamburgers, all loaded with bad fat.

Looking back, I wish I had stopped eating so much saturated fat long before my coronary arteries had become so plugged.

But I didn't know.

And neither did lots of my medical colleagues. As recently as 1983, a survey of physicians showed that only 28% knew that a high-fat diet has a large effect on coronary-artery disease! As late as 1986, only 40% of physicians knew this basic fact. Of course many more know about the dangers of saturated fat now and the awareness level has continued to increase among doctors and others following the Surgeon General's headline-producing report telling of the dangers of saturated fat. But unfortunately the awareness level hasn't increased fast enough.

You would certainly think patients admitted in 1988 to a major medical center because of plugged coronary arteries would be fed low-saturated-fat, low-cholesterol meals. I thought this basic principle would be strictly followed—until I was the patient and saw a big fat pork chop sitting on my hospital tray. I couldn't believe my eyes. Of course I didn't eat it, but I worried about others who didn't know better. Folks in a coronary-care unit served food like this may go home thinking this is the way to eat.

When I recounted my experience to Bill Castelli, he told me about one of his feisty patients who was served bacon and eggs for breakfast in the coronary-care unit of another leading medical center. This little grandmother had just had an angioplasty to open up her coronary arteries. She refused her breakfast because it was loaded with saturated fat and cholesterol. The nurse scolded her for not eating and sent for a resident doctor to encourage her to eat so she could "gain her strength." But this perky patient knew what was going on better than the staff. When the doctor arrived, she announced firmly, "I'm not going to eat this stuff. It will kill me. I just got my coronary arteries cleaned out and I'm not going to plug them up again!"

Hooray for this feisty grandmother!

I hope you will have as much spunk.

I made it through open-heart surgery with an unusually rapid recovery, thanks to prayers and excellent surgeons. There isn't any question about it, my life was saved. Besides getting a new chance to live, perhaps my going through all this will help you avoid heart surgery—or worse! If you learn to set safe limits of bad fat every day, there is a good chance you won't ever have to be a patient in a coronary ICU or have angioplasty or bypass surgery.

You can be sure I'm going to keep doing everything possible to beat the odds of having a heart attack—which for me means a good exercise program, taking aspirin and eating very little saturated fat and cholesterol. I don't want to have my rib cage sawed apart again.

Be smart.

Make good choices so the odds will be in your favor. Eat right and get the right amount of exercise. But, before starting on an intense exercise program, especially if you ever have had any chest tightness or discomfort, get a check-up. Depending on your age, this may include a stress test or Holter monitoring so you won't push your heart beyond the blood supply it has.

Please don't put this book down until you really know how to beat the odds of a heart attack. Then, together with your family, enjoy some great adventures in eating *without* all the bad fat so many people stuff into their bodies.

I also hope you will recommend *Good Fat, Bad Fat* to everyone you can influence . . . and help *them* beat the odds of a heart attack, too.

Glen C. Griffin, M.D.

1

Some People Just Don't Get Heart Attacks

The odds are 50-50 you are going to die of a heart attack or stroke.

Think about yourself having dinner with your best friend: one of you will likely die sometime because of fat plugs blocking a coronary artery, causing a heart attack.

These are lousy odds.

Plaques of bad fat probably have already started to form inside your coronary arteries. This isn't a pleasant thought. Another unpleasant thought is that three-fourths of the people in North America have fat streaks in their coronary arteries right now—and the problem gets worse every day.

The problem is serious.

But some people *don't* have fat plaques building up in their coronary arteries. Some people *don't* get heart attacks. In fact, people in most parts of the world do not get coronary-artery disease.

You can change the odds

You can be among those who don't—even living in a culture where much of the population will suffer and spend time in coronary-care units because of fat-plugged coronary arteries.

You can change these poor odds.

You have a choice

You have a choice every day—whether to let the fat plugging get worse, stay the same or do something that has a good chance to make it regress.

Your spaghetti-size coronary arteries carry blood to the walls of your heart—the muscle.

If fat plaques plug these vital passageways and blood can't get through, oxygen doesn't reach your heart. That causes a *myocardial infarction*—heart attack.

A major heart attack is gruesome.

It hurts!

And there is a significant risk of dying, especially before a heart-attack victim can reach a modern coronary-care unit.

Every morning you will want to wake up and ask yourself, "What can I do today to keep more fat from plugging up my coronary arteries?"

If you want to have clean and open coronary arteries, you can. You can make this decision and greatly decrease the risk of having a heart attack—especially if you don't smoke.

How?

It's simple—but not easy.

If you want to change the odds, the answer is to start living more like the people who almost never get heart attacks.

What people?

Among 20 industrialized nations, the Japanese have the fewest heart attacks. Other cultures with historically little heart disease from fat-plugged coronary arteries include other Asians, Eskimos, Africans, Mediterraneans and South Americans.

People from these cultures basically don't have heart attacks—at least very few of them do. And the ones who do, for the most part, live and eat like we do. Of course we are not suggesting that you move to Eskimo country, Asia or South America. But it might make sense to take a look at the varying lifestyles of these folks who don't get their coronary arteries plugged up with fat plaques called *atherosclerosis*.

Plaques disappeared

For a few moments let's go back to 1952 and listen in on an interesting conversation in a pathologist's laboratory in Belgium. Dr. Picard, the Professor of Pathology, was talking about a startling observation he had made.

"They are coming back!" Dr. Picard announces as he examines the inside of a dead man's coronary arteries.

"What's coming back?" asks a young medical student.*

"The fat plaques . . . just look at the atherosclerosis plugging up this 52-year-old man's coronary arteries. This is why he died of a heart attack. We have not been seeing coronary-artery *plaques* for a long time. They disappeared by 1942 and they have been gone for about 10 years. But now they are starting to come back. We saw them before the war in three-quarters of the people we autopsied. They were almost always there in the older people. Then they started to go away and not many seemed to die of heart attacks. The people lived longer and when they died, for whatever reason, their arteries were open and clear."

Dr. Picard and other pathologists continued to find coronary arteries lined with plaque buildups. Some coronary arteries were plugged all the way, blocking precious blood to the cells of the heart. These people died of heart attacks. Blood and oxygen could not get through to the cells, leaving sections of the heart muscle to die.

Why did the fat plaques go away during the war?

During those horrible war years something interesting happened. People couldn't get the rich foods they were used to eating. Meat was not available. Nor was

*The student was William P. Castelli.

3

milk or cream. Soldiers came to the farms with trucks and took the livestock for their own use.

During those war years the Europeans, rich and poor alike, were *deprived* of meat and cream. They had no choice. They lived on plain ordinary things like grains, vegetables and fruits—a diet rich in complex carbohydrates. The fat plaques disappeared by 1942 . . . and so did heart attacks!

Plaques start early in life

Pathologists have been seeing fat plaques for decades in North Americans, Argentinians, Scandinavians and others who consume heavy amounts of meat, cream and butter. Autopsies performed on American troops killed in the Korean War showed fat streaks in the coronary arteries of three-quarters of them. And most were young men with an average age of only 22.

Around the world

On the other hand, many cultures of the world have essentially no fat-plugged coronary arteries and almost no heart attacks.

If we are wise we will learn what we can about these cultures and make some changes based on what we learn.

Around the world people eat vastly different foods. But there are some interesting basic fundamentals. Each diet is built on some type of grain—wheat in the United States, Canada and Russia, rice in Japan and the Orient, and corn in Mexico, Central America and much of South America. A balance of grains and legumes provides essential protein building blocks called *amino acids*. But individual grains alone don't contain enough of some of the essential amino acids to make what is called a *complete protein*. The same is true of legumes such as beans. Fortunately, when both are in the diet (not necessarily in the same dish or even the same meal) in a ratio of 3 parts grain to 1 part legumes, a balance occurs so a complete protein results. Fish and seafood also supply the essential amino acids. Seafood or a combination of grains and legumes are good low-saturated-fat sources of the essential amino acids. They are the main diet components for people around the world who *don't* have heart attacks. Compare this with the quantities of meat, eggs and whole-milk products in the diets of people who *do* have heart attacks.

What about milk?

Another consistent dietary factor among many cultures with low heart disease is that, for the most part, *they are not heavy milk drinkers*. Of course cream, regular milk and cheese are loaded with butterfat.

"But isn't regular milk necessary in our diet? Isn't whole milk an essential food?"

We have all grown up learning that the answers to these questions are "yes." There isn't any doubt that whole milk contains many nutrients, including complete proteins with all the essential amino acids.

But after all these years of thinking that milk with butterfat is an essential food, maybe it isn't so. The editor of the *Yearbook of Pediatrics,* Dr. Frank Oski, points out that only 2% of the people in the world drink milk after they are weaned! Perhaps whole milk isn't essential after all—especially after childhood and especially as we consider how much bad, saturated fat there is in cream.

This doesn't mean we shouldn't use any milk. But the evidence suggests that after the milk-drinking years of childhood, a better choice may be to use non-fat milk, non-fat yogurt and tablespreads that are not loaded with saturated fats.

Is it a coincidence that the traditional Japanese who have so few heart attacks don't drink milk or eat much cheese or cream? Is it a coincidence that rice, fish and other seafoods are their basic foods?

There is good evidence that this *isn't* a coincidence. And what about the Eskimos and other people who usually don't have heart attacks? Eskimos don't consume much milk after the early years of life. Most of the protein in their diet comes from fish, seafood and meat of animals that eat fish.

Most cultures don't eat much bad fat

The traditional diets of most Africans and South Americans (other than in cattle-producing countries like Argentina and Uruguay where meat consumption is high) don't contain much bad, saturated fat. A high intake of pinto and other beans provides the protein balance along with healthy complex carbohydrates.

People from the Pacific Islands eat lots of fish and other seafood along with rice and tropical fruits.

Although people in Mediterranean countries consume some saturated fat in lamb, yogurt and cheese, their cooking oil is primarily olive oil. This contains mostly monounsaturated fat which, as we will see later, is much more healthful than bad, saturated fat.

You can be among the people who don't have heart attacks. You can significantly decrease the odds of having a heart attack, even after eating too much saturated fat all your life.

You don't have to move to the Arctic, Pacific Islands or other faraway places to join their healthy lifestyle.

"Well, what do I have to do?" you may be thinking. Even though many people have been wanting to cut down on saturated-fat intake, there hasn't been a simple game plan. How can we accomplish this in a culture where meat, milk, cheese and ice cream are such important parts of the diet?

We have a plan to help you. It's simple.

Why this book is different

You will quickly find this book is different. Some

may find it revolutionary. But it isn't.

One thing you may wonder as you read further is why we don't spend more time talking about not eating so much cholesterol, which has been the big emphasis in the last few years.

We will talk about *limiting* cholesterol. But, although limiting cholesterol is important, we will talk even more about not eating so much saturated fat.

Why?

Your blood cholesterol is caused more by the saturated fat you eat than by how much cholesterol you eat. Although both are important, people have not paid enough attention to saturated-fat intake.

Saturated fat is the culprit

Many people who think they are on a good low-cholesterol program are missing the boat and are getting into trouble. The problem is that the body makes cholesterol when we eat saturated fat. Obviously we want you to be concerned about how much cholesterol you eat. But you need to know that if you want to control your blood cholesterol and beat the odds of a heart attack, *no matter what else you do,* it is absolutely essential to limit how much saturated fat you eat.

You will be interested to know that if you limit the saturated fat in your diet, most of the time you will automatically limit the amount of cholesterol you consume. It's simple. The first thing is to learn about the different kinds of fats and how to limit the bad fat you eat. We'll show you the easiest way to control how much bad fat you eat—and if you will follow through, the rest will fall into place.

By changing from a pattern of eating too much bad, saturated fat and cholesterol, you can keep more plaque from forming in your coronary arteries. If you are really persistent, there is a chance that some of the plaque that has already formed may begin to disappear.

In 1987, Dr. David Blankenhorn of the University of

Southern California demonstrated convincing evidence in sequential angiograms. These showed that plaque formation can be slowed and reversed. His group reported that a significant drop in cholesterol will slow and can even reverse the formation of fatty deposits in arteries.

If you want to improve your odds, you probably have lots of questions. We'll answer these for you, beginning with an understanding about good fats and bad fats.

The Framingham Heart Study

In 1948 in Framingham, Massachusetts, an ongoing study commenced with 5127 men and women to evaluate the risk factors of coronary-artery disease. These folks represented one half of all the healthy adults—men and women—in that town. They have been examined and checked every two years since. Heart attacks, deaths and laboratory data have been carefully followed, providing valuable information about the risk factors related to coronary-artery disease.

After careful analysis of the data from Framingham, as well as collaborative studies from across the United States, there isn't any question that high cholesterol levels result in more heart attacks and strokes. Summing up these results shows that a 1% rise in cholesterol increases the chance of coronary-artery disease by 2% in both men and women.

Co-author William P. Castelli is the Medical Director of the Framingham Heart Study of The National Heart, Lung and Blood Institute (NHLBI).

2

Good Fats and Bad Fats

You may be thinking, "I know someone who should be eating less bad fat!"

Everybody knows *someone* who should be eating less bad fat. But most folks, maybe even you, think it's the *other* person who needs to cut down on saturated fat. Most of us think we are doing pretty well by not eating too much fried food. But, without a conscious effort, the grams of bad fat we eat every day add up like taxes or numbers on a gas pump.

Most people don't have any idea of how much bad, saturated fat is in the food they eat. Without thinking about it and adding up how much saturated fat foods actually contain, it isn't obvious at all.

Bad fat hides in lots of foods.

And incidentally, all fat isn't bad.

Fat is an essential part of our diet. Some fat is good. Everybody needs to eat some fat every day, but probably not anywhere near the amount you are eating.

Understanding about dietary fat does not need to be complicated and confusing. Because the quantity and kinds of fat we gobble up make such an important difference as to whether our coronary arteries stay open or not, you need to know about fats.

Identifying the Fats

Good Fat

Omega-3 Fatty Acids
  Fish
  Seafood
  Some plants
Unsaturated fats (oils)
  Monounsaturated
    canola (rapeseed) oil
    olive oil
    peanut oil
  Polyunsaturated
    safflower
    sunflower
    corn
    soybean
    cottonseed
    some fish

Bad Fat

Saturated Fats
  animal fats   ice cream
  avocados   lard
  butter   other milk
  cheese   products
  coconut oil   palm oil
  cream   palm-
                   kernel oil

Hydrogenated Fats
Solid margarine or butter substitutes. These fats have been transformed from liquid to a solid form. Process changes good qualities of some unsaturated vegetable fat into bad, saturated fat.

Cholesterol descriptions

Fat is an oily substance made up of chains of fatty acids.
Lipids are a basic fatty component of living cells. They may be in either a liquid or solid form.

Lipoproteins are a complex combination of fat and proteins, including cholesterol.

Cholesterol is a fatty substance found only in animal and human cells. Because it can be made in the body, it is not an essential dietary requirement. Large amounts of cholesterol are found in egg yolks, liver, brains, kidneys and fatty meats. There are good-fat cholesterols and bad-fat cholesterols. With all this "bad press" and negative publicity being given to cholesterol, you'd never get the idea that it is essential for the proper functioning of your body. But you don't have to eat any cholesterol to get all you need. About 75% of the cholesterol in your body is made in the liver. Cholesterol is used to make cell membranes. It is also used to produce steroid hormones in the sex organs and in the adrenal glands. And, as an ingredient in bile acids, it may aid digestion. Elevated blood cholesterol is a major cause of heart disease.

Low-density lipoprotein (LDL) is a particularly harmful form of fatty cholesterol. As blood and tissue levels of LDL cholesterol become elevated, the low-density cholesterols collect on the inside walls of the coronary arteries, starting a process of fat-filled cells and scar-like tissue called *plaque* that progressively blocks the flow of blood and oxygen to the heart muscles. An easy way to remember that LDL is a bad-fat cholesterol is to think of LDL as a *lousy lipoprotein*. High levels of LDL are associated with heart disease.

High-density lipoprotein (HDL) is a good kind of cholesterol—a good fat! High-density lipoproteins help move the bad kind of cholesterol out of the cells. High-density lipoproteins can be increased by exercise, by not smoking, and by using monounsaturated fats and omega-3 fatty acids instead of saturated fats. A helpful way to remember that HDL is a good-fat cholesterol is to think of it as a *healthy lipoprotein*. A low level of HDL is associated with heart disease. High levels of HDL indicate a lower risk of atherosclerosis and heart disease.

Triglycerides are the most common form of fat in the diet and in the human body. Too much of these fats puts a person at risk for *pancreatitis*—inflammation of the pancreas—as well as increased risk of getting a heart attack or stroke. Triglycerides are carried in the very-low-density lipoproteins (VLDL) which we can add to the other *lousy lipoproteins*.

Saturated fats are the characteristically hard fats found mostly in animal products such as lard, butter and animal fat. We usually consider all saturated fats as *bad* fats—and most are. Recent evidence seems to show that stearic acid, one of the saturated fats in meat, may not be so bad. It is important to know that the other saturated fats in meat *are* harmful. That's sufficient reason to eat small servings of very-lean meat. This is being made easier with the new system of FDA grading of beef. The grade that was called *good* is now being called *select*. This new *select* grade of beef is considerably lower in fat than other grades of beef that are marbled with fat.

Other common animal-fat sources of saturated fat are egg yolks, cream, cheese, ice cream and other milk products. Surprisingly, three vegetable oils (palm oil, palm kernel oil and coconut oil) are loaded with saturated fat—very bad fat. Another source of saturated fat is the hydrogenation or hardening process that converts some of the good unsaturated fat in vegetable oils into bad, saturated fat.

Hydrogenated fats are fats that have been transformed from a liquid to a solid form such as in margarine and shortening. Hydrogenation hardens the unsaturated fat, giving it a longer shelf life. The process also changes the good qualities of some of the unsaturated vegetable fat into bad, saturated fat.

Unsaturated fats are monounsaturated or polyunsaturated fats that come from vegetables or seafood. These are the preferred fats for the fat requirements in your diet—the good fats. But keep in mind, there are wise limits on many good things you eat, including the good fats.

Polyunsaturated fats are the predominantly good fats found in common vegetable oils such as safflower, sunflower, corn, soybean, cottonseed and walnut oils. Also, some of the fats in seafood are polyunsaturated. You will sometimes hear polyunsaturated fatty acids referred to as *PUFAs*.

Monounsaturated fats are the predominantly very good fats found in olive oil, peanut oil and canola (rapeseed) oil. While avocados are rich in monounsaturated fat, they also contain quite a lot of saturated fat that must be counted toward one's daily limit (which we explain in Chapter 4). In cultures where olive oil is the main fat source instead of saturated fat, the people are healthier and usually do not have heart attacks. Monounsaturated fats are our first choice of oils to use in food preparation, salads and cooking.

Omega-3 fatty acids are especially good fats. They are the healthful fatty acids found in fish, seafoods and in some plants. People who consistently eat fish and other seafood containing omega-3 fats instead of saturated fats seldom have heart attacks. If we were rating fats as good, better and best, the omega 3's would get a "best" rating. Supplements of omega-3 oils are sometimes prescribed in special bad-fat problems. We recommend eating fish and seafood as a regular source of omega-3 fatty acids.

Liquid vegetable cooking oils

When it became apparent that saturated fats were a problem, interest began to shift to vegetable oils because, for the most part, they are made up of unsaturated fats. But using vegetable oil is not enough because palm oil, palm kernel oil and coconut oil are loaded with saturated fat. To make things worse, these three are used *extensively* in food manufacturing—including baking—

as are lard and butter.

Have you ever wondered why cookies and bakery goods you buy at the store seem so fresh, even after being there a while?

The answer is the saturated fat.

Products made with bad (saturated) fats last longer than those made with other fats. That's why commercial breads, pastries and cookies baked with animal fats, or coconut, palm kernel or palm oil have a particularly long shelf life.

No wonder bakers like to use lard, butter, palm oil, palm kernel oil and coconut oil. Besides that, coconut oil is mild and pleasant. It doesn't have a strong odor. Coconut oil itself is almost tasteless—allowing it to pick up and enhance the flavors of the other ingredients. But as gram upon gram of saturated fat is eaten, the "shelf life" of the person eating the goodies may be decreased.

It is regretable that so much lard, butter, palm, palm kernel and coconut oil is used for making delicious croissants, pie crusts and other good-tasting things.

What about liquid vegetable cooking oils?

Cooking oils that contain mostly monounsaturated fat but little saturated fat are olive oil, peanut oil and canola oil—also known as *rapeseed oil*.

The oil with the longest historical track record in a culture with little heart disease is olive oil. Generations of people who have used olive oil as their main fat source have been particularly healthy and have not ended up with fat-plugged coronary arteries.

Such long-term results and safety records are reassuring, comforting and appealing.

Although some people may have the impression that olive oil has an odd odor and flavor, many varieties of olive oil are mild and delightful. You will find olive oil is especially good for cooking and in salads.

Canola (Puritan®) is a particularly mild-tasting, mostly monounsaturated oil.

The three most popular cooking oils containing predominantly polyunsaturated fats (PUFAs) and only a little saturated fat are safflower oil, sunflower oil and corn oil. All three are characterized by a particularly good flavor. These are followed by cottonseed and soybean oils.

A good balance may be to use mostly olive and canola oil in cooking and food preparation—together with a little polyunsaturated safflower, corn or sunflower oil.

The guidelines of the recent publication of the National Cholesterol Education Program recommend we balance our fat intake, cut saturated fats and eat some polyunsaturated fats for their essential fatty acids— without getting too much. We don't need much polyunsaturated oil. Probably a couple of teaspoons per day are sufficient—much of which may be obtained in tablespreads.

Tablespreads

One tablespoon of butter contains 7 grams of saturated fat and 30mg (milligrams) of cholesterol . . . a lot of bad fat!

Solid margarines and tablespreads are solid because the vegetable oil is hydrogenated. This increases the amount of saturated fat—taking away some but not all of its advantage.

There are usually about 2 grams of saturated fat per tablespoon in most solid margarines. Only 1 gram of saturated fat is in a tablespoon of the best soft (tub) tablespreads such as Weight Watchers Reduced Calorie Margarine,® Promise Soft Tablespread,® and Fleischmann's Soft Diet Margarine.® When it comes to margarines and tablespreads, *softer is better!*

There are U.S. laws governing the labeling of margarine. Look at the list of ingredients. The first word on that list is the clue to the predominant ingredient of that margarine. For example, if the first word is *liquid,* then most of the margarine is made of a liquid oil such as corn, safflower, sunflower or soybean oil. If the first words are *partially hydrogenated* or *partly hardened,* the margarine is made from oils that have been hydrogenated or hardened, meaning much of the oil has been changed into saturated fat. Avoid these margarines.

Actually the ingredient list of the best margarines starts with the word *water.* The best diet margarines have half the fat of the other margarines. To judge which are the best ones, look on the package to see how much saturated fat is listed per tablespoon.

The choice of tablespreads is very important. Your best choice is a soft diet margarine with only 1 gram of saturated fat per tablespoon.

Besides the choice of a tablespread, how the spread is used makes a considerable difference in the amount of saturated fat you consume.

If you usually spread a thick layer of margarine on bread or toast, that's way too much! Even a gram of saturated fat per tablespoon can add up—twice as fast if you use stick margarine, and seven times as fast if you use real butter!

A tablespread can accomplish its purpose on bread, toast or whatever when it is spread very thinly—maybe even missing parts of the surface. And, as you get used to eating with low-fat goals in mind, you may find, as we have, that bread can taste good with very little spread or by itself with no spread at all.

Changing eating patterns like this will take some thought and effort, but the good thing is you can enjoy tasty things without loading up on too much bad fat.

Because you probably want to know what all this has to do with cholesterol testing and what your cholesterol numbers really mean, we will help you become an expert in the next chapter.

School lunches
can be hazardous to kids' health

Before anyone knew that bad fats are a serious problem, various programs were instituted to provide lots of butter, cheese and milk products in public-school lunch programs. Such programs were undoubtedly begun with the best of intentions. But we now know that the tons of unhealthy, saturated fat that are fed to school children every day are a big problem. This adds to the already enormous problem of controlling the intake of saturated fat in kids whose favorite fast foods contain lots of bad fat. We are concerned about this pattern for two reasons. First, the process of fat buildup in the arteries begins early in life, as was discovered in the coronary arteries of young American soldiers killed in the Korean War. Our second concern is that eating habits made early in life are not easy to change later. Thus, the earlier healthy eating patterns can be established, the better—realizing that children eat more dairy products than adults.

Packing a healthful lunch for your child makes more sense than expecting him/her to choose low-fat meals when they are seldom offered.

Cholesterol Numbers

Cholesterol is measured in milligrams per deciliter (mg/dl). It is also measured in millimols per liter (mmol/L), sometimes termed SI for Système International d' Unités. So, when we use the number 150 without the mg/dl, it's to make for easier reading. It really is 150mg/dl.

We added the mmol/L figure in parentheses: 150 (3.9). What you are reading is 150mg/dl (3.9mmol/L).

Triglycerides are also measured in mg/dl and in mmol/L.

A table and formulas below will help you convert from one set of units to the other.

Cholesterol number conversion

mg/dl of cholesterol X 0.02586 = mmol/L of cholesterol

mmol/L of cholesterol X 38.67 = mg/dl of cholesterol

Triglyceride number conversion

mg/dl of triglyceride X 0.01129 = mmol/L of triglyceride

mmol/l of triglyceride X 88.496 = mg/dl of triglyceride

Cholesterol Conversion

mg/dl	mmol/L	mg/dl	mmol/L	mg/dl	mmol/L
120	3.1	220	5.7	320	8.3
130	3.4	230	5.9	330	8.5
140	3.6	240	6.2	340	8.8
150	3.9	250	6.5	350	9.0
160	4.1	260	6.7	360	9.3
170	4.4	270	7.0	370	9.6
180	4.7	280	7.2	380	9.8
190	4.9	290	7.5	390	10.1
200	5.2	300	7.8	400	10.3
210	5.4	310	8.0		

Additional conversion reference charts for HDL Cholesterol and Triglyceride are on page 32.

3

Your Cholesterol Numbers— and the Odds

You may already know your cholesterol numbers, but if you don't, we suggest you find out what they are right away. And why do we say *numbers* instead of *number?* Because there are different kinds of cholesterol and an important ratio to keep in mind—as described on the facing page.

Let's start with the single number called *total cholesterol.* "What should my total cholesterol number be?"

You were born with a total cholesterol level of about 70 (1.8), but as soon as you started eating, it started going up— probably reaching about 150 (3.9) by the time you had your first birthday.

After a child's cholesterol level reaches about 150 (3.9), it usually stays there until he or she is about 17-years old. Then the level usually starts going up again, often reaching 210 (5.4) to 220 (5.7)—the average cholesterol level of adults in the United States, Canada and similar cultures.

However, most people around the world don't have cholesterol levels that high. People in many parts of the world have total cholesterol levels around 150 (3.9)—and they don't get coronary-artery disease. The reason is that they don't eat as much saturated fat as most North Americans.

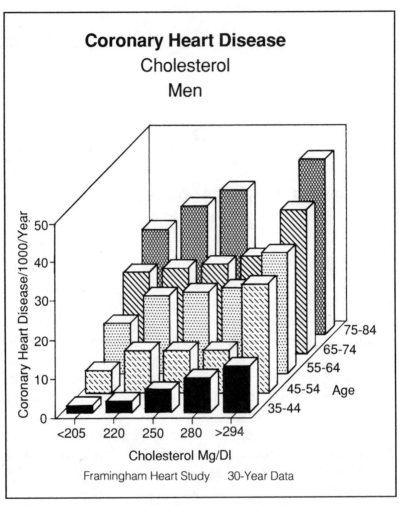

Figure 3-1—Heart attacks per 1000 per year in men versus total cholesterol. Higher cholesterol worsens the odds of heart attacks, especially as age increases. In every age bracket higher cholesterol correlates with a greater risk. The average level of men who had heart attacks is 235 (6.0). At any age the heart-attack rate rises 2% for each 1% increase in blood cholesterol.

While most adults around the world have cholesterol levels under 150 (3.9), half of the children in the United States and Canada already have a cholesterol level over that value.

The problem has been compounded because, until recently, many doctors did not become excited about a person's cholesterol unless it exceeded 300 (7.8). In the past, some cardiology textbooks said not to worry unless a person's cholesterol is over 250 (6.5). But we know from studies like the Framingham Heart Study that most people in our population who get a heart attack have a cholesterol level between 200 (5.2) and 250 (6.5).

Heart-attack rate rises with cholesterol

Much of our knowledge of how cholesterol relates to coronary heart disease comes from studies like the Framingham Heart Study. As figures 3-1 and 3-2 show, at virtually any age the heart-attack rate rises 2% for each 1% the blood cholesterol level goes up. This is even true for people over age 65.

The average cholesterol level of a man in the Framingham Heart Study who had a heart attack in the first 16 years of our study was 244 (6.3)—and now, 30 years later, that level is about 235 (6.0).

Some people in the Framingham Study didn't have a heart attack in the first 16 years. They had cholesterols between 180 (4.6) and 240 (6.2). The trick is to know where you stand when your total cholesterol level is over 200 (5.2). Are you headed for a heart attack—or will you escape?

More than one kind of cholesterol

This is where the *other* cholesterols in your blood come in. Your cholesterol consists of *five* different kinds.

Cholesterol is carried in little fat droplets in your blood. The largest is called a *chylomicron*. These

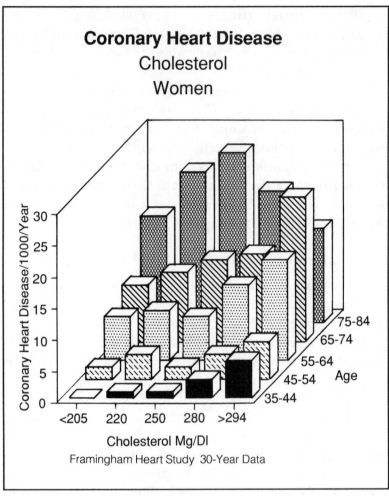

Figure 3-2—Heart attacks per 1000 per year in women versus total cholesterol. Higher cholesterol worsens the odds of heart attacks, especially as age increases.

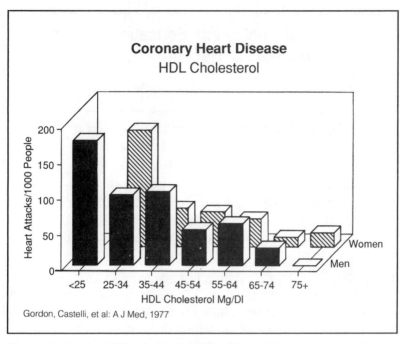

Figure 3-3—As HDL cholesterol increases, the heart-attack rate goes down sharply. This true for both men and women. This is a cross section for all ages. Chart courtesy of Framingham Heart Study.

chylomicrons appear in your blood after you eat fat.

The next-smaller-size particle is called a *very-low-density lipoprotein (VLDL)*. These carry *triglycerides.*

Until recently many doctors have thought that triglycerides are not very important in relation to heart disease. But you should know that some people with elevated triglycerides are headed for a heart attack, especially if their triglycerides exceed 150 (3.9) and their HDL cholesterol is less than 40 (1.0).

Hold on. We are getting ahead of our story.

The next smaller particles are the *intermediary-density lipoproteins* called *IDL.* They are dangerous if they

National Cholesterol Education Council
Summary of Recommendations*

Total Cholesterol	Recommendation	
Under 200 (5.2) Desirable	Follow prudent diet, quit smoking, lose weight if needed, exercise, relax, recheck in 5 years	
200 (5.2) to 239 (6.18) Borderline high	See your doctor for LDL check if you have any two of these risk factors: ✗ male ✗ high blood pressure ✗ smoke ✗ heart attacks in family ✗ HDL less than 35 (0.9) ✗ diabetes mellitus ✗ overweight	LDL under 130 (3.4) Low risk LDL over 160 (4.1) requires low-saturated-fat, low-cholesterol diet High risk
Over 240 (6.2) High	See your doctor for LDL check	LDL over 160 (4.1) requires low-saturated-fat, low-cholesterol diet High risk

*Refer to text for authors' suggestions that are designed to give you even better odds against heart attack and stroke.

Total Cholesterol/HDL Cholesterol Ratio

$$\frac{\text{Total Cholesterol}}{\text{HDL Cholesterol}} = \text{Ratio} \qquad \frac{150\ (3.9)}{43\ (1.1)} = 3.5$$

become elevated—but you probably don't need to worry about these—few people have this problem.

The next smaller particle is the most dangerous of all because it carries over half the cholesterol in your blood stream. This cholesterol is called low-density lipoprotein, or *LDL*.

You probably remember LDL is bad and is known as the *lousy lipoprotein* or *bad cholesterol!*

The four cholesterols we just described (chylomicron, VLDL, IDL and LDL cholesterol) are bad for you and tend to collect in your blood vessels.

Fortunately there is a fifth cholesterol—and it turns out to be good. This "good" cholesterol is called *high-density lipoprotein*, or *HDL cholesterol*. It apparently picks up the cholesterol from deposits all over the body and brings them back to the liver where 95% of the cholesterol is excreted.

No wonder HDL is known as the *good* or *healthy cholesterol!* As you can see from figure 3-3, the higher a person's HDL level, the lower the incidence of a heart attack.

We are now having a campaign in the United States to get everyone to find out their total cholesterol level. The National Heart, Lung and Blood Institute, part of the National Institutes of Health, has formed a dedicated group called *The National Cholesterol Education Panel* to get the message to the public. The first part of this important message is that everyone needs to know his or her cholesterol level because high cholesterol can lead to fat blockages of the arteries. This is also called *hardening of the arteries*.

What is a high cholesterol?

Well, remember we told you about the problem of a cholesterol level over 200 (5.2)? Some people with a cholesterol over 200 (5.2) are in serious trouble; some are not. The best way to tell if you are in trouble is to know your HDL, or "good cholesterol" level, and figure out a simple ratio by dividing the *big number*, total cholesterol, by the *little number*, good HDL cholesterol.

For example, if your total cholesterol is 200 (5.2) and HDL cholesterol is 50 (1.3), your ratio is 4, or 200 ÷ 50 = 4, which is very good.

But if your total cholesterol is 210 (5.4) and your HDL cholesterol is 30 (0.77), your ratio is 210 ÷ 30 = 7. If you are using mmol/L figures, it is 5.4 ÷ 0.77 = 7, which is bad.

Using the same math, if your total cholesterol is 150 (3.9) and your HDL cholesterol is 43 (1.1), your ratio is 3.5, which is very good.

An optimal ratio is 3.5, but for starters, we would be quite happy if you and everyone else in North America had total cholesterol/HDL cholesterol ratios under 4.5. To accomplish this would require about half the people in North America to stop eating so much saturated fat and cholesterol.

We know this is a major change for a lot of people. But because half the people in the United States and Canada are expected to die from plugged-up arteries, a change in eating patterns will be well worth it.

How to reduce heart-attack risk

From all the diet and drug-research studies ever done in the world to lower your blood cholesterol levels, we know that if you lower blood cholesterol level enough, you can significantly reduce the risk of a heart attack. If you consistently eat a low-saturated-fat and low-cholesterol diet and control your cholesterol levels for a long enough time, regression of the fat plaques may start to occur.

As we said, the best test to judge how you are doing when your cholesterol is over 200 (5.2) is to check the HDL-cholesterol level in your blood. Suppose we tell you that some people get heart attacks even though their total cholesterols are between 150 (3.9) and 200 (5.2). Indeed, once your total cholesterol is over 150 (3.9), you need to know your HDL level because, if your total-cholesterol/HDL-cholesterol ratio is over 4.5, you are still at an increased risk of having a heart attack.

This is also true of triglycerides. Once they are over 150 (1.69) you need to get your ratio under 4.5 and your HDL over 40 (1.03) or you could be in trouble.

Just as different people have different ideas about what the speed limit should be, there are different opinions about how to monitor cholesterol.

Not everyone uses the ratio of total cholesterol/HDL cholesterol, but it seems so helpful that we believe everyone's guidelines should be expanded to include it.

Get your cholesterol level checked

Certainly The National Cholesterol Education Program guidelines have been a great service in making people aware of the dangers of elevated cholesterol levels and bringing cholesterol-screening campaigns to towns all across the United States.

This is very good. In fact, this is a very important preventive health measure. Everyone needs to know his or her cholesterol level.

If you don't know what your cholesterol is, be sure to get it checked—by your doctor or at one of the cholesterol-screening campaigns in a local shopping mall, school, civic center, clinic or wherever. Don't take the attitude of "I don't want to know." And don't wait too long. If a campaign isn't going on, ask your doctor to check your cholesterol level. You need to know what is going on in your body so you can make informed decisions that will help *you* beat the odds of a heart attack.

What do they do in one of these cholesterol-screening programs? They run a blood test. Often the screening tests are done with a drop or two of blood from your finger, called a *finger stick*. Other times they may take blood from a vein in your arm. Whichever they do, it isn't a big deal at all.

Your cholesterol-screening report will place you in

one of the following categories. The accompanying recommendations are based on guidelines developed by The National Cholesterol Education Program:

The program outlines a series of recommendations:

If your total cholesterol is under 200 (5.2), that is called *desirable*. You will be given these recommendations: follow a prudent diet, quit smoking, lose weight if needed, exercise, relax and have your cholesterol checked again in five years.

If your cholesterol is over 240 (6.2), you will be told to see your doctor and have your LDL cholesterol measured.

If your cholesterol is between 200 (5.2) and 239 (6.18), you will learn that, according to these guidelines, this is potentially risky. You will be told to go to your doctor to get your LDL-cholesterol level checked—if you already have heart disease, have had a stroke or some other vascular disease.

You will also be told to go to your doctor for an LDL-cholesterol check if you have a cholesterol level between 200 (5.2) and 239 (6.18) and have any two of the following risk factors:

✗ you are a male
✗ you have high blood pressure
✗ you smoke cigarettes
✗ you have a family history where people have had heart attacks under age 55
✗ your HDL cholesterol is under 35 (0.9)
✗ you have diabetes mellitus
✗ you are overweight.

If you don't have a known history of an artery clogged with cholesterol or two of these risk factors, but your cholesterol is between 200 (5.2) and 239 (6.18), you will be told to follow a prudent diet, exercise, not smoke and have your cholesterol checked every year.

As we pointed out to our colleagues in the September 1, 1988 issue of *Postgraduate Medicine*:

"An interesting observation about these numbers is

frankly admitted in *The National Cholesterol Education Program Expert Panel's* report: 'These cutpoints are necessarily somewhat arbitrary.' One of the panel's decisions was to consider total cholesterol levels as *borderline-high* if they fall in the range of 200 (5.2) to 239 (6.18), and as *high* if they are 240mg/dl or more. The following statement of the panel about their cutoff levels is quite pertinent: 'The 240mg/dl cutpoint for total serum cholesterol is a level at which coronary-artery disease risk is almost double that at 200mg/dl, and is rising steeply.' Patients with cholesterol levels at or above this cutpoint have sufficiently high risk to warrant more detailed evaluation and possible treatment."

We go on to explain in our article that "the program is designed to discover the bulk of the people who will experience *coronary-artery disease* unless changes are made. However, experience in the Framingham Heart Study shows that the majority of heart attacks occur in people whose total cholesterol level is between 200 (5.2) and 250 (6.5). Unfortunately, most of these people fall into a *gray zone*—a middle or borderline group in which coronary-artery disease will definitely develop in some patients and will not develop in others."

These observations are important.

Social and economic impacts

Obviously judgment calls had to be made as to the cutpoints. The economic and social impact of these decisions and recommendations very probably weighed on the minds of the panel members as they made these decisions. And these are very important considerations. Just imagine the economic effect that their recommendations will make.

Health-care dollar costs will be enormous—at least at first when you consider all the additional equipment, supplies and personnel involved in cholesterol testing. Also consider the additional visits to doctors.

In the future these investments will be well worthwhile for everyone involved in paying for healthcare expenses—and that begins with you and me. It also includes governments, health-insurance companies and health-maintenance organizations (HMOs).

The impact on the food industry is also mind-boggling, which is probably why specific recommendations were left out of the U.S. Surgeon General's 1988 warning about the dangers of saturated fat.

We're not just talking about the economic effect on the dairy, egg, meat, baking and food-oil industries. Implications of the recommendations for a drastic cut in the consumption of saturated fat will also impact almost every aspect of the food industry, from production and distribution to groceries, markets, restaurants and fast-food businesses.

The National Cholesterol Education Program's expert panel is to be commended on making the bold recommendations it did. We know that if *our* recommendations are followed, the economic impact will be even greater.

LDL cholesterol check

If you are in one of the groups where you are told to go to your doctor because your cholesterol is over 240 (6.2); if you have a cholesterol level between 200 (5.2) and 239 (6.18) with two risk factors; or if you already know you have some plugged arteries, your doctor will probably have your LDL cholesterol checked.

Then what?

There are two new numbers to remember pertaining to these LDL cholesterols.

These numbers are 130 (3.4) and 160 (4.1).

If your LDL is under 130 (3.4), that's considered *low-risk*. You will be advised to follow a prudent diet, exercise and not smoke.

If your LDL is over 160 (4.1), you will be advised this is bad, bad, bad! You will be instructed that you need to go on a low-saturated-fat and low-cholesterol diet like we suggest. You may also find that medications are needed to get your LDL under 160 (4.1).

But if you already have cholesterol deposits in your arteries or if you have two of the risk factors, you will be treated with a low-saturated-fat, low-cholesterol diet. If necessary, medications will be prescribed to bring your LDL to under 130 (3.4).

So, in essence what The National Cholesterol Education Program is saying is that there are two goals, either 160 (4.1) or 130 (3.4).

You have just read about a lot of numbers. Almost everyone agrees that keeping your LDL-cholesterol level under 130 (3.4) is good. In such a case you are at a low risk. Almost everyone agrees that an LDL cholesterol over 160 (4.1) is much too high.

Because we are talking about *you*, let's take it a step further. *We don't want you to get lost in the shuffle*. We don't want *you* to have a heart attack.

What do you really need to do?

To some, success is getting the LDL under 130 (3.4).

To others, it is getting the ratio of the total cholesterol divided by the HDL cholesterol so it is less than 4.5.

We know it's better to combine the two standards: get your ratio under 4.5 *and* get your LDL cholesterol under 130 (3.4). This is what you should do if you want unimpeded flow of blood through your arteries.

The bottom line is that you should keep your total cholesterol under 200 (5.2) and your LDL under 130 (3.4) by eating less saturated fat and cholesterol.

We hope you and your doctor will monitor your HDL cholesterol level so the simple total-cholesterol/HDL-cholesterol ratio can be figured out and followed. Getting and keeping this ratio under 4.5 is one more step you and your doctor can take to improve the odds that *you won't get a heart attack*.

Heart attacks and strokes affect women, too!

Keep in mind—if you eat like a typical North American—odds are that you will die of a heart attack or stroke. And don't think this is just true for men. Because of the myth that women don't get coronary-artery disease, their symptoms of this disease are often not taken seriously—sometimes even by doctors. This is tragic because, especially after the menopause, women are at serious risk of heart disease. In fact, coronary-artery disease is the leading killer of women over 65—killing 250,000 women a year in the United States! This is seven times the number of women who die of breast cancer.

No one likes lousy odds in a bet, yet sometimes folks don't pay very much attention to lousy odds when it comes to themselves. All too many people think, "It won't happen to me." We hope you won't kid yourself into believing this dumb thought. Plugged-up coronary arteries can happen to you. So can a very untimely massive heart attack or stroke.

You can significantly change the odds.

HDL Cholesterol Conversion

mg/dl	mmol/L	mg/dl	mmol/L
20	0.52	55	1.42
25	0.65	60	1.55
30	0.78	65	1.68
35	0.90	70	1.81
40	1.03	80	2.07
45	1.16	90	2.33
50	1.29	100	2.59

Trigylceride Conversion

mg/dl	mmol/L	mg/dl	mmol/L
150	1.7	600	6.8
200	2.3	700	7.9
250	2.8	800	9.0
300	3.4	900	10.2
350	4.0	1000	11.3
400	4.5	1500	16.9
450	5.1	2000	22.6
500	5.6		

For additional information on cholesterol and triglyceride conversions, refer to page 18.

4

What's My Bad-fat Limit?

So what's my saturated-fat limit? Not very much. Preventing cholesterol levels from creeping up makes sense for everyone, but for high-risk people it is an absolute necessity to limit saturated-fat intake.

Almost everyone knows it is good to limit how much cholesterol we eat. But many don't know that when saturated fat is eaten, the body increases its production of cholesterol.

Until recently, few people paid any attention to how much saturated fat they ate. Those who tried had a difficult time finding out how much bad fat was in what they were eating.

People are becoming increasingly aware that it is easy to consume way too much saturated fat. The problem of eating too much bad fat is very real, very immediate and very serious.

For example, a big hamburger with cheese, an order of French fries and a milk shake contain 28 grams of saturated fat. That's as much bad fat as is in half a quarter-pound stick of butter!

Think about eating 1/8 pound of butter the next time you are tempted to order a big hamburger with cheese, a big order of fries and a large shake.

Can you imagine eating that much butter in one sitting? That's too much bad fat!

How much is too much saturated fat—and how much should you be eating?

This answer depends on several variables.

A farmer doing the most vigorous kinds of work, especially in very cold weather, needs a lot of calories. A lot of energy is required and many calories are expended. Under these conditions more saturated fat can be burned up by the body than in warmer or less-active circumstances.

The National Cholesterol Education Program's Expert Panel recommends as the first step of a heart-disease-prevention diet: consume less than 10% of the calorie intake in the form of saturated fat. In the second step: eat less than 7% of one's caloric intake of saturated fat.

So how much is this? It sounds complicated.

Well, it isn't really complicated—but it is a nuisance. And the more of a nuisance something is, the less likely a person is to follow it.

There is another problem about targeting an intake of saturated fat based on a percentage of the calories consumed.

We know a person concerned about cholesterol should consume less than 10% of his or her need in the form of saturated fat—and not 10% of whatever he or she decides or happens to eat in a particular day.*

For example, a sedentary person can eat far more saturated fat than is wise—and then eat even more to run up the number of calories on a particular day. The grams of saturated fat may still turn out to be only 10% of that day's calories.

Let's imagine you are an active adult and you burn up enough energy so you don't gain or lose weight on 2000 calories a day. Now just suppose that yesterday you had a big day—starting with a hearty breakfast, followed by lunch at a fast-food place with some friends, then you went out for dinner. Imagine that you *sort of* tried to keep the intake of saturated fat down—and that you did

* Castelli, W., Griffin, G., "A Simple Strategy To Limit Saturated Fat After Cholesterol Screening." *Postgraduate Medicine*, September 1, 1988.

only eat 44 grams of saturated fat. If your caloric intake that day was 2000 calories, 20% of your caloric intake was from saturated fat.

But if on this day you really consumed 4000 calories while eating the 44 grams of saturated fat, look what happens to the numbers! Running up the calories changes the percentage—so 44 grams of saturated fat is only 10% of the 4000 calories eaten that day. Someone might kid himself into thinking that this is meeting the goal.

It should be obvious that it isn't very healthful for a person who needs 2000 calories in a day to eat 4000 calories. And eating 44 grams of saturated fat isn't so good, either—even though it calculates to be only 10% of the calories eaten that day.

Anyone can beat the system, at least on paper!

If you really try to cut down on saturated fat so your coronary arteries will stay open, don't play paper games to make the numbers look good. It doesn't work that way.

The intent of the guidelines is to limit the amount of fat to 10% or 7% of the number of calories *needed* in a day—not the number of calories that someone happens to consume on a binge.

The way we see it, 44 grams of saturated fat is way too much if you eat 2000 calories, or even if you happen to eat 4000 calories on any one day.

Our easier way

As we explained in our *Postgraduate Medicine* article, "It seems to us that for simplicity, consistency and better compliance, *there should be* a specific limit on the number of grams of saturated fat to be eaten each day."

Using a certain number of grams of saturated fat as a daily guide is much easier than coming up with a lot of calculations at every meal.

Many people follow the North-American pattern of eating 100 grams of saturated fat or more each day with an average intake of saturated fat between 50 and 70 grams a day. So, the obvious question is, "What should the daily limit of saturated fat be for those concerned about cholesterol, especially those at high risk?"

Let's begin with the Step 1 and Step 2 recommendations of the expert panel of The National Cholesterol Education Program. We'll use these as a guideline to help answer this question as it applies to you.

How many calories per day?

The first thing you need to do is to decide on the maximum number of calories you should consume each day. Of course this depends on several factors.

If you ask your doctor—a very good idea—this is probably the kind of reasoning he or she will go through to help you figure this out.

How much do you weigh?

Is this about right—too much or too little? Have you been gaining, losing or staying about the same weight?

Do you do quiet sedentary work or are you the hardest-working lumberjack in the world?

Is it very cold where you spend most of your time, or is it relatively comfortable or extremely hot? People doing consistently heavy work, especially in cold weather, require more calories than sedentary folks, particularly where it is hot.

Are you large or small?

Are you a male or a female?

If you have no idea how many calories you should be eating each day, here are some general guides, assuming you are:

✔ average size and weight
✔ activity level about midrange
✔ between the ages of 23 and 50

If you are female, assuming the above factors, you are probably consuming around 2000 calories a day. If you are male, assuming the same factors, you should probably consume about 2500 calories per day.

After determining the maximum calories you should

be eating, it usually is not necessary to count calories every day just to control your cholesterol. If you have a problem with weight or with another medical problem, such as diabetes, you and your doctor need to know your daily caloric intake. If you don't have another problem, let's use your estimated caloric need to figure your daily limit of saturated fat.

How much saturated fat per day?

Unless there are some unusual variables, you may decide that you need somewhere between 1200 and 3000 calories a day. Your doctor can help you zero in on the number of calories best for you. Now, let's look at how needed calories relate to your saturated-fat limit.

Your caloric need:	10% of calories as saturated fat	7% of calories as saturated fat
1000 calories	11 grams	8 grams
1500 calories	17 grams	12 grams
2000 calories	22 grams	16 grams
2500 calories	28 grams	19 grams
3000 calories	33 grams	23 grams

As you can see, using the guidelines created by The National Cholesterol Education Program Expert Panel, the majority of folks on a cholesterol-control program need to limit their intake of saturated fat to somewhere between 11 and 28 grams per day.

Although detailed information isn't available, we estimate that people from various cultures whose total cholesterol levels average 150 (3.9) probably eat about 10 to 15 grams of saturated fat per day.

Perhaps you are at particularly high risk with an elevated total-cholesterol level. If your total cholesterol is very high and your total-cholesterol/HDL-cholesterol ratio is over 4.5, you and your doctor may decide to limit your intake of saturated fat to as little as 10 grams.

You need to make a decision as to how many grams

of saturated fat you are willing to eat or not eat a day—depending on the calories you should be consuming, your total cholesterol level and total-cholesterol/HDL-cholesterol ratio. You need to consider other risk factors such as any previous history of heart disease such as a heart attack or even angina, a family history of coronary-artery disease, high blood pressure, being a male or being a smoker.

By the time you come up with an answer, you may decide to limit your saturated fat to 10, 12, 15, 18, 20 or 28 grams per day—or some other level that seems appropriate depending on circumstances.

The important thing is that you can and will get out of the rut of eating 50, 60, 70 or 100 or more grams of saturated fat a day as you may have been doing.

We would like to see carefully done research studies to confirm the optimal daily amounts of saturated fat to prevent coronary-artery disease. But we think more than enough evidence exists now for you to make major changes in reducing the amount of saturated fat you have been eating.

Choosing your saturated-fat target

If you are trying to get rid of plugged-up coronary arteries, have already had a heart attack, or if you are in the high-risk category for any reason, we think you should choose a target close to 10 grams of saturated fat a day.

If you are having trouble getting your cholesterol down by adjusting your diet, or if you have already had a heart attack or bypass surgery, you might consider limiting your intake of saturated fat to less than 10 grams a day.

Borderline?

What if you are not in a high-risk category right now? If you don't have a high total cholesterol and if you have a high HDL cholesterol so your total-cholesterol/HDL-ratio is low, you don't have much to worry about. But what if your cholesterol level is border-line? Obviously you can, and are, going to eat as much bad fat as you decide. You might decide to eat between 10 and 20 grams or a little more saturated fat a day. That would be pretty good, certainly better than most of your friends and neighbors.

But recall the eating patterns of folks who don't get heart attacks—those who eat mostly fish and rice, and lots of grains and legumes. Their saturated-fat intake is probably 10 to 15 grams a day. For anyone concerned about cholesterol, limiting saturated fat to 10 to 15 or even up to 20 or 28 grams a day is a lot smarter than eating 28 grams of saturated fat in one meal.

Get motivated

Cutting down on excessive saturated fat makes sense. How much you cut down depends on a lot of variables, including your own motivation.

We know that scaring people about health consequences is not the most powerful motivator in the world. It should be a good motivator, but it isn't always.

Why?

Because, all too often, folks rationalize behavior and activities. They think, "People really should wear seat belts, stop smoking, not do drugs, have pap smears taken, but I'll do it later—because it won't happen to me!"

People sometimes think they are invincible—that things happen to everyone else—but not to them.

The fat-plaque story we've been telling you is real. *It can happen to you.*

The odds are terrible.

But you can improve the odds. A big step toward doing so is to cut down significantly on the amount of saturated fat you eat.

"Well, I'm almost convinced, but how do I do it?" A

good beginning is to choose extra-lean select beef. This means no regular hamburger, bacon or sausage that is loaded with bad fat. When you want ground meat, choose only the leanest meat to grind—with no visible fat. When you choose a roast or steak, make it very lean select grade without any marbling. Even after you choose very-lean, select-grade meat, you or the butcher will trim off all the fat you can see. Even after getting rid of this obvious fat, it is wise to eat very-lean meat sparingly in 3- or 4-ounce servings instead of in 6- to 14-ounce portions. You should also eat fish and seafood meals frequently. Get a kitchen scale so you can check the weight of portions you are serving.

Egg yolks are a major problem

Because egg yolks contain so much cholesterol (as well as saturated fat), eat egg substitutes and cook with egg whites only, no yolks. Even if you are not in a high-risk group, limit eggs to one or two a week—or fewer.

Choose non-fat milk products

Adults who need to cut down on their saturated-fat intake should choose non-fat yogurt, non-fat cottage cheese, non-fat milk and very-low-fat cheese. Buttermilk and 1% milk are not as good as non-fat milk. They do contain less fat than whole milk so you may choose them occasionally. If you have a cholesterol problem, avoid whole milk, cream, ice cream, ordinary cheese or other dairy products containing butterfat.

"But how do I determine how much saturated fat to limit myself to?"

Start by keeping a running count of the grams of bad fat you eat in a day. This isn't hard to do.

Just count the grams of saturated fat in the things you eat.

"But isn't this a bother?"

Sure it is. However, it's lots easier than counting

calories and calculating percentages, too. We said this program would be *simple,* but we never said it would be *easy.*

We'll help you so it won't be as bad as you think. If you are convinced you will have a longer and more pleasant life, it is worth doing something a little different. To cut down on the saturated fat you eat requires *planning ahead.* It requires *thinking.* It requires *making some new choices.* It requires *doing something* about it.

Eat well while limiting your fat intake

However, this plan doesn't mean you can't eat good things.

But it does mean choosing different kinds of good things, eliminating the bad things you and most other people eat. This takes effort, but it is well worth it.

Limiting the amount of saturated fat you consume is one of the most important things you can do to prevent fat from plugging up your arteries. And you can do it while eating delicious and enjoyable food.

Eating enjoyable food while limiting the intake of saturated fat to 10 to 15 or even 20 to 28 grams a day means a whole new way of shopping, cooking and eating.

Of course, it is entirely up to you—entirely!

If you have a total cholesterol of 150 (3.9), an HDL cholesterol of around 43 (1.1) so your total-cholesterol/HDL ratio is about 3.5, you probably have been limiting your saturated-fat intake. Or, you may have a fortunate genetic makeup. If so, on the basis of what we know right now, you probably don't have much to be concerned about at this time.

If you choose to eat 30 or 40 grams of saturated fat a day, you will be doing better than most people. But you probably don't want to be like most people. You don't want fat plugging up your coronary arteries.

If you have any reason whatsoever to be concerned about cholesterol, limit your saturated-fat intake to between 10 and 28 grams per day. But, the more "at risk" you are, the closer you should strive toward a 10-grams-per-day limit.

If you carefully limit the saturated fat you eat to around 10 to 15 grams or so a day, you will probably not eat too much unsaturated fat, either. But just because we are not suggesting you count up all the grams of unsaturated fat you eat, please don't go overboard. Don't start consuming big amounts of corn or other oils—even if it is mostly unsaturated. And don't invent recipes for ice cream or other things that use huge amounts of oil, even if the oil is a *preferred* one.

Make a commitment

Now we hope you will make a commitment to limit your saturated-fat intake to a certain number of grams per day. Exactly how many grams is for you to decide.

You know, or can find out, enough information to make a very intelligent decision. Do it.

Recheck your cholesterol level

After two months, have your cholesterol levels checked again. If your total cholesterol or triglyceride levels do not come down to healthy levels—and if your total-cholesterol/HDL-cholesterol ratio does not drop to less than 4.5—set a new lower daily saturated-fat limit.

Stick with your new limit and check your numbers again in another 60 days. With your doctor's help, the Fatgram Tables, clues and recipes in this book, you will probably be able to get your cholesterol numbers looking quite respectable. If you can't, your doctor can help you with medications.

But it all starts with an ongoing low-saturated-fat eating program.

Good sense is very important. Use it!

5

Keeping Track of
Your Bad-fat Intake

Think about all the saturated fat so many people are cramming into their bodies and how quickly these grams of bad fat add up. Then think about the limit of saturated fat you will set for yourself.

How do you keep track of your bad-fat intake?

No one wants to go on a diet.

No one wants to change or eat foods that are not good. We know you won't eat things you don't like.

We also know that most families eat a regular pattern of relatively few foods. Although each culture has its own typical meal pattern and typical menus, there is also a wide variation of favorite menus and dishes within each.

Unfortunately, the repetitive meal patterns most people eat are usually loaded with saturated fat. And this may be happening in your kitchen and dining room today.

It is pointless to try to convince you to limit yourself to anyone else's favorite dishes. The two of us enjoy some of the same basic foods, but our favorite meals differ.

No change is easy. But as long as you have an opportunity to change and have wide enough choices, it isn't difficult.

It would be useless for us to pick out a menu for you

day after day. You wouldn't like it—so we won't.

But we will help you figure out how easy it is to count *fatgrams* along the way—and then help you come up with some ideas about different ways to choose and prepare foods that are not loaded with bad fat.

One fun way to discover new favorite recipes is to refer to the recipe section, page 135, then have low-fat potluck dinners with different groups of friends. This is a good way to exchange favorite recipes.

"But can't I ever have a big hamburger, French fries and milkshake again?"

Yes, you can have big hamburgers, French fries and milkshakes three times a day, every day for the rest of your life if you want. You can also eat straight lard and pounds of butter if you choose. Or, when you want a hamburger, you can choose to make your own out of select lean beef without any visible fat.

It is your choice

You can choose to eat all that bad fat—and choose to have a heart attack and not feel as well along the way. Or you can choose not to have a heart attack.

How much saturated fat have you eaten in the last 24 hours? Because it is very important for you to know how much bad fat you eat, it will be very helpful for you to stop and figure it out.

If this is a typical day for you, write down everything you ate. If it hasn't been typical, write down what you usually eat for breakfast, lunch and supper—and don't forget the snacks, all of them. Write down anything and everything you have had to eat and drink other than absolutely plain water. Use the Bad-Fat Tally, page 58.

Write down everything . . . *everything!*

Put each different food on a separate line.

Then check the Fatgram Tables, page 106, for the number of grams of saturated fat and the milligrams of cholesterol in each and every thing you have eaten today.

Then add up the numbers.

How much saturated fat and cholesterol do you think you usually eat in a day? You may be surprised at the real totals.

It isn't necessary to weigh and measure everything you eat, but ask your butcher to show you samples of various portions of different kinds of meat and fish weighing three, five, six and eight ounces. You can then estimate the weight of a piece of meat just by looking at it. It is even better to get a kitchen scale so you will know the exact weight of the the portion sizes you are creating.

The tables indicate typical servings of various foods. If you eat much more or less than an ordinary serving, change the amount of fat accordingly. You'll be interested to see how much fat you consume. Many North Americans eat over 100 grams of saturated fat a day—which is a lot of bad fat!

But let's get back to figuring out how much bad fat you are eating.

By the time you finish calculating the quantity of saturated fat you consumed in the past 24 hours, we think you will be ready to do something about changing your eating habits.

Keeping track

As you shift into a pattern of eating less bad fat, keep track of the grams of saturated fat and milligrams of cholesterol you consume for the next three days, preferably including two weekend days. Your Bad-Fat Tally will help make this easier. Once you get an idea of what foods you can eat to achieve the daily limit of fat you choose, you probably won't need to write down everything every day.

Even after you get into the system, you will probably find it helpful to keep a Bad-Fat Tally of everything you eat one day a week or so. We suggest choosing a Saturday or Sunday. If you keep a tally at least one day a week for several weeks, it will make it easier to learn how much saturated fat is in the common foods you eat. You will then begin to get a pretty good "handle" on how to eat wisely.

Pick some of the non-fat and low-fat recipes in the recipe section—or some others you know about or figure out. If you choose to have oatmeal and a serving of legumes such as navy or great northern white beans every day, these complex carbohydrates will start dropping your cholesterol. As you fill up on these things along with apples, oranges, bananas and other fresh fruits and vegetables, you should be well on your way to being much healthier—and looking ahead to having no fat plaques in your coronary arteries.

Keep track. Jot down the grams of fat every time you eat. This may be one of the most important things you have done in a long time. Just do it—and keep it up.

No one will check on what you are doing. You are on the honor system. The entire program is up to you. It's *your* heart—and *your* life. Cheaters are buried.

If you keep track of the amount of saturated fat and cholesterol you are eating, it will make it easier to limit the bad fat that gets into your body. It's simple.

Let's look at several popular foods and add up the numbers: Suppose you had a breakfast of two sunny-side-up fried eggs, two strips of bacon, a piece of toast spread with butter and a glass of milk or a cup of coffee with 1 tablespoon of cream. How much saturated fat and cholesterol did you eat?

	Saturated Fat (grams)	Cholesterol (mg)
2 eggs	3.4	550
1 tsp butter	2.3	10
3 strips bacon, thin	3.3	16
1 piece toast	0.2	0
1 tsp butter	2.3	10
Coffee with tbsp light cream	2.0	10
Totals	13.5 grams	596mg

This is 13.5 grams of saturated fat—and 596mg of cholesterol—and the day has just started!

Compare this with a breakfast of oatmeal and sugar, non-fat milk, orange juice, 2 pieces of toast with a low-fat diet spread and jam, and a cup of non-fat chocolate milk or coffee with a low-fat creamer.

	Saturated Fat (grams)	Cholesterol (mg)
1 cup rolled oats	0.4	Trace
Sugar	0	0
Non-fat milk	0.3	Trace
1 cup orange juice	0	0
2 pieces toast	0.4	0
1 tablespoon soft diet spread	1.0	0
2 tablespoons jam	0	0
1 cup of no-fat chocolate milk	0.8	10
Totals	2.9 grams	10mg

This only adds up to 2.9 grams of saturated fat—with almost no cholesterol.

That's quite a difference.

You may grimace at the prospects of oatmeal instead of sunnyside-up eggs and bacon—but doesn't it sound better than all that fat plugging up your coronary arteries?

And with an intake of only 2.9 grams of saturated fat for breakfast, there is still some room for a little fat at lunch and dinner—for flavor and proper nutrition.

But don't get so cocky about doing so well for breakfast that you blow all the good down the drain at lunch.

Think about some alternative lunch menus.

And coming up with some good ideas for dinner is going to take some imagination, too.

Here's another practical example: you saw the differences in the amount of saturated fat in the two breakfasts. Let's look at a typical fast-food lunch consisting of a hamburger with cheese, French fries and a chocolate shake. While this particular burger doesn't have the most fat, it has a lot:

	Saturated Fat (grams)	Cholesterol (mg)
Big hamburger with cheese	15	100
French fries (in unsat. fat)	7	0
Chocolate shake	6	30
Totals	28 grams	130mg

Now suppose you try a safer lunch like a chicken-breast sandwich? A broiled, roasted or microwaved chicken-breast sandwich cooked without skin or extra fat contains only 2 to 3 grams of saturated fat and between 70 and 100mg of cholesterol.

Suppose you eat this sandwich and have a glass of chocolate skim milk and an orange for your lunch? How many grams of saturated fat are you eating?

	Saturated Fat (grams)	Cholesterol (mg)
Chicken breast 3 oz.	1.0	70
Whole wheat bread (2 slices)	0.6	0
Lettuce	0	0
Fresh bean sprouts	0	0
Chocolate skim milk	0.8	10
Orange	0	0
Totals	2.4 grams	80mg

Here's another idea that may seem strange at first. How about a bean sandwich?

"A bean sandwich?"

Sure! It's delicious.

You're probably thinking we are crazy, but it's an adaptation of the Mexican Burrito served in the Southwest. Try it, we think you will like it.

Begin with *cooked* great northern, navy, pinto or other beans—cooked vegetarian style *without added meat or fat*. Combine 1 cup drained beans with 2 chopped small onions. Mash the beans and onions. Do this in a blender or food processor if you wish. Cover two slices of low-fat whole-wheat bread with a layer of romaine lettuce. Spread the bean mix on top. Add salsa, tomato sauce or mustard to taste. Salt and pepper are optional. You could add a layer of bean sprouts. Top with bread, completing the two sandwiches. If you want to add spice, stir chopped green chilies into the bean mix. These are available in mild or hot varieties. To make a burrito, roll the beans in a flour tortilla. Be sure to buy the new flour tortillas that are made with vegetable oil instead of lard. Always get that kind, of course!

If you eat both these sandwiches and have a glass of chocolate skim milk and an orange for your lunch? How many grams of fat will you get in this lunch?

	Saturated Fat (grams)	Cholesterol (mg)
Beans	trace	0
Whole wheat bread (4 slices)	1.2	0
Lettuce	0	0
Fresh bean sprouts	0	0
Chocolate skim milk	0.8	10
Orange	0	0
Totals	2.0 grams	10mg

Besides tasting good and being filling, this lunch gives you plenty of protein and other nutrients—and look how little fat there is.

Or you might choose a lunch of French Onion Soup, page 149, or one of the many other soups, salads or other gourmet dishes in the recipe section, or a fruit plate with rolls and a jam sandwich with juice.

These lunches contain 25 grams or so less saturated fat than a lunch like the hamburger with cheese, fries and a milk shake.

How about supper?

Let's see how much fat is in an all-too-typical supper, at least for some—a 9-ounce sirloin steak, hash-brown potatoes, peas, milk and a piece of pie.

	Saturated Fat (grams)	Cholesterol (mg)
9-oz. sirloin steak (marbled)	33	270
Hash Brown Potatoes* (cooked in preferred oil)	6	trace
Green peas	0	0
Butter 2 teaspoons	4.7	20
Milk, 1 cup	5	33
Pie	4	30
Totals	52.7 grams	353mg

Just look at the numbers.

But instead of all this fat for supper, take a look at what happens if you choose a 3-ounce piece of very-lean flank steak. Soak the meat in Worcestershire sauce, then sprinkle it with coarse or freshly ground pepper. Then broil it over a charcoal, electric or gas grill.

	Saturated Fat (grams)	Cholesterol (mg)
3-oz. very lean flank steak	4	50
Baked potato	0	0
Green peas	0	0
Soft diet margarine, 1 tbs.	1	0
Choice of soup		
Russian Borscht*		
Navy Bean*		
Spiced Tomato*		
Minestrone*		
Cauliflower Curry*	trace	0
Juice	0	0
4 Oatmeal cookies*	trace	0
Raspberry sorbet*	0	0
Totals	5 grams	50mg

* see recipes in recipe section

If during the past 24 hours you ate this meal, the chicken sandwich lunch and oatmeal breakfast, how much saturated fat and cholesterol do you think you would have consumed?

The results add up to 10.3 grams of saturated fat and 140mg of cholesterol . . . for the entire day!

On the other hand, if you ate the three typical high-fat meals we described, you would have consumed 92.4 grams of saturated fat and 1079mg of cholesterol—in just one day!

Look at the difference.

Here's another example of how much bad fat and cholesterol can be eaten so easily in a day—compared to how little bad fat and cholesterol can be eaten by making different choices.

Another meal comparison is on the next page.

By now you can see why three-fourths of North Americans and many others who eat high-saturated-fat diets have fat plaques starting to plug up their arteries. Most of these people have no idea this is happening!

But you do. And maybe you are a little worried. We hope you are.

One thing for sure, we are worried about you—and we hope you are worried enough to want to do something about it.

The recipes in the recipe section are a big help, but it takes a significant amount of initiative, thought, planning and effort to avoid overeating fat.

Watch your cholesterol intake, too

While you are watching the saturated fat, also keep your cholesterol intake to less than 300mg a day. Or, even better, less than 200mg per day with very few exceptions—especially if you are in a high-risk group.

If you are in a high-risk group and decide to use a day's limit of cholesterol and more for an egg, remember the yolk alone contains 275mg of cholesterol. All that cholesterol is in the yolk, whether you eat it alone or use the egg in something you cook. We recommend not eating yolks very often. How often? If you are not in a high-risk group, don't eat more than one or two eggs a week.

Comparison of two daily meal plans

	High-saturated-fat meals			Low-saturated-fat meals	
	Sat. fat (gm)	Chol. (mg)		Sat. fat (gm)	Chol. (mg)
Breakfast					
1 c orange juice	0	0	1 c orange juice	0	0
3 strips bacon	3	15	1 c oatmeal with		
1 egg	1.7	275	raisins	0.4	0
2 slices toast	0.6	0	Skim milk for cereal	0.3	0
1 T butter	7	30	1 plain bagel	0.3	0
1 c coffee/tea	0	0	1 t soft diet margarine	0.3	0
1 T cream	2	20	1 T strawberry jam	0	0
			1 c coffee/tea	0	0
			2 t low-fat creamer	1	0
Lunch					
1 large cheeseburger	15	100	Tossed salad with		
1 serving French fries	7	15	salsa	0	0
10-oz. strawberry			Great northern beans with		
milk shake	6	30	barbecue sauce	Trace	0
1 piece cherry pie (made			6-oz. broiled skinless		
with veg. shortening)	4	0	chicken breast	2	140
			Mushrooms	0	0
			1 T olive oil to sauté		
			mushrooms	2	0
			2 slices non-fat bread	0	0
			1 T soft diet margarine	1	0
			12-oz. orange freeze	0	0
Supper					
1 c cream of mushroom			1 c consommé	0.3	0
soup	3	20	6 oz. orange roughy	0.2	30
6-oz. sirloin steak			1 T rapeseed oil to		
(marbled)	13	150	sauté fish	1	0
Hash-brown potatoes			Seafood sauce	0	0
(fried in vegetable oil)	6	Trace	Baked potato w/chives	0	0
Broccoli	0	0	Green peas with		
2 T Hollandaise sauce	4	15	lemon pepper	0	0
2 baking powder			3 slices regular bread	1	0
biscuits	2	Trace	1 T soft diet margarine	1	0
1 T hard margarine	2	0	Spinach and tomato salad,		
1 avocado	5	0	with vinegar dressing	0	0
2 brownies	4	30	Angelfood cake with		
			strawberries and glaze	0	0
Snacks					
2 glazed donuts	10	20	1 apple or banana	0	0
1 serving creamy fruit			1 serving low-fat/non-fat		
yogurt	5	30	yogurt	0.3	0
Totals	100.3	750		11.1	170

T, tablespoon; t, teaspoon; c, cup.
Sat. fat = Saturated Fat
Chol. = Cholesterol

Figure 5-1

If you are in a high-risk group, use egg whites or an egg substitute such as Egg Beaters® instead.

Eggs taste good, but they certainly run up the cholesterol in a hurry. Fortunately egg whites alone or with Egg Beaters® can be used in many recipes without a noticeable difference in taste. Besides the 275mg of cholesterol, each egg yolk also has 1.7 grams of saturated fat. Incidentally, no egg yolks are used in any of our 200 recipes.

Fat is hidden everywhere

Remember, globules of fat are everywhere—well, almost everywhere. Fat abides in so many foods most people eat today that it takes careful planning to avoid consuming large amounts of it.

One gram here, five grams there. Keep track of each.

The key is to keep saturated-fat intake to around 10 to 28 grams a day or less. Remember, much of the fat you eat should be monounsaturated fat or omega-3 fat.

Just as it is fun and a challenge to improve on your golf or bowling score, it can be just as much fun to figure out how to eat enjoyable foods without too much fat.

Eating out

Dining at home and away while escaping the fat trap can be an intellectual challenge.

It means lots of thinking because foods and snacks don't jump out of the refrigerator or off the table with a number of fatgrams written on them. It's not that hard to figure out—and you will soon remember how much fat common foods contain.

Turn to Chapter 10 for tips on eating out.

Snacks

Look out! There are sneaky sleepers such as chocolate which comes with lots of saturated fat, non-dairy creamers loaded with coconut oil and peanut butter made with coconut oil. Then there's the little package of peanuts with a notation on the package saying: "Roasted in peanut or coconut oil." There is a big difference. Peanut oil is mostly monounsaturated. Coconut oil is saturated. If you don't know which oil the manufacturer used for *that* package, choosing to eat those peanuts may provide a lot more saturated fat than you really want. Incidentally, "roasted" in the case of nuts means deep-fried.

A good alternative to munching peanuts, chips and other snack foods made with saturated fat is to eat fresh or dried fruits.

Breads

The same problem of innocent-looking foods being overloaded with saturated fat occurs with bakery goods. Many content labels say "Baked with lard, vegetable, palm, palm kernel or coconut oils." When a label says this, assume the worst. It probably *is* cooked with undesirable, saturated fat.

What about the bread you usually eat?

Unfortunately, most commercial bread is baked with lard, palm, palm kernel or coconut oil, so most loaves of white bread and whole-wheat bread found on grocers' shelves contain saturated fat.

Although traditional French bread is made without any fat, all too often French bread is made with butter or another saturated fat. Classic French Bread, page 196, is made without oil.

The grams of saturated fat in ordinary bread add up if a lot is consumed—especially with too much spread. It's worse if the spread is butter or cream cheese.

You need to read labels to know for sure about how much saturated fat your favorite brand of bread contains. Many breads contain 0.2 to 0.3 gram of bad fat per slice. This doesn't sound like much until you observe how many slices of bread some people eat at a sitting— not to mention the tablespreads that go on it. And then there are baking-powder biscuits that may contain a full gram of saturated fat. Croissants are even worse. Doughnuts may top the list at about 4 grams of saturated fat each.

The amount of fat in plain bread is not the main fat problem. Under the best programs you are going to eat some bread that contains a little saturated fat.

But there is a way around getting too much saturated fat in bread.

You can bake bread with unsaturated fat. Or, if you look hard enough, you may find some high-fiber, low-calorie breads made without any fat!

How can you tell?

Read labels—just be sure the label doesn't say it is baked with butter, lard, animal fat, palm oil or coconut oil. We are looking forward to the day when more bread will be made without saturated fats—but in the meantime it takes looking and choosing to avoid saturated fat in bread.

Some English muffins and some English muffin breads don't contain any bad fat. It depends on the recipe.

Did you know that plain bagels usually contain only 0.2 gram of bad fat?

There are egg bagels, too, that are much higher in cholesterol. Bagels are often served with a big portion of butter or cream cheese, even when the bagels themselves are almost fat-free. You can make a very good non-fat cream-cheese substitute. See Yogurt Cream Cheese, page 301.

Obviously the total amount of saturated fat is what counts—and lots of things are much worse than most kinds of bread. But unless you choose real French bread or other completely non-fat breads, the bad fat can add up if you eat a lot of bread.

There are delicious homemade-bread recipes in the recipe section that you can make with preferred oils, especially those containing mostly monounsaturated fat or the ones that contain mostly polyunsaturated fat.

You probably didn't want to know about all this. Maybe you are thinking it would be easier to close this alarming book and to forget about the whole thing.

Well, that certainly is the easiest thing to do. But remember your coronary arteries. Consider the saturated fat that already may be starting to coat the inside walls of your coronary arteries.

You can do what many others do and ignore the whole thing.

Ignoring the bad fat in croissants, cheese, ice cream, hamburgers, fries and other food doesn't remove the fat—and it certainly doesn't help make it go away.

The fat is there, even if you don't pay attention to it. There are some very good ways you can avoid all this hard, white fat. It doesn't need to get in your coronary arteries. You don't need the stuff.

The grams of fat in bread add up a gram or so at a time—unless you happen to pick up some of the specialty breads, such as croissants or muffins which are typically loaded with butter, lard, coconut oil and other saturated fats. Then the fat adds up much faster.

Be careful!

Along with a very nice low-fat, low-cholesterol breakfast served on a flight from Boston, a delicious-looking croissant sat there on the tray just asking to be eaten. What would you do if you came face to face with a croissant on an airplane? There was also one of those little plastic containers of strawberry jam. The solution? The jam went on one small corner of the tasty-looking croissant. One small bite. A really tiny one. Then the rest of the jam went on a second little bite—and that was it. The rest of the croissant went back on the tray with napkin, empty juice cup and dirty dishes.

Think about it. You will find it challenging and even fun to make new choices.

Other hidden Fat

You may be surprised to learn that fat is hidden in other foods. Extra fat is often added to frozen turkeys and even to some fresh ones to enhance the flavor—and, maybe to increase the weight.

Carry your label-reading habit to the meat and frozen-food sections of the market. If all the frozen brands have had butter or other saturated fat added, look for a fresh turkey that has not been pre-basted with butter or other saturated fats.

It's up to you

It doesn't make much sense to cheat yourself!

What have you been eating these past 24 hours—or what do you usually eat in a typical day?

Stop right now and write down everything you have eaten in the past 24 hours on the following Bad-Fat Tally Be honest! Include meals, snacks and munching.

Add up the grams of saturated fat you have eaten during that time. It will only take a few minutes. Then add up the milligrams of cholesterol.

How much of these two things have you eaten?

The results will surprise you.

Record your Bad-Fat Tally for the past 24 hours (or a recent typical day) on the chart on the following page. Or, copy the chart if you prefer.

It's your life!

Bad-fat Tally

Date_____

Food Description	Amount Saturated Fat	Cholesterol
_____	_____ grams	_____mg
_____	_____ grams	_____mg
_____	_____ grams	_____mg
_____	_____ grams	_____mg
_____	_____ grams	_____mg
_____	_____ grams	_____mg
_____	_____ grams	_____mg
_____	_____ grams	_____mg
_____	_____ grams	_____mg
_____	_____ grams	_____mg
_____	_____ grams	_____mg
_____	_____ grams	_____mg
_____	_____ grams	_____mg
_____	_____ grams	_____mg
_____	_____ grams	_____mg
_____	_____ grams	_____mg
_____	_____ grams	_____mg
_____	_____ grams	_____mg
_____	_____ grams	_____mg
_____	_____ grams	_____mg
_____	_____ grams	_____mg
_____	_____ grams	_____mg
_____	_____ grams	_____mg
_____	_____ grams	_____mg
_____	_____ grams	_____mg
_____	_____ grams	_____mg
_____	_____ grams	_____mg
_____	_____ grams	_____mg
_____	_____ grams	_____mg
_____	_____ grams	_____mg
_____	_____ grams	_____mg
_____	_____ grams	_____mg
_____	_____ grams	_____mg
Totals	_____ grams	_____mg

Today's Bad-fat Tally

	Saturated Fat	Cholesterol
Breakfast		
	grams	mg
Lunch		
	grams	mg
Dinner		
	grams	mg
Snacks		
	grams	mg
TOTALS		
	grams	mg

Today's Bad-fat Tally

	Saturated Fat	Cholesterol
Breakfast		
	grams	mg
Lunch		
	grams	mg
Dinner		
	grams	mg
Snacks		
	grams	mg
TOTALS		
	grams	mg

Make copies so you can use these forms to keep track.

6

It Doesn't Have to be Loaded with Bad Fat to Taste Good

Fat enhances the flavor of foods.

But too many things we eat contain bad, saturated fat, are cooked in, or topped with bad fat to make them tasty and appealing.

There are ways to get around eating patterns that include eating too much bad fat.

We are not saying the new ways of cooking will exactly take the place of the old ways. The changes we suggest will mean some sacrifices. But the extra years you will live and the better quality of life you will enjoy during your extended life will be worth it.

The course you are setting is your own.

We'll give you some ideas—but it is up to you what you choose to eat and not eat.

We hope you will try our non-fat and low-fat recipes. You'll find a variety of enjoyable appetizers, salads, soups, entrées, breads, desserts, fruit drinks and treats.

Develop your own recipes, too

Be creative and come up with your own low-fat recipes. After enjoying some oatmeal cookies, we discovered that the recipe contained a half cup of oil—which seemed like quite a lot. Even though the amount of oil per cookie was moderate, the grams of bad fat added up when several cookies were eaten.

So, our recipe expert Helen Fisher invented a completely new recipe using only a small amount of peanut butter instead of oil. What really amazed us was the new recipe produced better-tasting cookies than the original.

We like these oatmeal cookies so much that we suggest the first new low-fat recipe you try be Delicious Oatmeal Cookies, page 281.

How about sour cream?

What about foods that are traditionally topped with butter or sour cream? Borscht is a hearty thick soup that looks and tastes better with a topping of sour cream. The creamy flavor and texture make the soup even more delicious. But a big spoonful of sour cream has too much fat and too much cholesterol to make it acceptable.

You may be able to find low-fat sour cream with only 1 gram of fat per tablespoon serving. An even better alternative to sour cream can be made by combining equal parts of non-fat cottage cheese and non-fat yogurt, whipping them in a blender until smooth and adding a touch of lemon before serving.

Or you may find plain non-fat yogurt with lemon juice is very satisfying. Another alternative is to make a cream-cheese substitute out of non-fat yogurt. A simple recipe is on page 301.

What to put on potatoes?

What about something to go on potatoes? Use the low-fat sour cream—or soft diet margarine. Just don't use too much.

You might wonder about using a commercial white substitute for sour cream. Unfortunately, you'd lose because most of these are hydrogenated or have palm, palm kernel or coconut oil that contain bad, saturated fats.

Plain non-fat yogurt combined with salt and pepper

can make a good topping for baked potatoes. Sprinkling some non-fat powdered Butter Buds,® Dash,® or Molly McButter® on top of the yogurt topping may make it even tastier. For variety add a small amount of grated Parmesan cheese.

Mashed potatoes can be enhanced with yogurt, or try our recipe for whipped potatoes.

Non-fat yogurt is made from skim milk—1% or 2% fat yogurt is not the same. These so-called *low-fat* yogurts are not the *"non-fat"* yogurt you should use.

Likewise, cottage cheese made with 1% and 2% milk is marked *low-fat cottage cheese*. These indeed contain less fat than creamy cottage cheese with 4% butterfat. But why settle for getting rid of part of the butterfat when very good non-fat yogurt and non-fat cottage cheese are available?

Speaking of non-fat yogurt and non-fat cottage cheese—or a blended mixture—these are a good base for dips and toppings. And either of them or a mixture can be used to create various salad dressings and sauces. Don't hesitate to add onion, garlic, mustard or salsa.

Yogurt is a good non-fat dessert

Keep yogurt in mind as a dessert. Non-fat yogurt is becoming more popular and more available all the time. Incidentally, if you want a product you don't see, tell your grocer or supermarket manager. When enough of us speak out, these foods will become more readily available.

Fresh, canned or frozen fruit can be added to plain non-fat yogurt for a variety of refreshing desserts, which can be sweetened to taste with sugar or a sugar substitute. You can make desserts just as good as the commercial yogurts—without the fat—at lower cost.

Then, if you wish, your fruit-flavored yogurt can be put in an ice-cream freezer and whipped into a creamy non-fat ice-cream-like frozen dessert.

Also, mixing fresh, canned or frozen fruits with non-fat yogurt in a blender can create a delicious, refreshing drink without the saturated fat from milk, cream or eggs.

Icy Orange Cooler, page 303, is a simple and delicious non-fat frozen drink. Make it by blending frozen orange juice or sections of oranges along with plain or frozen non-fat yogurt. This thick orange drink is similar to a popular orange drink, but without the saturated fat from eggs and milk.

More desserts

The frozen gourmet concoctions you can make with non-fat yogurt are limitless. Try some. You'll see.

Fresh-fruit ices and sorbets are excellent alternatives to milkshakes and malts. Try our frozen desserts. They are made with fresh strawberries, raspberries, pineapple, lemon, lime, or other fresh, frozen or canned fruits or juices. The amount of ice and time in the blender determines the thickness. They can range from a thin slush to an almost-solid sorbet. If you want to make a frappé, scoop the thick slush into paper or plastic cups and place in the freezer.

Enjoy guilt-free, fat-free frozen desserts and cooling drinks.

Fried foods soak up fat

"But what about my taste for fried foods?" Obviously some oil penetrates deep-fat-fried foods—or even those that are pan-fried. Of course, using predominantly unsaturated-fat oils is important. It is also important to learn to fry with very small amounts of oil.

Deep-fat frying—even with primarily good fats—adds quite a bit of saturated fat to what you eat. For example, a potato starts out with no fat. When it is chopped into 20 French fries, the surface area increases so more oil is soaked up as the potato strips cook in oil.

Then, if you slice another potato very finely into 40 potato chips and deep-fry them in oil, you greatly increase the surface area and oil that enters the potato.

How much fat have you added?

Compared to no fat in the original potato, 20 fries soak up 5.2 grams of saturated fat. The 40 potato chips soak up 8 grams of saturated fat. This is true even if the fries and chips are cooked in a preferred oil.

Of course, it is worse if the chips or fries are deep-fat-fried in lard or coconut or palm oil.

There are ways to beat the odds of a heart attack and enjoy low-fat gourmet dining. However, it requires discovering new techniques and skills, along with some willingness to be creative.

Broiling is best

Broiling boned-and-skinned chicken-breast strips on top of a grill makes a delicious entrée. Cook them plain or seasoned with lemon juice, Cajun seasoning or lemon pepper. Seafood strips can be prepared the same way, as can very-lean beef.

Although there is reason to be concerned about the amount of saturated fat in the usual cuts of pork, lamb and beef, there is a way to enjoy small servings of red meat without feeling guilty and without plugging up your coronary arteries. The idea is to start with extra-lean meat, using the FDA's new classification of beef. Choose the *select* grade. This grade used to be called *good*. Select grade contains less than 7% fat as compared with *prime,* which—with its marbling—can contain 32% fat.

Choosing a low-fat, select grade of beef is just the beginning. Trim off any remaining fat before cooking. This is also important in preparing chicken or turkey because as the meat cooks, a considerable amount of fat melts and soaks into the meat. Broiling is the best way to cook meat; some of the fat you may have missed or could not trim off will drip away.

How much beef?

As with everything we have been talking about, how much select lean beef you choose to eat—and how often—is up to you. We suggest limiting servings to 3 or 4 ounces. Even so, you should not do this very often because there is still more saturated fat in lean beef than you would get from seafood or skinless chicken breasts. But, if you carefully keep track of all the saturated fat you eat, you can enjoy extra-lean select beef from time to time while staying within your guidelines.

Soufflés

Do you like soufflés?

Maybe you have never had a soufflé. It is a delicious oven-puffed creation of eggs. It may include cheese. Why even talk about it when egg yolks and cheese are both on the "don't-use" list?

You can make a delicious puffy salmon soufflé, without egg yolks and cheese, that will bring lots of compliments. You'll find Salmon Soufflé on page 241.

If you like salmon and puffy gourmet things, you will love this hot dish.

There are plenty of other choices. The point is: Food doesn't have to be loaded with fat to taste good.

Don't snack on cheese

While trying to keep down your intake of meat, it's easy to think about the protein in cheese for snacks and main-course entrées. But most cheeses are *loaded* with saturated fat. For example, there are 6 grams of saturated fat in a 1-ounce serving of Cheddar cheese, plus about 30mg of cholesterol.

This 6 grams of saturated fat might be a large part of an entire day's allotment of saturated fat if you are trying to keep saturated fat to a minimum.

The worst part of this is that we are talking about a small serving. Most of us are used to eating several ounces of cheese at a time, on pizza, in cheese sauces, cheese crackers or cheese soup. This is discouraging.

Low-cholesterol, low-fat brands of imitation cheese, such as Lo Chol,® are now available. It contains only 3mg of cholesterol instead of about 30; only 0.3 gram of saturated fat per 1-ounce serving. That's very good!

Weight Watchers' Swiss-Flavored Cheese Product® contains less than 1 gram of saturated fat and 2mg of cholesterol per 1-ounce slice! Borden's Lite Line® cheese has similar fat and cholesterol content.

With a little ingenuity, a 1-ounce serving of one of these specially made imitation-cheese products can be stretched even more. Shred or cut up a 1-ounce slice. Sprinkle the pieces on a couple of pieces of bread that weren't made with lard or coconut or palm oil. Sprinkle basil or oregano over the cheese. Broil the bread with the bits of cheese on it. As the cheese melts, it spreads over the bread. By using the special low-fat cheese and then making it go twice as far by shredding it, you can enjoy two cheese sandwiches with only a small intake of saturated fat.

Special low-fat cheeses can be included in many other favorite recipes, so your enjoyment of cheese doesn't have to be sacrificed altogether. However, don't expect your taste buds to be fooled. The tastes and textures of these imitation cheeses are still a long way from the real thing.

Once you start thinking about good foods that are not filled with saturated fat, you will come up with more and more wonderful ways to fix them.

Remember that millions of people in the world eat good things every day that are not packed with fat. North Americans and a few others have become accustomed to eating lots of saturated fat—and it isn't necessary—not at all!

Food doesn't have to be loaded with saturated fat to taste good.

7

Fill Up on Complex Carbohydrates

Apples.

Apples.

Apples.

Apricots, bananas, mangoes, melons, peaches, pears, prunes, raisins, potatoes, yams, corn, rice, wheat, beans, and many other fruits, vegetables, grains and legumes contain lots of complex carbohydrates.

These are the good guys.

When you start eating less bad fat, you may lose some weight unless you make a conscious effort to eat more of other kinds of food. If you need and want to lose weight, great! If you don't, be sure to fill up on *complex carbohydrates*.

You can lose weight and feel better on a decreased intake of saturated fat, but be certain to keep your energy level up with a good balance of fruits, vegetables and legumes.

If you are about the right weight—or once you get to the weight you want to be—go ahead and fill up on complex carbohydrates.

By complex carbohydrates we mean foods like those listed above. These have various carbohydrate chains rather than simple sugars and starches.

Sugars and sugar substitutes in moderation are fine for most people. But don't fill up on candy or other straight sugar sweets. They are not only terrible for your teeth, but when they are eaten in great excess, too much of these simple carbohydrates may actually raise your LDL cholesterol and triglyceride levels. This is exactly what you don't want to happen.

Let's go back to the complex carbohydrates that include many of the good, wholesome, basic high-fiber grains and legumes.

Granola is a very-popular breakfast cereal. Because it contains grains, many people think of it as a health food. But as healthy as granola is thought to be, it has a big problem. It contains lots of saturated fat from coconut, one of its main ingredients. Unfortunately, granola may also contain coconut and palm oil.

A better choice is a high-fiber cereal with something other than coconut.

Oats help reduce cholesterol!

Oats are particularly helpful in reducing total cholesterol and the unwanted low-density lipoprotein (LDL) cholesterol levels. Additionally, oats probably increase HDL cholesterol. Some people call it the *miracle food* because of the role it can play in reducing cholesterol.

So, if you are in any way concerned about cholesterol, or have high triglycerides, eat a sizable serving of oatmeal or another oat cereal every morning. Or eat the same amount of oats in other things such as low-fat oatmeal cookies or oat-bran muffins. Instead of serving oatmeal with regular milk or cream, use non-fat skim milk. Try other combinations of oatmeal with equal parts of applesauce. Or cut up fresh fruit with sweetener added to taste. By the way, raisins make an excellent sweetener for oatmeal. Another variation is to pour maple syrup on the oatmeal or serve it with jam or preserves. Two other ways to serve oatmeal without milk are with sugar and sprinkled with grated orange rind or cinnamon.

Eating whole-grain cereals like oats and wheat used to be a standard good old-fashioned breakfast. Somehow many people got away from this very healthy habit. Let's face it, the aroma of bacon and eggs cooking is very enticing—and along with biscuits and butter, they taste wonderful. But, wow, are they loaded with saturated fat and cholesterol—particularly egg *yolks*. When folks started choosing bacon or sausage and eggs instead of old-fashioned rolled oats, the cholesterol problem really started picking up steam.

One of the problems today is that many people don't eat oats and other whole-grain cereals for breakfast. Fortunately, many are getting the word and are going back to eating oats for breakfast.

But the tide has just begun to turn—and not nearly fast enough.

It's as if oats were a big secret!

Oats are a very good source of protein, but interest has focused lately on the fact that oat fibers help to lower the LDL (bad) cholesterol and raise the good, HDL cholesterol.

People got away from eating oats for breakfast because it seems easier to slap an egg and some sausage or bacon on a muffin—and go off to work, to school and to play. The big hurry people are in, the availability of cold cereals and the impression that it takes a long time for oatmeal to cook are also reasons why oatmeal's popularity waned. It is coming back strong!

Oats manufacturers have microwave and stove-top instructions on their boxes. Add raisins or other fruit before cooking. Sprinkle some of your favorite 7-grain cereal, sugar or Grape-nuts® cereal on top of your oats for flavor and crunch!

Concoct whatever combination you want—as long as you get the oats—and don't ruin everything by putting cream or butter on the top!

Oatmeal costs only a few cents—far less than you'd pay for an egg on a muffin!

All oats are not the same.

It's not hard to figure out.

Oats start out with a tough outer husk that is scoured off. Then the oats are partially cooked with steam and crushed in a roller, so they are called *rolled oats*.

If rolled oats are chopped, sliced or cut up so the cereal cooks faster, they are called *one-minute* or *quick* oats. Rolled and quick oats are packaged without additives. Both rolled oats and quick oats contain oat bran. You can buy oat bran as a flour made from the outer seed casing or bran of the whole-grain oat. It can be cooked as a cereal or incorporated as an ingredient in many recipes.

Watch out! Some "instant oats," especially individual-serving packages, may contain added oils—frequently coconut, palm or palm kernel oil, plus salt and extra vitamins. You don't want any of these oils because they have the highest saturated fat content of all the oils! Some instant oatmeals contain almost a gram of saturated fat per serving.

It's back to reading labels. Be sure your oats are just plain—without coconut oil.

Cheerios® and oat-based cereals without added fats are excellent choices if you want to enjoy the benefits of oats without cooking. Here again, read the labels to make sure the oil used in maunfacturing is not coconut, palm or palm kernel oil.

Other complex carbohydrates

Other complex carbohydrates include wheat, rice, beans, peas, other legumes and grains. These complex-carbohydrate foods contain essential proteins. These are the foods that sustain millions of people throughout the world who eat little or no meat or other saturated fats.

Eating high-fiber complex carbohydrates helps to lower cholesterol, as does oatmeal. So it also helps to eat high-fiber complex carbohydrates such as beans, split peas or other legumes.

Many people who are not accustomed to eating legumes every day may find these dishes enjoyable as well as healthful.

Fruit is a great group of complex carbohydrates. Unfortunately, candy bars and other such snacks that contain lots of saturated fat have taken the place of fresh fruit as treats for many children and adults.

Imagine you were a director of a large advertising agency and someone offered plenty of money wanting you to create a series of radio or television commercials for an *apple*—not the computer, the fruit!

With a little thought and imagination, you could create a fantastic commercial—because the product is so perfect. Think about it—a self-contained, crunchy, delicious snack!

The trouble is, kids don't know this—and lots of grown-ups have forgotten.

Can you imagine what you could do with enough resources to create a commercial for oranges, pears, bananas, strawberries and other fruits?

When you really think about it, fresh fruits are more appealing than candy or almost any snack or fast food.

After a distinguished doctor's talk about reducing the fat intake for children to prevent coronary-artery disease, someone asked the question: "Which are the best fast foods for kids—McDonald's, Wendy's, Burger King's or Arby's?"

Unfortunately the speaker really missed the boat. What a perfect opportunity to answer, "Apples, bananas, oranges, grapes, pears!" But he didn't.

These and other high-fiber, complex-carbohydrate fruits help accomplish the goal of this book—to prevent the plugging of coronary arteries with fat. But high-fiber foods also help digestion. When these fruits and raisins, prunes or figs are eaten wisely, problems such as constipation may disappear and the risk of cancer of the colon decreases.

Fruits, legumes, vegetables and grains rich in high fiber and complex carbohydrates can provide multiple benefits. These are real *natural health foods*.

8

Don't Forget Seafood

If you thought we forgot fish, we didn't.

Remember, Japanese, Eskimos and others who consume a lot of fish and seafood don't typically have heart attacks from fat-plugged coronary arteries.

One of the factors in seafood that helps is omega-3 oil. It seems to help prevent the platelet cells in the blood from getting sticky, cutting down on the tendency for blood clots to occur.

You have probably heard the recommendation for fish and seafood dishes to be served twice a week.

Well, if it is good for us to eat fish or seafood twice a week, why not more often? Why limit the benefits?

Different seafood and even different types within the same group have different amounts of omega-3 oil. Salmon, mackerel, herring, sardines and, to some extent, trout have the most omega-3 oils.

Although you may frequently choose salmon or one of the other seafoods with high omega-3 oils, it makes good sense to eat a variety of seafoods.

What kinds of seafood are OK ?

You may have heard that a diet to control cholesterol excludes shellfish. But we say it is OK to eat all kinds of shellfish—within limits.

There are two groups of shellfish. The group that doesn't move includes clams, mussels, oysters and scallops. They simply lie on the bottom of the ocean and suck in *phytoplankton*—the vegetables of the sea. Like vegetarians everywhere, these creatures contain a very small amount of cholesterol. Shellfish were once thought to have a high cholesterol content, but we now know that the old cholesterol-measuring tests measured some fish and plant components as cholesterol—which they are not. And, shellfish are very low in saturated fat. Even if you have no desire to become a vegetarian yourself, you can eat a vegetarian from the sea.

It is also OK to eat the other group of shellfish—those that move. These include crabs, crayfish, shrimp and lobsters—officially called *crustaceans*.

Although crustaceans contain some cholesterol, they are quite low in saturated fat. Six medium-size shrimp (weighing about 100 grams or 1/4 pound) contain about 120mg of cholesterol, but only 0.3 gram of bad, saturated fat. When you consider both factors and compare shrimp to the same amount of skinless chicken breasts, the minuses are about the same.

The obvious good answer is that fish, clams, mussels, oysters and scallops are best. It's OK to eat a reasonable amount of chicken or turkey breasts, shrimp, crab, crayfish or lobsters. This means that an all-you-can-eat shrimp dinner isn't a good idea. But a half-dozen boiled, broiled or grilled shrimp may be just fine.

Don't get trapped into thinking just because something is seafood it is all right no matter how it is fixed. Preparation is very important.

Hold the butter!

Many people choose the right entrée, but choose shrimp drowned in deep fat or cooked as scampi in butter. Other fish are served or topped in butter or a cheese sauce.

The cod in "fish and chips" is a great choice—but the batter often contains saturated fat. And the fish fillets and chips are often fried in melted lard, thereby defeating the purpose of eating seafood.

Even if the fish and chips are deep-fried in an oil containing mostly unsaturated fat, the fish and batter soaking in the oil pick up a lot of saturated fat.

Instead of deep-frying fish or other seafood, it's better to grill or poach it.

Crab and lobster are commonly served with a dish of melted butter into which the seafood is dipped. Many grams of saturated fat can come from doing this. Skip the butter, please!

What can you put on fish?

One of the many good alternatives to cheese sauces, butter toppings and butter dips for seafood is seafood cocktail sauce made of catsup or chili sauce and horse-radish. Although seafood cocktail sauce is customarily served with cold shrimp, crab or lobster, it is delicious with almost any kind of hot seafood.

Some people like fish with malted vinegar.

Others prefer lemon or lime on their seafood.

Butter-flavored sauces and toppings can be made with non-fat Butter Buds® or Molly McButter.® These can be sprinkled on directly without any other preparation.

Others think just a little salt and pepper provides the perfect seasoning for seafood. Others prefer very spicy seasonings on seafood like the Cajun pepper used to prepare Blackened Redfish. Fish and seafood recipes start on page 227.

Which fish?

Some fish are more oily than others, but the omega-3 fats in them are beneficial.

If you haven't been accustomed to eating fish and seafood, begin with some of the milder varieties such as cod, haddock, orange roughy and halibut. When fresh or freshly frozen and thawed, they have a mild taste. Many people mistakenly believe cod has a strong taste because they remember the taste of cod-liver oil from their childhood. Yuk! Back then no one thought of putting the contents in a capsule or making a vitamin pill. Cod is a mild-tasting fish. Orange roughy and halibut join cod in being so mild that almost everyone who tries these fish likes them.

Trout is another delicious and mild fish with the added advantage of more omega-3 oil.

Salmon has even more omega-3 oil than trout. When fresh or smoked properly, salmon is mild and delicious—having a very distinctive taste. Salmon and trout are the mildest of fish with abundant omega-3 oils.

Crab, shrimp, scallops and lobster are also mild and tasty—and almost everyone who gives them a fair try likes them. There is a lot of psychology in tastes and eating preferences.

Serve seafood regularly

Hopefully seafood will become more popular in families so children will learn to enjoy it regularly instead of eating foods that are loaded with saturated fat.

Seafood is a wonderful source of protein. People who eat it regularly instead of meat are less likely to have plugged coronary arteries or heart attacks.

9

Balance What You Eat

You may be surprised to learn that most people exist on a repetitive course of eating. Most eat the same things day after day, alternating their meals among about 10 choices.

That does not represent very many main-course recipes! If you really want to beat the odds of a heart attack, which we think you do, look for new recipes from which you can choose your 10 favorites—or more if you want to expand your menu choices.

One way to do this is to get together with friends who share your enthusiasm for healthful eating. How about having a neighborhood potluck dinner for 10 families? Each family can bring one special low-fat recipe found in this book or from their own recipe files. Some can bring main courses, breads and salads, vegetables and legumes; others can bring desserts.

Each family should know something about the things we have been talking about so everything brought to the dinner will be low in saturated fat and cholesterol.

As you get together you will find that some recipes appeal to you more than others. Exchange recipes to get the ones you like. Then do the same thing again next week. After doing this for a while you will have the opportunity to taste 100 or so recipes. Chances are you will find really good recipes you and your family will enjoy. Then this won't be as difficult a change in your life as if you had to follow a rigidly planned meal-by-meal diet.

Choosing delicious foods that are not loaded with saturated fat will be a great new adventure.

There is no reason to go without good food.

It is just a matter of being selective.

There are lots of good foods we can eat without ending up with a heart attack.

Finding foods not loaded with fats can be fun. A challenge? Yes. But, it is up to you. We encourage you to try many of the recipes in this book—and then be creative.

Make up your own recipes

You will soon be adapting and making up your own non-fat and low-fat recipes. Look at the recipes in your favorite old recipe books and on notes and cards that have been handed down from the great cooks in your family and from friends. Don't think that just because something has always been done a certain way that it has to continue to be done that way. Substitute non-fat yogurt and skim milk for cream and sour cream. When you substitute a preferred oil for lard and butter, you may even make some improvements in your old recipes. When substituting oil for a solid shortening you can generally use 2/3 cup of oil for each 1 cup of solid shortening. But remember that even with preferred oils, 2/3 of a cup of oil in most family-size recipes is a lot of saturated fat per serving. You should expect to experiment to get the amount of oil to a minimum—while making the food taste just as you like it.

More helpful substitutions are listed on page 304.

Obviously not everything is going to work. Some things you create, just like some of the recipes we tried, may not be acceptable. But that won't happen very often.

Each of the recipes in our book lists the amount of saturated fat and cholesterol in a usual serving. You must judge if you eat more or less than an ordinary serving.

Until you get on a consistent low-saturated-fat eating pattern, keep notes every day. Write down how much cholesterol and saturated fat you've consumed. Keep a running total through the day and have a contest with yourself to see how well you do.

It's up to you to choose whether or not you are going to have a heart attack and the problems that follow as a result of the food you eat!

Obviously we are trying to get you to focus on the fats in your diet. The emphasis in this book is probably quite different from other things you have read about fats and cholesterol. For one thing we've made it simple and easy to understand.

We want to be sure you know that: **Your blood cholesterol level is what it is today more because of the saturated fat you have been eating than because of the cholesterol you have been eating.**

This is very important. It is so important, let's say it again. If your blood cholesterol is up more than it should be, it is more because of the large amounts of saturated fats you have been eating than how much cholesterol you have been eating.

Of course, you shouldn't eat too much cholesterol. But you know that even if you don't, your body manufactures too much cholesterol if you eat too much saturated fat.

We want to help you stop this excessive internal cholesterol production. We also want to help you do away with the fat plaques that have already formed in your arteries.

We want you to keep saturated fats out of your diet. If you cut down on these, you will automatically cut down on the amount of cholesterol you eat without really having to think about it.

Eat a balanced diet

When it comes to eating properly there are other things to think about besides avoiding saturated fats. You also need to be sure you get enough of the other right things like proteins, vitamins and minerals that you need to maintain good health.

People have been concerned about nutrition for a long time, but there has been an explosion of interest in the past 60 years. During the '30s and '40s many things were discovered about good nutrition. Dreaded diseases like pellagra, scurvy and rickets developed when people failed to eat a balanced diet. This was especially true in cities as people got away from growing and raising much of what they ate.

During that time there was a significant turnaround as people began to pay more attention to good nutritional principles which are now accepted as logic and common sense. Although the experts had some right answers, there were many wrong answers—especially about how much meat and dairy products were needed.

In addition to getting more citrus and other fruits to prevent vitamin-C deficiencies and scurvy, people who could afford to eat "properly" started eating so many eggs and so much milk, cheese and meat that it got way out of hand. Other errors and confusion on the part of the experts and public alike got things out of balance. No wonder there has been room for many wild and un-proved health practices, schemes, regimes and ideas—many of which prevail today.

Rules for good nutrition

But now we can safely focus on correct principles of nutrition, correcting the excesses of the past. There are a few rules to understand.

As the principles of nutrition were figured out, it became obvious that by eating foods from various food groups, many problems could be avoided and controlled. Foods were put into *four basic groups:*
- milk
- meat
- bread/cereal
- vegetable/fruit.

What was not so obvious was the correct balance in the consumption of these foods.

And when people were told these were "essential" food groups, they thought that if foods from the four basic groups were "essential" they must be "wholesome." And if they were "essential and wholesome," then more of them would be better than less. This was a big mistake, especially with butterfat and animal fat.

Even today most people still don't know how to enjoy eating a balance of foods in a healthful way.

Actually a better way to group foods is in *seven basic food groups:*

  ❦ Fish, poultry, legumes and meat
  ❦ Leafy green and yellow vegetables
  ❦ Citrus fruits, tomatoes and salad greens
  ❦ Potatoes, other vegetables and non-citrus fruits
  ❦ Grains, breads and cereals
  ❦ Fat
  ❦ Milk

Some foods from each group, or substitutes, are needed every day. Now that you know how important it is to cut way down on saturated fats, it should be obvious that *the amount of food needed from the different groups is certainly not equal.*

You can obtain a good nutritional balance by eating a good selection of food from each of the food groups every day. Of course this includes the fat group, which you are learning how to manage.

Milk in your diet

You probably are aware of healthy people such as the Japanese who do not drink milk.

But what about the milk group?

Milk is an excellent source of protein, calcium, vitamin D and other nutrients. Some people don't drink milk for cultural reasons; others because of allergies or intolerances. We speak out firmly about avoiding excesses of saturated fat in milk, cream and cheese. But, unless there is an allergy or a lactose intolerance that can't be controlled by adding a lactase enzyme, we encourage you to include non-fat milk products in your diet every day. Even if you don't like drinking skim milk, there are many ways to use non-fat milk products in making delicious desserts, shakes, drinks and other recipes with non-fat yogurt, non-fat cottage cheese, non-fat skim milk and now some very tasty low-fat cheese products. If there is an allergy or other reason that milk products are prohibited, other foods will need to be included. These occur naturally in the diets of the healthy cultures of the world where milk is not consumed.

Calcium

What about calcium in your new eating plan that includes limited milk and milk products? We are recommending a major change—because as you visualize the amount of saturated fat in cream, cheeses (other than the intentionally made low-fat imitations), ice creams, etc., you will find the grams of fat add up fast. It may not mean you can't ever have any of these foods, unless you are in a high-risk category or if you have a *hyperlipidemia* problem—too much fatty substance in the blood. But if you are in a high-risk group, you'll probably want to use non-fat milk products almost exclusively.

Even if you are not in a high-risk category, after learning how fat plugs up arteries, you might find yourself eating little bites and tastes. Eating big servings of ice cream and rich cheeses as you may have done in the past may no longer be appealing.

What about calcium?

There is calcium in non-fat yogurt, non-fat cottage cheese, low-fat cheese products and skim milk. It is reassuring to know there is calcium in green vegetables (especially broccoli, kale, mustard and turnip greens), potatoes and citrus fruits. For example, there is as much calcium in a cup of mustard greens as there is in a cup of milk.

Where do cows get their calcium?

They certainly don't get it from drinking milk. Cows get their calcium from grazing.

Calcium and other minerals will come from non-fat milk products and a variety of vegetables, grains, fruits and seafood.

Protein in your diet

Now, let's think about protein. Everyone needs some every day.

You are probably getting more protein than you need. Most North Americans eat about 100 grams of protein a day, probably too much and actually unhealthful. What you need as an adult is approximately *60 grams or a little more of protein a day.* Plan on getting about 20 grams of protein at each of three meals a day. It doesn't have to be exact and it usually won't be. You don't need to go around counting grams of protein at every meal. You have enough to do keeping track of fat intake.

However, think about this for a few more minutes— and then just keep the general plan in the back of your mind so you won't short yourself from getting enough protein.

A big bowl of oatmeal with skim milk will give you about 15 grams of protein. Add two pieces of whole-wheat toast and you will get a total close to 20 grams.

If you don't quite make it for breakfast, you probably will get a little more than 20 grams for lunch and again at supper. Just think about choosing other foods, especially legumes (navy beans, split peas, etc.), seafood and white chicken and turkey, as you selectively avoid choosing as much red meat as you used to eat.

When it comes time for lunch, most sandwiches with tuna, chicken, beans or a little lean meat will exceed 20 grams of protein. Or a bowl of split-pea or bean soup, brown rice, and other legumes and grains will add protein to your diet.

You will get over 20 grams of protein at dinner even if you are eating only 3 ounces or so of seafood, chicken or very-lean meat.

Essential amino acids

As you eat less meat and less whole-milk products, if a meal does not include seafood, it is important to plan a *combination* of legumes and grains. These will provide all eight of the essential amino acids.

By eating seafood or meat, you can get all eight essential amino acids in well-balanced amounts—but not so when it comes to eating any one grain or legume such as wheat, oats, rice, lentils, split peas, navy beans, pinto beans or lima beans.

Grains and legumes—except for soybeans—contain lower amounts of one or two or three of the essential amino acids. So, when you serve beans, also serve rice, corn or wheat. The combined amino acids of these incomplete proteins supply a more complete protein than either one does alone. Complementary proteins may be cooked together in the same dish or served separately, and not necessarily at the same meal.

A combination of oats and whole wheat such as a breakfast of rolled oats and whole-wheat toast provides a balance of essential amino acids.

Beans and cornmeal also provide a good balance. And so do navy beans and rice.

Even though it is possible for an adult to eat a nutritious vegetarian diet, this is difficult to accomplish. We would rather you include fish and seafood regularly in your diet so you won't miss out on the benefits of the omega-3 fats and other nutrients in fish and seafood that help avoid plugged-up coronary arteries and heart attacks.

Variety is the key

As you plan your meals and grocery shopping,

choose a variety of different things to provide yourself and your family with a balance of nutrients.

Don't get in a rut.

Fruits and vegetables add fiber

If you let yourself get locked into a pattern of eating the same few things—you may not get a good variety of grains, beans and other legumes, fruits and vegetables.

We hope you put seafood on your menu almost every day. Choose a variety of foods including oatmeal, whole wheat and beans of one kind or another almost every day, with a good balance of the other legumes and grains such as brown or wild rice.

You will need three or four servings of vegetables daily. Try for three or four servings of fruit each day—apples, pears, oranges, bananas and others. When choosing fruit juice be sure it is *real* fruit juice and not just something with a little juice and a lot of water. When you prepare juice, don't throw away the pulp. Whenever possible, squeeze your own orange and grapefruit juice and keep the pulp. Likewise, grape and pineapple juice with the pulp provides valuable fiber that is missed when it is strained and filtered out. Fortunately, the pulp fiber is usually left in prune juice and apricot, guava and pear nectars.

Fiber contained in fruit, beans, and other legumes, grains and vegetables is needed several times a day. In addition to other benefits derived from these various nutrients, fiber helps prevent cancer of the colon. Be sure to eat a variety of raw fruits and vegetables. Consider the cruciferous vegetables such as broccoli and cauliflower. Only cook vegetables until they are tender-crisp.

Other kinds of fiber in fruits—such as pectin in apples—also help to lower cholesterol.

When you cook from scratch, rather than using overcooked or processed foods, you will discover delicious new flavors. Experience new adventures in eating as well as feeling better.

Rice

People cheat themselves by using instant or minute rice that has lost much valuable fiber. Brown rice, which really isn't brown, contains all these valuable fibers as do other wild rices.

Instant rice is so popular because of its convenience. It simply saves time. We're used to popping a little box or bag of rice into boiling water and having it ready in very little time. But we've paid for this convenience in terms of lost nutritional value. Regain this value by using brown rice and a little more time.

Once your rice is cooked, add a little salt and pepper along with soft diet margarine and you are all set.

If you'd like more "zip," fix Brown Rice with Vegetables, page 209. Also try other modifications you'll think up using whole wheat and other grains.

Be creative.

Another delicious and interesting variety is *wild rice* which has long, thin, dark-brown (almost-black) grains. When cooked, a white interior explodes from the wild-rice grains.

It is surprisingly simple to cook wild rice or whole wheat for a main course or side dish. Many variations and combinations of these wholesome basic foods are possible. They can be served for pennies with lots of nutrition, *no* saturated fat and *no* cholesterol.

Balance

The bottom line is balance.

And that is the top line, too.

We have purposely not devised a scheduled list of meals for you to eat. No one likes to be told exactly what to eat and when to eat it.

This is why we want you to know what's going on

along with some ideas about how to fix your own no-fat and low-fat recipes—so you can be on your own.

And, as you make choices at the market, restaurant and in your own kitchen, *think creatively*. Put some variety into what you choose, buy, cook and eat.

And remember the "b" word—*balance*.

Children and milk and low-fat diets

You are in a wonderful position to make a big difference. You can help to stamp out coronary-artery disease in the lives of your children.

By seeking the best guidance as your children grow, along with the principles you are learning and some common sense, you will be able to help them grow up with clear coronary arteries.

For the first several months of their lives, babies get 100% of their nutrients from milk. Many used to think that whole milk continued to be essential throughout life. As we look at the problems caused by saturated fats, we don't think adults should drink much whole milk—if any— or eat much ice cream or genuine cheeses loaded with saturated fats.

Infants and toddlers up to age 2 need this butterfat.

When we talk about limiting milk products mostly to non-fat yogurt, non-fat cottage cheese, non-fat skim milk and avoiding ice cream, we are not talking about these very-young children.

It makes sense to feed children more seafood and meat without fat, and in sensible portions. There is wisdom in feeding children healthy, basic foods like grains, legumes, fruits and vegetables, as well as whole milk. Our guidelines for limiting daily intake of saturated fat to a certain number of grams a day are for adults. Children need a reasonable amount of whole milk. Babies and young children should not be fed non-fat skim milk.

On the other hand, many infants and children get far too much milk every day. Some babies and toddlers become blubbery, gaining huge amounts of weight because they drink too much milk. An excess of butterfat fattens them up. Being blubbery is definitely not healthful—even for a baby. Check with your doctor about your individual youngster's needs as you pay attention to fat intake and other nutritional principles.

10

Tips on Eating Out

You will soon find that eating a limited-fat diet is rather easy at home. But it becomes more challenging when eating out. It takes real effort to eat out without consuming a lot more fat than you should.

Choosing a buffet or restaurant that offers an extended salad bar makes an eating-out experience easier than a fast-food establishment with standardized menus. More and more buffets and salad bars are including foods containing complex carbohydrates and proteins. These often include cold pastas, peas and beans as well as a wonderful assortment of fruit, vegetables and traditional salad components. A good salad bar can provide excellent meal choices, especially when an all-you-can-eat salad bar is loaded with fruits and vegetables—so you get a complete meal with fruit as a dessert.

Although some restaurants are offering low-saturated-fat items on the menu, many don't. Even if they don't, restaurant people are usually very helpful in preparing salmon or whatever you order broiled instead of fried, and with lemon instead of butter sauce.

Tell the waiter exactly what you want

When asked, chefs will leave potatoes and vegetables "dry," or without butter, sour cream or cheese sauces. If you are creative in your suggestions it is surprising how often alternatives can be found.

So what do you put on potatoes or vegetables at a

restaurant? Tell the waiter or waitress what you want. More and more resturants have soft diet margarine available for the asking. Chopped chives, Butter Buds,® Molly McButter,® corn-oil margarine or Mrs. Dash® seasonings may also be available. You could slip a package of your favorite seasoning in your pocket or purse before you go out to eat.

Another topping to request in restaurants for your baked potato is a small amount of cooked chopped broccoli or cottage cheese. Fresh chopped tomato is also very good. Or, if the restaurant serves non-fat or low-fat salad dressings, you might want to try one of these as a tasty topping for your baked potato instead of sour cream or butter.

Low-fat salad dressings

Lemon or lime wedges are usually available to squeeze on vegetables or salads. Most restaurants also have salad vinegars—often more than one variety.

A typical Italian salad dressing contains 2 grams of saturated fat per tablespoon. Instead of a heavy greasy salad dressing, some restaurants now offer light no-oil dressings. Others offer low-calorie dressings with only a gram or so of total fat and only a trace of saturated fat. In their absence, and if you don't want to use lemon or lime juice or a salad vinegar, ask for salsa or picante sauce. Or ask for chopped onion or chili pepper. When none of these happen to be on hand, almost every eating establishment has catsup and mustard that can be used in a variety of ways.

Another good salad topping that most restaurants have on hand is seafood cocktail sauce. It is made by combining catsup with a little horseradish and coarse pepper. This sauce is one of the things many people like about shrimp cocktails. This same sauce tastes good on a lettuce or spinach salad!

You might find you like one of these alternatives even better than the regular thousand-island or bleu-cheese dressing. At home the choices of commercial non-fat or low-fat salad dressings or recipes for new dressings and toppings are endless.

As you carefully follow a low-saturated-fat diet while others eat such things as steak, cheese, ice cream and other things, you might feel cheated. But the problem is more one of how you think about it than anything else.

You can think about things you should not eat—or you can think of things you can enjoy. It's like the perspective of a glass being half-full or half-empty.

It comes down to attitude.

Airline meals

The standard airline meal is loaded with more saturated fat than anyone should eat in a day. And it may not be very appetizing, either.

When you make your reservations ask your travel agent or the airline for a low-saturated-fat, low-cholesterol meal. Or, a vegetarian, fruit or seafood meal may be available. What you get may not be exactly perfect, but usually it will be much closer to your low-fat diet than if you had not asked for a special meal. Just don't eat the pat of butter that may somehow end up on your tray.

Be sure to place your special meal requests a day to a week before the flight, depending on the airline. It isn't reasonable to expect a special meal by asking for it the same day as the flight. Although the airlines are pretty good about making sure your special meal is on board, there are times when it doesn't happen. Let the airline know if you change your flight plans so food isn't wasted.

Fixed menus

When you are eating out and there is a fixed entrée, what do you do?

You can choose to eat what is served or you can choose to eat only a small portion. Choosing not to eat everything is hard for some of us who were taught to clean our plates and not waste a thing. It is even harder when you are hungry and a big juicy steak is put in front of you. Sending it back or just leaving it untouched may seem unthinkable. But the question is: Is it more wasteful to eat something that will load your coronary arteries with fat—or send it back to the kitchen uneaten? Ask the waiter or waitress whether it might be possible to get fish, chicken or a vegetable or fruit plate instead of the chosen entrée. You won't be the first—or last—to ask for such treatment.

When there really isn't another choice, the best approach is to just eat a little of what is served. You can cut very thin slices of the steak or entrée. Take tiny bites of these small pieces, chewing them slowly. You can eat a few bites of the lean part of the steak. The vegetables, bread and salad will then add up to a pretty good meal.

You don't have to eat all that is served.

Another very good choice is to eat a small portion and to ask for a doggie bag to take the rest home. This eliminates the need for excuses or explanations. People don't ask to take home things they don't like.

What to do about chicken?

At home you can prepare white chicken meat by trimming off the skin and fat. In restaurants chicken is often served with the fat-laden skin left on. What do you do?

Just because chicken is served with the skin doesn't mean you have to eat it. Chicken skin contains considerable saturated fat—made even worse if it is fried. It is certainly acceptable to trim off the skin and fat and eat some of the chicken that is served.

If chicken or seafood has been deep-fat fried, the crusty fried skin is very flavorful, especially if it has been dipped in a seasoned batter. There is a large amount of fat in this crust. Some oil penetrates into the chicken or fish as it is being fried in deep fat. Peeling off this crusted outer skin solves most of the problem and is a pretty good solution when there's no other entrée choice.

Improvising

If obviously low-fat entrées are not listed on a menu, you have several choices. You can blow your diet and eat lots of fat. Or you can improvise like one of us did when a group was enjoying an evening at a delightful Italian restaurant. The menu listed pizzas, lasagna, fettuccine and an assortment of other delicious-looking pastas loaded with cheese. The other entrees were steak, French-fried shrimp and fish and chips.

The menu also included sandwiches, soups and giant salads. But there wasn't a main entrée on the menu that wouldn't push the saturated fat beyond a day's limit. There weren't even any fatless side dishes.

Hunger created ingenuity. When the menu was studied, fish-and-chips was considered—but even peeling off the fried batter would leave oil in the fish. Slipping out to another restaurant wasn't an option. Going without eating wasn't a very good idea, either.

But wait. On the sandwich list a "Turkey Club Sandwich" looked like a possibility, but the mayo and bacon would be a problem.

If the club sandwich were ordered, when it arrived at the table the bacon could be taken out and some of the mayo could be scraped off. But what if the sandwich were ordered without mayonnaise, without butter and without bacon?

Farther down the menu was a Reuben sandwich. Reubens have ham and cheese, but they also have sauerkraut. What if sauerkraut were ordered as a side dish? Then, what if some plain spaghetti were ordered—with clam sauce, tomato sauce or marinara sauce?

At least there were some foods in the kitchen that could be eaten by someone who wanted to restrict his fat intake. The next problem was to communicate all this so the waitress and then the cook would understand. This was a bigger problem than usual because of so many people at the party having so much fun. Shouting all these requests or instructions across the table didn't sound appropriate or practical, so a simple note was written and quietly handed to the waitress. It read:

> *Turkey club sandwich*
> *No mayo*
> *No butter*
> *No bacon*
>
> *Side order sauerkraut*
>
> *Side order spaghetti*

The waitress read the note and looked up and asked, "Are you serious?" A simple "yes" answer was given.

She looked at the note again and said, "I don't know if we have any sauerkraut!"

"The menu lists Reuben Sandwiches, so you probably do. Could you ask the cook?"

"Sure."

As the meals were served, the waitress brought out a delicious club sandwich without bacon, without butter and without mayonnaise. There was a serving of sauerkraut. The spaghetti enhanced with marinara sauce was filling. Along with a relish dish of fresh vegetables, this turned out to be a pretty good meal. Maybe you don't like sauerkraut, but that isn't the point. The idea is that if the restaurant has something you can eat in the kitchen, you can get it. Just be imaginative—then ask.

Options are usually available

Usually there are more options than are listed on a menu. Waitresses, waiters and cooks are usually more than willing to help you get something that pleases you.

You might choose to explain you are on a low-fat diet, or just let them figure it out. Restaurant people have every reason to encourage your business. So just ask.

To keep things at a low key, or if you want to improve the chance the waitress or waiter will get the instructions conveyed correctly to the cook, write out a dinner order on the back of a business card or on note paper. This is an excellent way to get the message across.

Plan ahead

Sometimes you know ahead of time about a dinner that's sure to have a fixed entrée. Ask the organizers what menu choices are available for people who need special meals. You'll be surprised at how often your needs can be accommodated.

Eating out without overloading on saturated fat is much more possible—and maybe easier—than most people think.

And when you have a choice of restaurants, choose carefully. Then study the menu.

Build on something standard by choosing items from things that are probably on hand for other dishes.

Be creative.

Don't be afraid to ask for vinegar or slices of lemon to squeeze on steamed vegetables, salads or seafood.

Or ask for salsa to substitute for a usual high-fat topping for salads, potatoes, rice, pasta and vegetables.

And keep in mind a seafood sauce for salads even without shrimp or other seafood.

Be imaginative.

Apologies are never necessary.

And of course, be appreciative.

Eating out can be fun and fat-less.

11

Keep Your Body Moving!

Do you really have to exercise?

No.

You don't *have* to do anything.

But if you want to have maximum control of your cholesterol levels, feel the best and take care of your heart, you *will* exercise.

If you already are walking or jogging, or doing some other regular aerobic exercise, great! Keep it up! If not, don't be intimidated by the word *exercise*. After getting a thorough medical checkup, get started on a program of walking or riding an exercise bike every day. Begin slowly, adding a little every day rather than beginning an immediate intensive program of running.

A definite correlation

There is definitely a correlation between cholesterol reduction and vigorous aerobic exercise. Exercise helps increase the high-density lipoprotein (HDL) which is the healthy or *good* cholesterol. This is important because, as the healthy cholesterol goes up, bad cholesterol (LDL or VLDL) is picked up out of the cells and dumped—so the bad-cholesterol levels go down. But—exercise is needed regularly to do any good.

We are not suggesting that you run marathons or even jog. We recommend a sensible program of vigorous exercise every single day unless there is a specific medical reason to do otherwise.

Exercise doesn't always have to be something that is done for that reason alone.

Some people prefer to accomplish something while they are exercising rather than just running or walking around a track. Many use walking and jogging as productive think time. Others use a reading stand on an exercise bike or treadmill so they can read while exercising.

Aerobic exercise does not have to be meaningless work like a rat running on a treadmill.

If you want to do something constructive like heavy gardening, chopping wood or something else productive, great! Or if you want to walk to work or to the market, fine. The point is, don't fail to do some aerobic exercising every day because you can't stand to do something dull. On the other hand, if you want to walk somewhere and just enjoy the beauty of nature, hooray!

If you want to use your exercise bike, you might enjoy reading as you do your workout. Or, use your exercise time to watch TV or listen to music.

How much exercise?

How much vigorous exercise do you need?

This depends on your age, health and other circumstances. Begin your increased activity gradually with guidance from your doctor after a thorough check-up. But walking down the driveway to get the mail probably won't be enough—unless you have some major physical problems or a very long driveway!

As you think about walking, plan to walk to places you already go or to do things that are worthwhile, unless you just like going around the block.

For example, if you drive to work, park farther away rather than closer to where you are going. Does this sound crazy? Maybe so, but it might even be fun! Spaces in the parking lot that are the farthest away are more likely to be available—and because others may not want to park there, you may get some other advantages like fewer nicks in your car doors!

Another way to build exercising into your daily life is to use stairs instead of riding elevators. Or, if your floor is way too high to walk all the way, at least at first, take the elevator part of the way. Then walk the rest of the way.

In other words, go out of your way to exercise during your work day.

Exercise regularly

The important thing is to begin a program of regular exercise—and keep it up. Exercise needs to be more than a token effort. If you are a healthy adult, we recommend gradually and wisely increasing your activity enough to push you more than you may think you want to be pushed right now. Plan on a lot of stairs, a lot of blocks, a lot of laps, lots of exercise-bike pedaling or a lot of tough physical work.

You may find that you need to be walking 2 miles or so a day, or perhaps 3 miles three times a week.

But whether you choose walking, bicycling, swimming, riding an exercise bike or working doesn't matter—just as long as you accomplish sufficient vigorous activity every day. If not every day—exercise vigorously at least three or four times a week . . . and keep it up!

12

How Much Fat Is in
Everyday Food?

Add up the numbers.

You can choose how much saturated fat *you* put into your coronary arteries.

Keep in mind that the following figures for saturated fat and cholesterol in various common foods are approximate. Variations exist in serving sizes. There are vast differences in the amount of saturated fat and cholesterol in different grades and cuts of meat. Big differences also occur in types and species of seafood. Then there are all sorts of consumer food products— from restaurants and fast-food establishments to the wide variety of fresh, frozen, dried and canned goods available in grocery stores and markets. Some saturated-fat and cholesterol differences in these products are obvious and some are not obvious at all.

All charts don't agree

So when you compare lists showing the grams of saturated fat and cholesterol in foods and food products, don't be surprised to see different figures. Most of the time differences are relatively small. Don't worry about it. The idea is to get the big picture and to get on a course that will help keep your arteries from getting plugged up with fat plaques.

The more you get into this and the more creativity

and ingenuity you use, the more ways you will discover to prepare delicious foods without loading up on too much saturated fat.

Rules of thumb to figure fat content

Read labels. Most labels tell you how many total grams of fat are in a serving. Unfortunately, the saturated-fat content is not always given. Two general rules of thumb may help. In figuring how many grams of saturated fat are in a beef product, you can estimate that *half* of the total fat is saturated fat. That's easy enough.

Here's another one that's almost as easy.

To determine how many grams of fat are in a serving of a milk product, figure that 2/3 of the total fat per serving is close to the amount of saturated fat. For example, the label on a particular type of whipped ice-cream dessert says there are 12 grams of total fat per serving. Using the 2/3 rule, estimate that 8 grams of saturated fat are in each serving.

Amount of the product per serving

Another thing that is important to pay attention to is the amount of the product for which the fat is listed. Sometimes the numbers look attractive until you realize that the specification is for 1 ounce and an ordinary serving is 8 ounces. Example: A popular frozen yogurt contains 1 gram of fat—per ounce! The 2/3 rule checks out with the company's label claim of 0.7 oz. per 1 oz. But a typical serving of frozen yogurt is 8 oz. That adds up to 5.6 grams of saturated fat. A better choice is to choose a non-fat frozen yogurt such as Dannon,® Honey Hill Farms® or Yoplait.®

Read the fine print on those labels. Ask for product information if it is not on the package. And refer to our charts frequently until you get to know the total and saturated-fat contents of the most common foods you eat. Use the charts to help you choose new favorites.

There's more to this than knowing that there are 4 grams of saturated fat in a piece of pie. You need to know how many grams of saturated fat you actually eat each day.

You don't want to have to run an accounting audit of what you eat every day for the rest of your life—but, unless you do it enough times to get to know about how much fat you are eating in your usual meals, you will never know. It would be like writing checks on your checking account without keeping a current balance.

The difference between learning about your pattern of eating and your checking account is that you won't have to keep writing down everything you eat, like you would to keep track of how much money is left in the bank.

So, study these lists—and then keep track of your Bad-Fat Tallies at least for the next three days . . . and then at least one day a week until you are on a solid low-fat pattern of eating for the rest of your life.

Is it worth it?

It is if you don't want a heart attack.

You can keep more fat from plugging your coronary arteries—if you start right now on limiting how much saturated fat *you* put into your body.

It's up to you.

Fatgrams: Saturated Fat and Cholesterol in Everyday Foods

Food	Saturated Fat (grams)	Cholesterol (milligrams)
Beans and Legumes, 1 cup cooked without meat		
Navy, lima, black, pinto, great northern beans	trace	0
Split and black-eyed peas	trace	0
Bread Group		
Bagels—egg	0.5	5
Bagels—plain	0.3	0
Baking powder biscuit	1	trace
English muffin—no fat	0	0
English muffin—regular	0.3	0
French bread (made with oil)—slice	0.3	0.3
French bread (traditional without oil)—slice	0	0
Hamburger/hot-dog bun, hard roll, brown & serve	0.5	0
Homemade white bread—slice	0.2	0
Light Oatbran Bread	0.2	0
Pinto Wheat Bread	0.2	0
Pita bread	trace	0
Pumpernickel, rye, Italian	0.2	0
White soft bread—slice	0.2	0
Whole-wheat bread—slice	0.3	0
Butter and Tablespreads—per tablespoon		
Butter	7	30
Fleischmann's Diet® (soft tub)	1	0
Fleischmann's Light®	2	0
Margarine—corn, soy, cottonseed	2	0
Margarine—safflower	2	0
Promise Tablespread®	2	0
Promise Tablespread® extra light	1	0
Weight Watchers® Reduced Calorie	1	0
Cakes—per slice		
Angel food—with applesauce or strawberries and Danish glazing	0	0
Chocolate bakery	4	40
Devil with chocolate frosting	3.5	40
Fruit cake	1.5	20
Pound cake	3	35
White with white frosting	3	20
Yellow with frosting	4	20
Candy		
Candy bar—typical	6	20
Carmel 1 oz.	2	trace
Chocolate 1 oz.	5.4	10
Gum drop 1 oz.	0	0
Hard candy 1 oz.	0	0
Taffy	3	trace
Cereals 1 cup		
Bran cereal 1 oz. = 1/3 cup	0.1	0
Cheerios® 1 oz. = 1-1/4 cups	0.3	0
Corn flakes 1 oz. = 1-1/4 cups	trace	0
Farina	trace	0
Granola 1 oz. = 1/3 cup	3.3	0
Oatmeal, rolled, quick, and some instant	0.4	0
Most cold cereals	0.2	0

(If homogenized milk is used, add 3 grams saturated fat and 20mg cholesterol)

Food	Saturated Fat (grams)	Cholesterol (milligrams)
Cheeses		
Most cheeses per 1 oz. slice	6	30
Cottage cheese		
Creamed 4% fat, 1 cup	6.5	35
2% fat, 1 cup	3	20
Low-fat 1% fat, 1 cup	1.5	10
Non-fat, 1 cup	0.3	0
Cream cheese, 1 oz.	6	30
Dorman's Light Lo Chol® Imitation Semi-Soft Cheese	0.32	3
Mozzarella—part skim 1 oz.	3	16
Parmesan, grated 1 tablespoon	1	5
Weight Watchers® Swiss-flavored Process Cheese Product—1 oz. slice	<1	2
Yogurt cream cheese (non-fat, page 301)	0.3	0
Cookies (per one cookie)		
Brownie squares	2	15
Chocolate Chip cookie	1	5
Delicious Oatmeal Cookie (see recipe section)	trace	0
Fig Newton cookie	trace	5
Lorna Doone cookie	1.2	trace
Gingersnaps	trace	0
Oatmeal cookie—commercial	0.5	trace
Crackers—12 grams of crackers		
Soda crackers, 4 ordinary	0.4	trace
Soda crackers, 4 made with vegetable fat	trace	trace
Oyster crackers	trace	trace
Rye crackers, 2 wafers	0.3	0
Graham plain, 2 crackers	0.3	0
Wheat crackers, 5 thin or 3 thick	0.7	trace
Cheese crackers, 12 small crackers	1.1	6
Custards, Puddings and Gelatins		
Egg custard, 1 cup	7	275
Danish desert	0	0
Gelatin deserts	0	0
Instant pudding with non-fat milk	0	0
Instant pudding with homogenized milk	2.2	15
Egg and Substitutes		
Egg, 1 large	1.7	275
Egg yolk	1.7	275
Egg white	0	trace
Eggbeaters®, egg substitute	0	0
Egg white with 5 drops of yolk	trace	trace

Fast Foods

Please note that the following are examples of the wide range of saturated fat content. This varies depending on serving size, the type of fat or oil used in the preparation of the food, and the spreads, sauces, and flavorings used on the product. Most fast-food and restaurant chains test and publish the fat content of their products. They will share this with customers who ask for it.

Food	Saturated Fat (grams)	Cholesterol (milligrams)
Burrito (large meat)	10	50
Cheeseburger (regular)	7.3	45
Cheeseburger (4 oz. patty)	15	100
Chicken club sandwich	12	100
Chicken fillet, fried, sandwich	18	90
Chicken nuggets, fried, (9)	14	125
Chicken, roasted, sandwich (skinless breast)	3	100
Enchilada	8	30
Fish, fried, sandwich	6	90
French fries	7	trace

Food	Saturated Fat (grams)	Cholesterol (milligrams)
Fast Foods, (continued from previous page)		
Hamburger, double, with cheese	24	130
Hamburger (small)	4.4	35
Hamburger (4 oz. patty)	7	70
Hot dog (broiled) with mustard, catsup etc., but without mayonnaise or butter	5.3	30
Hot dog (fried) with mayonnaise etc.	8	45
Onion rings, French-fried	10	0
Pizza 1/4 of 12-inch plain mozarella cheese pizza	4	50
Pizza 1/4 of 12-inch cheese and pepperoni pizza	5	70
Roast beef, regular	3.5	55
Roast beef, large	11	60
Stuffed potato with cheese etc.	27	70
Taco	4	20
Fish and Seafoods		
Catfish, broiled, 3 oz.	1	50
Clams, 3 oz. (6)	0.2	55
Cod, broiled, 3 oz.	0.15	50
Crab, Alaskan, boiled/broiled, 3 oz.	0.1	45
Crab, Blue, boiled/broiled, 3 oz.	0.2	85
Flounder or sole, broiled, 3 oz.	0.3	60
Halibut, broiled, 3 oz.	0.4	60
Herring, broiled, 3 oz.	4	85
Lobster, boiled or broiled, 3 oz.	0.1	60
Mackerel, broiled, 3 oz.	3.5	60
Orange Roughy, broiled, 3 oz.	0.1	15
Oysters, 3 oz. (6)	1	90
Salmon Red Sockeye, broiled, 3 oz.	1.2	60
Salmon Pink, broiled, 3 oz.	0.5	45
Salmon Coho, broiled, 3 oz.	1	35
Sardines, 3 oz., oil drained off	1.5	130
Scallops, 3 oz. (6)	0.1	30
Shrimp, boiled or broiled, 3 oz. or cocktail	0.3	160
Shrimp, French-fried, 3 oz.	3	170
Snapper, broiled, 3 oz.	0.5	40
Trout (Rainbow), broiled, 3 oz.	0.7	60
Tuna, 3 oz., in oil	1.4	55
Tuna, 3 oz., in water	0.3	50
Fruit		
Avocado, medium	5	0
Olives, 4 medium	trace	0
Most other fruits	0	0
Ice Cream and Frozen Desserts		
Banana split	8	30
Custard, Frozen 1 cup	14	150
Fruit bars, frozen	trace	0
Ice cream, 1 cup	9	60
Ice milk, 1 cup	3.5	15
Ice cream, soft, 1 cup	3	15
Icy Orange Cooler (page 303)	0	0
Milk shake (medium)	11	40
Milk shake (thick and large)	17	70
Sherbet, 1 cup	2.5	14
Sorbet—commercial	1	0
Yogurt, frozen, made from non-fat milk	0.3	0

Food	Saturated Fat (grams)	Cholesterol (milligrams)
Meats and Poultry		
Beef		
Ground beef lean, 15% fat, 3 oz.	5	50
Ground beef regular, 27% fat, 3 oz	7	80
A 3-oz. hamburger patty is 3 inches in diameter and 5/8-inch thick before cooking; a big hamburger patty weighs 5 or 6 oz. before cooking.		
Liver, 3 oz.	3	410
Roast or steak, marbled, 3 oz.	11	90
Roast or steak, lean, 3 oz.	4	50
A piece of uncooked meat 1/2-inch thick and 3 x 3 inches weighs 3 oz. A typical small dinner steak is twice this size.		
Soy meat substitute	trace	0
Veal cutlet, 3 oz.	4	110
Lamb		
Lamb roast or chop, lean, 3 oz.	4	70
Lamb roast or chop, lean plus fat, 3 oz.	8	85
Pork		
Bacon, 3 slices	3.3	16
Ham (lean and fat), 3 oz.	6	53
Ham (lean only), 3 oz.	2.4	35
Pork roast or chopped lean, 3 oz.	4	60
Pork roast or chopped lean plus fat, 3 oz.	9	80
Sausage links, 3 oz. (There is considerable variation in fat)	4.2	35
Poultry—Chicken and Turkey		
Chicken à la king, 1 cup	3	50
Chicken and Noodles, 1 cup	6	50
Dark meat without skin, 3 oz.	2	80
Dark meat with skin, 3 oz.	4	90
Light meat without skin, 3 oz.	1	70
Light meat with skin, 3 oz.	2.5	80
Rabbit		
Rabbit, 3 oz.	1.6	54
Rabbit Italian Style, 3 oz.	1.6	54
Rabbit Stew, 3 oz.	1.6	54
Variety Meats		
Bologna, beef, 1 slice	3	15
Braunschweiger, 1 slice	3	45
Ham, chopped, 1 slice	1.2	10
Hot dog—frankfurter	5	30
Lunch meat, lean, 1 slice	2.4	15
Salami, 1 slice	2	20
Milk and Cream		
Buttermilk, 1 cup	1.5	10
Chocolate milk, 1 cup	5.5	30
Cream, heavy, 1 tablespoon	3.5	20
Cream, half and half, 1 tablespoon	1	6
Cream, light, 1 tablespoon	2	10
Dessert topping, non-dairy, 1 tablespoon	1	trace
Eggnog, 1 cup	11.5	150
Homogenized milk, 1 cup	5	33
2% milk, 1 cup	3	18
1% milk, 1 cup	1.5	10
Non-fat (skim) milk, 1 cup	0.3	trace
Sour cream, 1 tablespoon	2	5
Sour cream, imitation, 1 tablespoon	2	0
Yogurt creamy, 1 cup	5	30
Yogurt low fat 2%, 1 cup	2.3	15
Yogurt non-fat, 1 cup	0.3	trace

Food	Saturated Fat (grams)	Cholesterol (milligrams)
Nuts		
Almonds, dry, 2 tablespoons = 15 nuts	0.8	0
Almonds, oil roasted, 1/2 oz.	2	0
Coconut 1/4 cup, 0.7 oz.	7	0
Peanut butter (pure), 1 tablespoon	1.5	0
Peanuts, dry, 1/2 oz.	1	0
Peanuts, oil-roasted, 1/2 oz.	2	0
Pecans, 1/2 oz.	1	0
Sunflower seeds, 1/2 oz.	1	0
Walnuts, 1/2 oz.	0.5	0
Oils and Shortening, 1 tablespoon		
Canola oil (Puritan®)	1	0
Coconut oil	11.8	0
Corn oil	1.7	0
Olive oil	1.8	0
Palm oil	6.7	0
Peanut oil	2.3	0
Safflower oil	1.2	0
Soybean/cottonseed oil blend	2.4	0
Sunflower oil	1.4	0
Pancakes, Waffles and French Toast		
French toast	2	110
French toast with Eggbeaters® and non-fat milk	trace	0
Pancake	1.5	15
Pancake with Eggbeaters® and non-fat milk	trace	0
Waffle	4	100
Pantry Supplies		
Honey	0	0
Imitation Bacon Bits	0.5	0
Jam & Jelly	0	0
Sugar	0	0
Syrup (without added butter)	0	0
White flour, 1 cup	trace	0
Whole wheat flour, 1 cup	trace	0
Pasta		
Macaroni and most other plain pasta	trace	0
Macaroni and cheese	9	45
Noodles, egg, 1 cup	0.5	50
Spaghetti, plain	trace	0
Spaghetti with cheese sauce	3	20
Spaghetti with meat sauce	4	80
Spaghetti with tomato sauce	trace	0
Pastry, Pies and Donuts,		
Cake donut	3	20
Chocolate Eclair (filled)	9	80
Danish pastry	4	10
Glazed fried donut	4	20
Pie, per slice,		
add for cream, custard or meringue	4	20
Potatoes, Rice and Stuffing		
Baked potato, plain	trace	0
French-fried potatoes	6	15
Hashed brown potatoes, 1 cup	6	trace
Mashed potatoes, milk & butter	6	trace
Potato chips, 10	2	0
Potato Salad with mayonnaise and egg	6	170
Rice	trace	0
Stuffing	6	60

Food	Saturated Fat (grams)	Cholesterol (milligrams)
Salad Dressings, 1 tablespoon		
Bleu-cheese salad dressing		
regular	1.5	5
low-calorie	0.5	trace
French dressing		
regular	1.4	trace
low-calorie	trace	trace
Italian		
regular	1.3	trace
low-calorie	trace	trace
Kraft Light®	1	5
Mayonnaise	2	5
Miracle Whip®	1	5
Miracle Whip Light®	1	5
Thousand Island	1	4
Weight Watchers® Low-Fat Mayonnaise	1	5
Snacks		
Corn chips	2	0
Popcorn, air-popped, plain, 1 cup	trace	trace
Popcorn, air-popped + Butter Buds®, 1 cup	trace	0
Popcorn, with vegetable oil and buttered, 1 cup	1.4	trace
Potato chips, 10 chips fried in vegetable oil	2	0
Rice cakes	trace	0
Soups—Be sure to read labels		
Canned—mixed with equal parts of milk:		
Clam chowder, 1 cup	3	10
Cream of chicken, 1 cup	5	27
Cream of mushroom, 1 cup	5	20
Canned—mixed with equal parts of water:		
Bean with bacon, 1 cup	1.5	5
Beef broth, bouillon or consume, 1 cup	0.3	trace
Beef noodle, 1 cup	1	5
Minestrone	0.5	trace
Split pea	1	0
Tomato	0.4	0
Vegetable beef	1	5
Vegetable	0.3	0
Homemade—low-fat (see recipe section)		
Dehydrated—mixed with water		
Chicken-noodle	0.2	0
Onion	trace	0
Tomato-vegetable	0.3	0
Vegetables		
Most vegetables (without butter or sauce)	0	0

13

It's All Up to You

There is no easy way to make a cholesterol or triglyceride problem go away.

It takes effort.

It takes motivation.

It means cutting way down on the amount of saturated fat you eat. It takes being smart enough to follow through. But you can do it and we think you will—because the alternatives are terrible.

Even if your cholesterol levels are not high enough for you to be specifically told to cut down on the amount of saturated fats you eat, we still think you should.

We think you will want to protect yourself like the folks are protected around the world who don't plug up their coronary arteries with fat like North Americans, Scandinavians and others do.

Recheck your cholesterol

After you have been on your low-saturated-fat diet for a while, you may want to know when to recheck your cholesterol again to see how you are doing. Well, it takes time. A person's cholesterol levels stay more or less constant, usually taking two weeks or so to change after dietary changes are made. In some people noticeable changes are even slower, taking a month or so before cholesterol levels change appreciably. This is why blood cholesterol levels can be checked without any need for fasting beforehand.

So, after beginning a new program of eating, we recommend waiting a couple of months before rechecking your blood cholesterol levels. Then if progress hasn't occurred, more changes may be needed.

On the other hand, triglyceride levels go up and down almost immediately, depending on what you do or do not eat. Getting a meaningful triglyceride level requires fasting for 12 to 14 hours before getting blood drawn for a test. Even then, if someone who runs high triglycerides eats a lot of bad fat, it may take a few days for the triglyceride level to come back down to a more acceptable level.

Cutting way down on the saturated fat you consume should help. It will probably make a big difference. However, it is possible that even carefully limiting saturated fat may not be enough. If LDL-cholesterol or triglyceride levels can't be controlled by reducing the intake of saturated fat, it is encouraging to know that medications almost always can.

Medications to lower cholesterol

People with very-high cholesterols over 300 (7.8), or triglycerides over 400 (4.5) often have an inherited tendency to over-manufacture cholesterol in their bodies. Low-fat and low-cholesterol diets are often not enough to reduce high levels in these people without the help of the excellent new prescription medications.

Some of these are: clofibrate (Atromid-S®), gemfibrozil (Lopid®), lovastatin (Mevacor®), colestipol (Colestid®), cholestyramine (Questran®) and probucol (Lorelco®).

Sometimes nicotinic acid (niacin) is used alone or in combination with one of the newer medications. However, "High dosages over long periods may cause liver damage or aggravate a stomach ulcer," according to Winter Griffith, M.D., in his book *Complete Guide to Vitamins, Minerals and Supplements*. He also points out that niacin should not be taken without consulting your doctor, especially if you have diabetes, gout, gallbladder or liver disease.

We think that if a medication is indicated, the right choice and right dosage for you is obviously important— as is proper monitoring and follow-up. These decisions are not like choosing a dandruff shampoo, mouthwash or deodorant. What happens inside your arteries in the weeks and months ahead will determine how long you will live—and we hope that will be for a long time.

Low-saturated-fat diet is the foundation

However, every plan to control high cholesterols and high triglycerides is built on a solid foundation of an ongoing low-saturated-fat diet.

Exercise is also extremely important.

Not smoking is absolutely necessary.

Close monitoring of elevated total cholesterols, LDL cholesterols and triglycerides, and of low HDL cholesterols by an interested and informed physician is very important. Your doctor's goal is to help you accomplish the best control possible with a low-saturated-fat diet along with exercise—and to help you stop smoking. Then, if these measures do not reduce the high levels of fat in your blood, your doctor can choose the best medication for the situation.

The ultimate goal

The ultimate goal of this program is to keep the blood flowing through your coronary arteries without restriction.

Blood flow to your heart should not be slow, otherwise you'll experience painful angina.

You definitely don't want *silent myocardial ischemia,* either. What is that? Silent myocardial ischemia is a significant lack of oxygen supply to the heart muscle without the typical angina chest pain.

And you certainly don't want blood flow to be

totally blocked by fat plaques so oxygen cannot reach your heart muscles, causing a heart attack.

We don't think you want to die prematurely.

Maybe you have already been through bypass surgery. If you have, you definitely don't want to go through it again. If you haven't, you certainly don't want to go through this experience as long as you can stop fat-plaque build-up in time.

If you feel as we do, your motivation level is high. We are so convinced of what we are suggesting that we have been eating low-saturated-fat meals for some time now—and we fully intend to keep doing so.

We don't want to die prematurely.

And we don't like the idea of being a patient in a coronary-care unit—nor spending several hours on the operating table undergoing bypass surgery, followed by the uncomfortable experiences during recovery.

If you have a serious problem

If fat plaques have already built up so there is a major blockage in your coronary arteries, surgery may be necessary to provide an adequate blood supply to your heart muscle to prevent a massive heart attack. Or, if a heart attack does happen, it may be necessary to employ surgical measures to provide a better blood flow after the situation is stabilized.

Increased blood supply is accomplished surgically in two different ways. A decision to do either of these procedures is made after careful evaluation of the situation with the help of a coronary-artery angiogram. This is done in a coronary-catheterization lab by a cardiologist or heart surgeon.

After a local anesthesia is injected into the skin and soft tissue of the thigh, a small incision is made and a tiny catheter tube is slipped into an artery. The catheter is passed up through the aorta and into the coronary arteries. A radio-opaque dye is put in through the tubing.

As the dye passes into each coronary artery the doctor can clearly see on a video monitor if there is a block-age and if so, how much and where. This is recorded on film or videotape. It can be replayed and carefully eval-uated as many times as is necessary by all the doctors in-volved in the decisions. Usually, the patient and family also want to see this very interesting recording.

Several important things are learned by studying a coronary angiogram. Any and all obstructions are indi-cated, as well as how much the blood flow is restricted at each obstruction and exactly where the obstructions are located.

Under some circumstances the recommendation is to perform an *angioplasty*, which is somewhat like the coronary angiogram. A tiny inflatable balloon on the end of a catheter tube is slipped up into the coronary artery. The blockage is opened up with skillful manipulation. The video monitor lets the surgeon observe what is hap-pening.

Bypass surgery

The other choice is coronary-artery-bypass surgery. The decision to do this or angioplasty depends on many variables, including the condition of the patient and the situation at the time. However, if the blockages are mul-tiple, numerous, extensive or in certain locations, bypass surgery may be the best thing to do.

Coronary-artery-bypass surgery is amazing.

It is frightening because it is necessary to stop the heart. A mechanical pump is used to supply blood and oxygen to the brain and the rest of the body while the surgeons carefully hook up new pathways for blood to flow around the blocked coronary arteries.

Although the idea of having one's heart stopped and restarted is frightening, in skilled hands the procedure usually goes very well. Although there are risks, these are relatively small—especially now as compared to when surgeons were first learning how to do this and other open-heart-surgery procedures.

What is meant by a coronary-artery bypass?

Let's compare your coronary arteries to a water pipe going to a water heater. Suppose the pipe got corroded and clogged with lime and other deposits. Water just couldn't get through to the water heater. If this happened the plumber would first turn off the main water supply. If he didn't, water would gush out when he worked on the pipe. This is similar to what happens in the operating room. The difference is that the body can't get by without a continuous blood supply carrying oxygen to the brain and other cells.

Tubes are inserted to carry the blood to an outside pump that maintains blood flow during the operation. Then big clamps temporarily close the large vessels going in and out of the heart so the delicate surgery can proceed.

As for bypass surgery itself, a new passageway needs to be added to carry blood around the blockage. In the case of a water pipe, the plumber just cuts out the blocked pipe and puts in a new one. Because it is not practical to cut out a blocked coronary artery, a new passageway is made around the blockage.

If the artery that goes to the soft tissue of the left breast is clean and open, this artery is often disected away from where it usually goes. An opening is made in the blocked coronary artery past the major blockage. The end of the internal mammary artery is carefully stitched into this opening.

If another coronary artery is blocked (there may be as many as eight obstructions), the other bypasses are done with sections of veins usually taken from a leg. An incision is made and the vein is tied off above and below where it will be removed. Then a spaghetti-like section of vein is taken out.

When a vein is used, an opening must be made above and below the coronary-artery blockage. Both ends of the vein are carefully stitched into place. This is repeated for all obstructions.

Thus, bypass surgery is referred to as a *single, double, triple* or *quadruple bypass,* depending on how many obstructions must be bypassed.

After this delicate surgery is completed, the heart is restarted as the tubes and clamps are removed. A pacemaker wire is placed on the heart in case rhythm irregularities occur during the recovery period. The chest is closed, but chest tubes are left in place for drainage.

This may be more than you wanted to know about coronary angiography, coronary angioplasty and open-heart-bypass surgery. But, you should know about them because they can be lifesaving procedures. If you or someone close to you already has major obstructions in the coronary arteries, you may be looking ahead to these space-age procedures. Also, knowing what's involved in such surgery should give you additional incentive to restrict your bad-fat intake.

On the other hand, if the fat plaques have not formed this much in your coronaries, knowing the alternatives may convince you to do something about significantly limiting your cholesterol and saturated-fat intake.

The alternatives

A much worse alternative to coronary angioplasty or open-heart coronary bypass surgery is dying prematurely of a massive heart attack before you can get to a modern coronary-care unit. This frequently happens. Many people die quickly and suddenly. Some people tell us, "Well, this isn't such a bad way to go. In fact, I kind of like the idea of going in a hurry. Because everybody has to go sometime, I'm going to keep eating all the ice cream, cheese, red meat and fried stuff that I always have—and if I die of a heart attack, that's OK."

You might be thinking the same thing.

There's just one thing wrong with this line of reasoning. Lots of these folks die of massive heart attacks prematurely—long before their time.

We don't think this is what you want to happen to you—or those close to you.

Yes, we all are going to die, but why do things that create such crummy odds?

We want to help you turn the odds around so they are in your favor. If this is what *you* want, *you can do it!* Obviously, it is your choice. It's up to you.

Beating the odds—pleasantly!

If you want to beat the odds of an early heart attack, we also want to help you do so pleasantly. We want to help you find a lifestyle you will enjoy and continue to follow.

Being a non-smoker is a very important part of not having a heart attack. Not smoking also improves the odds against getting emphysema or lung cancer, too. So this is a big one. But it's *your* choice.

As you should now know, it is very important to control your cholesterol and triglycerides. The very most important basic thing in controlling cholesterol is to avoid eating too much saturated fat. Always remember that just controlling the amount of cholesterol you eat is not enough. You must also control how much saturated fat you eat.

Limiting saturated fat and cholesterol is not something to fiddle around with for a few days now and then.

Now and then isn't good enough. Fat plaques will just keep building up. Sooner or later they will probably cause decreased blood flow to your heart, which means *ischemia* and a heart attack.

Try the recipes in the recipe section. Of course there's no way that every recipe will please everyone. But these recipes are a beginning. Pretty soon you'll be figuring out low-fat things to fix on your own—and you will really be into it.

A life-long commitment

Remember, this is not a 2-week program.

It is not a one-month plan, either.

And it isn't even an 8-week cure!

There's no such thing as an 8-week cure.

By doing the right things you may be able to get your cholesterol levels down to a normal range in two months. To us, a *cure* means that you do something and the problem goes away without you having to do anything else.

You can't go on any program to *cure* a cholesterol problem in 8 weeks.

So *cure* is the wrong word.

A much better word is *control*.

You very likely can get things in control in two months—providing you follow through. But this problem is one that lasts a lifetime. And this plan is for a whole new life—so you can have a very good chance to beat the odds of a heart attack and live a longer, healthier life.

The simple plan is based on eating a variety of delicious and wholesome basic foods from the different food groups. Grains, legumes, seafood and vegetables of different kinds, along with fruits, will provide you enjoyable meals without excessive fat at every meal.

Well, that's it.

You can beat the odds of a heart attack. Remember there are 28 grams of saturated fat in a big hamburger with cheese, large order of fries and a milk shake.

Every time you eat such a meal, it adds up to eating as much saturated fat as is in a half stick of butter.

Instead of all this bad fat, you can enjoy some very good non-fat and low-fat meals and snacks.

We hope you choose to limit the amount of saturated fat you eat every day to a reasonable number of grams. We want you to limit your fat intake to the omega-3 fats in seafood and for the most part to the monounsaturated fats in olive oil and canola oil with some polyunsaturated fat products such as soft diet margarines made with safflower oil, sunflower oil, corn oil oil or soybean oil.

Keeping track

As you get used to this new way of eating, keep track of your saturated-fat intake every day. You will find Fat-gram Tables showing how much saturated fat and cholestesterol are in typical servings starting on page 106 and a simple Bad-Fat Tally, page 58.

How long do you need to keep a daily tally of the bad fat you eat?

However long it takes to get a pattern going—and to keep it going. This might take a few days, a month or two, or maybe it will take a year or longer.

It will probably take at least a few days of recording what you eat to get an idea of how to limit your fat intake to these amounts. But, however long it takes for you to feel comfortable about limiting the amount of fat to your own personal goal, we suggest doing it. You will probably find that recording what you eat and logging the fatgrams at least one day each week for a while will help you stay on target.

Then, if you are worried about slipping, just keep a running tally—like you were keeping a record of your golf scores.

Keep your cholesterol intake below 300mg a day, even better, below 200mg a day, especially if you are in the high-risk group. You will probably do much better than this because once you choose foods without egg yolks (except on a rare occasion) and with a limited amount of extra-lean, *select*-grade beef, the amount of cholesterol you eat should be remarkably simple to control.

Be sure to eat oatmeal, beans and other grains and legumes. Remembering the cultures who don't have heart attacks, eat plenty of fish and seafood for the omega-3 fat. Choosing fruit, especially apples, prunes, raisins and others with plenty of fiber, shouldn't be difficult. Instead of things filled with bad fat, think about fruits as special treats and snacks.

Also think about *oats, beans* and *fish* as important everyday foods that can be prepared in enjoyable ways.

If you keep your cholesterol/HDL ratio under 4.5, your LDL cholesterol under 130 (3.4), your triglycerides under 150 (3.9), and don't smoke and do excercise, you will very probably never have a heart attack.

Chances are you will feel better than you have felt in a long time, with more energy and get up and go.

By the way, you'll also save money on your grocery bill. But the most important thing is that plaques of fat won't be clogging up your coronary and other arteries.

What's next?

If you haven't figured out exactly what saturated-fat limit to set for yourself, refer back to Chapter 4 and come up with a number. This will be the number in grams of saturated fat you will allow yourself to consume per day. Chances are the number will be between 10 and 28 grams per day.

The higher your total cholesterol or triglycerides level and the higher your cholesterol/HDL ratio is above 4.5, the more you must limit your saturated-fat intake.

Keep in mind that these numbers are *starting points*. If your total cholesterol or triglycerides level (or both) doesn't come down to healthy levels, set a lower level. The same is true if your cholesterol/HDL ratio does not drop to less than 4.5. If you are in a high-risk category you should probably set an initial saturated-fat limit of close to 10 grams per day.

If you faithfully keep on a low-saturated-fat intake every day and you can't get your cholesterol numbers down far enough, don't be discouraged. Excellent medications are available. Ask your doctor.

Remember, no matter what else you do, the foundation of controlling cholesterol is to continue a low-saturated-fat eating habit.

You can do it.

Some really good non-fat and low-fat recipes follow. We want to keep you out of the coronary-care unit—unless you are a visitor. But maybe we can help keep your friends and family out of there, too, so you won't even need to be a hospital visitor.

It's all up to you!

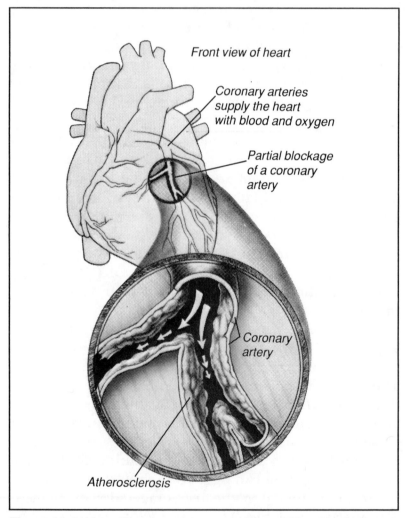

Front view of heart

Coronary arteries supply the heart with blood and oxygen

Partial blockage of a coronary artery

Coronary artery

Atherosclerosis

Figure 14-1 When there's a decreased flow of blood to the heart, the heart muscle may be damaged. Drawing courtesy of American Heart Associaton.

14

Heart Attack, Stroke and Risk Factors

This chapter is reproduced with permission from the American Heart Association's Fact Sheet on Heart Attack, Stroke and Risk Factors.

What is a heart attack?

The human heart basically is a muscle that pumps blood. It has its own blood vessels, the coronary arteries, that nourish it and keep it alive. In most cases when a heart attack occurs, fatty deposits (composed mostly of cholesterol) have lined the coronary arteries. As these deposits build up, they progressively narrow the arteries and decrease or stop the flow of blood to the heart. When there's a decreased flow of blood to the heart, the heart muscle may be damaged, but when there's a complete blockage of the flow of blood so that the heart can't get the oxygen and food it needs, a part of the heart may actually die. This is a heart attack.

A heart attack most often results when a blood clot forms in a narrowed artery and blocks the flow of blood to the part of the heart muscle supplied by that artery. Doctors call this form of heart attack a *coronary thrombosis, coronary occlusion* or *myocardial infarction.*

When a heart attack occurs, the dying part of the heart may trigger electrical activity that causes ventricular fibrillation. Ventricular fibrillation is an uncoordinated twitching that replaces the smooth, measured contractions that cause blood to be pumped to the organs of the body. In many cases, if trained medical professionals are immediately available, they can get the heart beating again by using electrical shock and/or drugs.

If the heart can be kept beating, and not too much heart muscle is damaged, small blood vessels may gradually reroute blood around the blocked arteries. This is the heart's own way of compensating for the clogged artery, and it's called *collateral circulation*.

The key to surviving a heart attack is promptly recognizing the warning signals and getting immediate medical attention.

How to recognize a heart attack

If you feel an uncomfortable pressure, fullness, squeezing or pain in the center of your chest (that may spread to your shoulders, neck or arms) and your discomfort lasts for two minutes or longer, you could be having a heart attack. Sweating, dizziness, fainting, nausea, a feeling of severe indigestion or shortness of breath also may occur, although not all symptoms necessarily occur. Sharp, stabbing twinges, on the other hand, usually *aren't* signals of a heart attack.

When a person has these symptoms, it's natural for him or her to deny what's happening. No one wants to think that he might be having a heart attack. But before you shrug off the symptoms, it's important to know that more than 300,000 heart-attack victims died before reaching the hospital last year, many of them because they refused to take their symptoms seriously.

What should you do if you think you might be having a heart attack? If you're uncomfortable for two minutes or more, call your local emergency medical service (EMS) immediately. If the EMS isn't available, get to a hospital offering emergency cardiac care as soon as possible.

Know in advance which route from home or work

will take you to the hospital the quickest. You might even discuss your possible choices with your doctor. Another option is to call the American Heart Association and ask which recognized emergency medical service and hospitals cover your area. Keep emergency information where you will find it easily and develop a "buddy system" with someone you know.

Recovery and rehabilitation

When people are hospitalized because of a heart attack, they often become depressed and anxious about whether they'll be able to resume full physical, social, professional and sexual activities. Usually there's no cause for worry. Unless the heart attack was extremely severe, most heart attack victims in time and with the proper care can function as well as they did before their heart attack.

What is a stroke?

A stroke occurs when the flow of blood to the brain is blocked. In order to function, brain cells must have a continuous, ample supply of oxygen-rich blood. If the brain cells don't get this supply of blood, they die. One of the frequent causes of stroke is the blockage of an artery by a clot that has formed inside it. When this happens, it's called a *cerebral thrombosis,* and a part of the brain doesn't receive the oxygen and nourishment it needs.

It's rare for a clot to form in a healthy artery, but when the inner walls of arteries become lined with thick, rough deposits of plaque (a condition known as atherosclerosis), the arteries are narrowed, the flow of blood slows, and clots are more likely to form. The reason is that blood is designed to clot when it comes in contact with foreign substances, and as the plaque builds up, the blood treats the plaque as an alien substance. Clotting results.

Sometimes a wandering clot is carried by the bloodstream until it lodges in one of the arteries of the brain and chokes off the flow of blood. This is called a *cerebral embolism*.

When a clot, either a thrombus or an embolus, plugs up a cerebral artery, the result is called a *cerebrovascular occlusion,* or more commonly, a *stroke.*

Stroke also occurs when a diseased artery in the brain bursts, flooding the surrounding tissue with blood. This is called a *cerebral hemorrhage.* (When a blood vessel on the surface of the brain bursts and blood floods the space between the brain and the skull, a subarachnoid hemorrhage occurs.) When these events happen, cells nourished by the artery are deprived of blood, while at the same time they're squeezed by the pressure that builds up inside the skull. The result is that they can't function. An added problem is that the accumulated blood from the ruptured artery soon forms a clot, which may displace or destroy brain tissue and interfere with brain function, causing physical disability.

Although cerebral hemorrhages don't all result from the same cause, they're more likely to occur when a person suffers from a combination of atherosclerosis and high blood pressure.

Hemorrhage of an artery in the brain also may be caused by a head injury or a burst aneurysm. Aneurysms are blood-filled pouches that balloon out from weak spots in the artery wall; they're often associated with high blood pressure. Aneurysms don't always cause trouble, but if one bursts in the brain, a stroke results.

When a stroke occurs, nerve cells in the damaged area of the brain can't function. Then the part of the body that's controlled by this area of the brain can't function, either.

The usual result of a stroke is *hemiparesis* (paralysis of one side of the body). A stroke can also result in aphasia, which is the loss of the ability to speak or to understand the speech of others. Loss of memory can be another result of stroke. When the brain is damaged by stroke, the effects may be slight or severe, temporary or permanent, depending on which brain cells have been damaged and how widespread the damage is. Effects also depend on how well the body restores its blood supply.

Because injured brain cells can't heal or create new cells, the prevention of stroke by modifying risk factors is very important.

How to recognize the early signals of stroke

The primary signal of a stroke is a sudden, temporary weakness or numbness of the face, arm and/or leg on one side of the body. Other signals include: temporary loss of speech, or trouble speaking or understanding speech; temporary dimness or loss of vision, particularly in one eye; unexplained dizziness, unsteadiness or sudden falls.

Many strokes can be prevented by diagnosing and controlling hypertension (high blood pressure), because hypertension is a leading cause of stroke. Sometimes major strokes are preceded by transient ischemic attacks, or TIAs. These are "little strokes" whose effects are similar to the symptoms of a major stroke, except that they only last for a very short time. TIAs can occur days, weeks or months before a severe stroke, and so should be considered warning signals. Prompt medical or surgical attention to these symptoms can prevent a major stroke.

The stroke profile

A person who's most likely to have a stroke will probably have high blood pressure and/or a history of brief, intermittent stroke episodes. A thorough medical examination often shows the presence of atherosclerosis (hardening of the arteries), too. Diabetic individuals have a greater chance of stroke than other people. Increased cholesterol levels and other fats in the blood also add to the risk of stroke. Gout (elevated uric acid) and heavy smoking are less well-documented risk factors.

How to reduce your risk of heart attack and stroke

There are several ways to lower your chance of having a heart attack or stroke. The following advice, if you heed it, could save your life:

Have your blood pressure checked once a year. High blood pressure is a major risk factor in heart attack, and it's the major risk factor in stroke.

Don't smoke cigarettes. Smoking increases the risk of heart attack.

Eat Nutritious Food in Moderate Amounts. Eat a well-balanced diet that's low in cholesterol and saturated fats. Fatty foods contribute to atherosclerosis, which itself is a major contributor to heart attack and stroke.

Have regular medical checkups. Risk factors such as high blood pressure, elevated cholesterol, excess weight, lack of exercise and cigarette smoking call for medical supervision to prevent a heart attack or stroke.

What you can control with medical supervision

Blood cholesterol—Cholesterol is a fatty substance that's found in everyone's living tissue. People need some cholesterol, and they get it in two ways. First, a person's body automatically manufactures most of the cholesterol it needs; but second, people increase their cholesterol levels by eating foods that contain it or that stimulate the body to increase its production or cholesterol. Too much cholesterol isn't healthy, however, because when it's carried by the blood it can build up on the walls of arteries. When this happens, the arterial passageways are narrowed, the blood supply to the heart or brain is decreased, and the stage is set for a heart attack or stroke. If excess cholesterol is a problem, your doctor can prescribe dietary changes and drugs to keep your blood cholesterol within a normal range.

High blood pressure. Modern medicine hasn't identified the cause of most cases of high blood pressure. But even though the cause isn't known, fortunately there are ways to treat and control it. If necessary, your doctor can suggest changes in lifestyle and medication to keep your blood pressure in check.

Diabetes. Diabetes, or a hereditary tendency toward it, is linked with an increased risk of heart attack and stroke. Your doctor can detect diabetes and prescribe a program to control your diet and weight if necessary. Exercise and drugs also may be prescribed to keep diabetes in check.

What you can't control

Heredity. Although there's no hard scientific evidence that heart attack and stroke are hereditary, it's true that some families have a higher incidence of these diseases. In such cases, reducing other risk factors (which can be controlled) becomes even more important. Race is also important. Blacks in the U.S. are almost 33% more likely to have high blood pressure than whites. Statistics also show that they are more likely to suffer strokes at an earlier age and with more severe results.

Sex. Young women have a much lower death rate from heart attack than men. After menopause, apparently because of hormonal changes, the rate of heart attack for women increases sharply, although it never reaches that of men.

Age. More than one fifth of all heart-attack deaths occur before age 65. Stroke, generally a disease of the elderly, also strikes younger people at an alarming rate. In fact, about one in seven people who die from stroke is under age 65.

(Estimates based on 1985 provisional statistics for the United States.)

Prevalence[1]—64,890,000 people in the U.S. have one or more forms of heart or blood vessel disease.
- High blood pressure: 59,130,000.
- Coronary heart disease: 4,870,000.
- Rheumatic heart disease: 2,150,000.
- Stroke: 1,990,000.

Cardiovascular disease (CVD) Deaths—991,300 in 1985 (47.6% of all deaths).

More than one-fifth of all persons killed by CVD are under age 65.

Other 1985 mortality: cancer 457,700; accidents 92,100.

Heart attack—caused 540,800 deaths in 1985.
- Heart attack is the leading cause of death in the U.S.
- 4,870,000 people alive today have a history of heart attack, angina pectoris (chest pain), or both.
- More than 300,000 people die each year before they reach the hospital; studies indicate that 50% of heart-attack victims wait two hours or longer before getting to a hospital emergency room.
- This year as many as 1,500,000 people in the U.S. will have a heart attack and about 540,000 of them will die.
- Based on the Framingham Heart Study, 5% of all heart attacks occur in individuals under age 40, and 45 percent occur in individuals under age 65.

Stroke—killed 152,700 in 1985; approximately 1,990,000 stroke victims are alive today.
- Based upon the Framingham study, approximately 500,000 people in the U.S. suffer strokes each year.
- Stroke is the third largest cause of death behind heart attack and cancer.

High blood pressure[2]—afflicts an estimated 59,130,000 people in the U.S. aged six and older.

- Many people who have high blood pressure don't get treatment.
- Only a minority of people with high blood pressure have their problem under control.
- Although the cause of 90% of the cases of high blood pressure isn't known, high blood pressure is easily detected and usually controllable.

Rheumatic heart disease—afflicts 100,000 children and 2,050,000 adults.
- Rheumatic fever and rheumatic heart disease killed about 6,200 in 1985.
- Modern antibiotic treatment has sharply reduced mortality; in 1950, for example, more than 22,000 people in the U.S. died of these diseases.

Congenital heart defects—35 recognizable types of defect.
- About 25,000 babies are born every year with heart defects.
- Infant mortality from heart defects was estimated to be 6,000 people in the U.S. in 1985.

Atherosclerosis—was a leading cause of many of the 693,500 heart attack and stroke deaths in 1985.

Coronary care units (CCU)—most of the 6,000 general hospitals in the U.S. have coronary care capability.
- Specialized coronary care for heart-attack victims can reduce in-hospital deaths by about 30%.

Coronary artery bypass surgery—an estimated 230,000 of these operations were performed in 1985; 74.8% were performed on men.

CVD cost—the cost of cardiovascular disease in 1988 is estimated by the AHA at $83.7 billion. This figure includes the cost of physician and nursing services, hospital and nursing home services, medications and lost productivity resulting from disability.

Research—from 1949 through the 1986-87 fiscal year, the American Heart Association has given more than $691 million in support of research.

- By policy, AHA allocates 60.5% of its National Center budget to research.
- AHA affiliates allocate at least 15% of their gross divisible income to research.
- In fiscal year 1986-87, the AHA contributed $60 million to research.

1. The total number of cases of a given disease in a population at a specific time.
2. These figures are consistent with recommendations of the 1984 Report of the Joint National Committee on Detection, Evaluation and Treatment of High Blood Pressure.

15

Low-fat, Low-cholesterol Recipes You'll Enjoy

**Recipe development by
Helen Fisher, Publisher, Fisher Books,
in conjunction with the Authors.**

Acknowledgements

We wish to thank Susan Deeming, Ph.D., R.D. for the use of her recipes: Jamaican Bean Pot, Brunswick Stew, Spanish Rice & Bean Pie, Lentil-Tomato Soup, Pinto Wheat Bread and Oriental Pocket Sandwiches.

Appetizers

Enjoy appetizers as a relaxed way to introduce the meal to come.

Start with something light and not too filling. Serve a dip with fresh vegetables cut in convenient sizes to replace a heavier fried food.

Enjoy our Bean Dip with jícama or carrot sticks, or Bean Tostadas as a prelude to a Mexican dinner. If you are in the mood for Chinese food, begin with Turkey Bundles. Serve your appetizer with your favorite beverage.

Whatever you choose, relax with family or friends with a complementary appetizer before dinner.

Chili-Onion Dip

2/3 cup non-fat
   cottage cheese
4 tablespoons skim
   milk
2 tablespoons
   Worcestershire sauce
1 teaspoon paprika

3 onion bouillon cubes or
   instant onion bouillon
   mix
1 tablespoon dehydrated
   onion flakes
1 (4-oz.) can chopped mild
   green chili peppers
Assorted fresh vegetables

Mix all ingredients except vegetables in blender or food processor until smooth. Serve with crisp celery, radishes, cauliflower, etc. This dip makes a delicious topping on fish or baked potatoes. Refrigerate in container with a tight fitting lid. Makes 1 cup.

❤ Each serving contains:
   Saturated fat   Trace   Cholesterol   None

Vegetable Dip

1 cup non-fat plain yogurt
1 tablespoon grated
   onion
1 tablespoon chopped
   parsley

1 teaspoon dried dill weed
1 teaspoon Bon Appetit
1 tablespoon capers
Assorted fresh vegetables

In a small bowl, combine all ingredients except vegetables and chill. Serve with your favorite fresh vegetables. Makes about 1 cup.

❤ Each serving contains:
   Saturated fat   Trace   Cholesterol   None

Bean Dip

1/2 cup non-fat plain
  yogurt
1/2 cup Fresh Salsa, page
  140
1/2 teaspoon garlic powder
1/2 teaspoon chili powder

1 cup drained, cooked,
  pinto, kidney or black
  beans
Toasted no-lard tortillas or
  pita bread
Assorted fresh vegetables

In a small serving bowl, combine yogurt, Fresh Salsa, garlic and chili powders. Mash beans slightly; stir into yogurt mixture. Serve with tortillas, pita bread and/or raw vegetables. Makes about 2 cups.

❤ Each serving contains:
  Saturated fat   Trace   Cholesterol   None

Turkey Bundles

1/2 cup (3-oz.) shredded, skinned, cooked turkey breast
1/4 cup finely chopped apple
2 tablespoons chopped celery
1 tablespoon chopped green onion
1 tablespoon chopped green bell pepper
3 tablespoons chopped crystallized ginger
1 tablespoon soy sauce
1 tablespoon rice or cider vinegar
1/2 teaspoon sugar
8 lettuce or spinach leaves

In a small bowl, combine turkey, apple, celery, onion, pepper and ginger. Stir together soy sauce, vinegar and sugar. Pour over turkey mixture; mix thoroughly. For each bundle, place 2 to 3 teaspoons of mixture on lower edge of lettuce or spinach leaf. Roll over, tucking ends in, envelope-style. Place seam side down on small serving tray. Serve at once, or cover and refrigerate until serving time. Makes 8 bundles.

Variation

For individual salads, double amounts above. Shred lettuce or spinach leaves and top with turkey mixture.

❤ Each serving contains:
Saturated fat   Trace   Cholesterol   10mg

Bean Tostadas

12 appetizer-size corn
  tortillas
1-1/2 cups cooked pinto
  or black beans, drained
1/2 teaspoon chili powder
1/4 cup chopped green
  onion
Salt and pepper

3 small tomatoes, chopped
1 tablespoon chopped
  cilantro (Chinese parsley)
  or parsley
3 tablespoons grated
  Parmesan cheese
6 to 8 radishes, sliced

Preheat oven to 350F (175C). Spread tortillas in 1 layer on a baking sheet. Toast in oven 5 to 7 minutes. Remove; set aside. In a saucepan, combine beans, chili powder, onion, salt and pepper to taste. Stir and mash beans as they heat. Remove from heat. Place about 1 tablespoon bean mixture on each tortilla. Top with tomatoes, cilantro, Parmesan cheese and radishes. Serve at once. Makes 12 servings.

❤ Each serving contains:
  Saturated fat   0.3 gram   Cholesterol   Trace

Fresh Salsa

1 cup chopped tomatoes
1/3 cup chopped fresh
  roasted or canned
  chilies
3 green onions, chopped
1/2 teaspoon dried
  oregano leaves

1 tablespoon chopped
  cilantro (Chinese
  parsley)
Salt and pepper
Toasted corn-tortilla or
  pita wedges

In a small bowl, combine all ingredients except tortilla or pita wedges. Cover and chill. Serve with tortilla or pita wedges. Makes about 1-1/2 cups.

❤ Each serving contains:
  Saturated fat   Trace   Cholesterol   None

Smoked-Salmon Spread

1/4 cup Yogurt Cream
   Cheese, page 301
1/4 cup non-fat cottage
   cheese
1 teaspoon lemon juice
1 tablespoon light
   mayonnaise
2 tablespoons chopped
   pimiento-stuffed olives

1/4 teaspoon garlic powder
2 green onions, chopped
1/4 teaspoon lemon
   pepper
3/4 cup flaked smoked
   salmon
Celery sticks
French bread

In a blender or food processor, combine Yogurt Cream Cheese, cottage cheese, lemon juice and mayonnaise. Blend until smooth. Scoop mixture into a serving bowl and stir in remaining ingredients except celery sticks and bread. Chill at least 2 hours before serving. Spread on celery sticks or toasted French bread. Makes about 1-1/2 cups.

❤ Each tablespoon contains:
   Saturated fat   Trace   Cholesterol   None

Crab-Stuffed Mushrooms

24 large fresh mushrooms
1 (6-oz.) can crabmeat or
   6 oz. fresh cooked
   crabmeat
2 green onions, chopped
1 celery stalk, finely
   chopped

1 teaspoon horseradish
2 teaspoons Yogurt Cream
   Cheese, page 301
1/2 teaspoon paprika
3 tablespoons chopped red
   bell pepper or pimiento
Salt and pepper

Remove stems from mushrooms; wipe caps clean with a damp cloth or paper towel. In a small bowl, combine remaining ingredients. Season to taste with salt and pepper. Fill mushroom caps with mixture. Serve. To serve hot, place on baking sheet and bake in 350F (175C) oven about 12 minutes. Serve at once. Makes 24.

❤ Each serving of 3 contains:
   Saturated fat   Trace   Cholesterol   5mg

Jícama Sticks

1 jícama, about 1/2 lb., or
   2 cucumbers
3 tablespoons orange-
   juice concentrate,
   undiluted

2 teaspoons grated orange
   peel, if desired
1/2 teaspoon chili powder
1/4 teaspoon garlic powder
Salt and pepper

Peel jícama; cut into 1/2-inch sticks. If using cucumbers, peel, cut and remove seeds. Combine orange-juice concentrate, orange peel, if desired, chili and garlic powders. Stir to combine. Season with salt and pepper to taste. Pour over jícama or cucumbers; toss to coat. Chill 1 to 2 hours before serving.

❤ Each serving of 3 contains:
   Saturated fat   None   Cholesterol   None

Stuffed Cherry Tomatoes

24 cherry tomatoes
1 (6-oz.) can cocktail
   shrimp, drained, or 6 oz.
   fresh cooked shrimp
1/4 cup cooked rice or
   orzo (riso) pasta
2 teaspoons curry
   powder

1/4 teaspoon dry mustard
1/4 cup cooked petite
   peas
2 teaspoons lemon juice
Salt and pepper

Slice tops from tomatoes. With a melon baller or sharp small spoon, scoop out pulp and set aside. Chop tomato pulp and shrimp. Combine with rice or orzo, curry powder, mustard, peas and lemon juice. Season with salt and pepper to taste. Fill tomato shells with rice mixture. Cover and chill before serving. Makes 24.

❤ Each serving of 3 contains:
   Saturated fat   Trace   Cholesterol   40mg

Turkey-Stuffed Mushrooms

1/4 lb. skinned turkey
  breast, ground
1 tomato, seeded, chopped
1 teaspoon garlic powder
2/3 cup fresh French bread
  crumbs

2 tablespoons parsley
1 teaspoon imitation
  bacon bits
2 egg whites
Salt and pepper
18 large fresh mushrooms

Preheat oven to 375F (190C). Spray a 13 x 9-in. baking sheet with vegetable cooking spray. Set aside. Spray a skillet with vegetable cooking spray. Cook turkey until no pink color remains; stir with fork to crumble. Remove from heat. Add tomato, garlic powder, bread crumbs, parsley, bacon bits and egg whites. Thoroughly combine. Add salt and pepper to taste. Brush mushrooms with a dry cloth; remove stems. Place about 1 tablespoon filling in each mushroom. Place in prepared pan. Bake uncovered about 20 minutes. Serve hot. Makes 18.

♥ Each serving of 3 contains:
  Saturated fat   0.3 gram   Cholesterol   16mg

Soups

Homemade soup brings back memories of home and good, simple meals. We have a variety from which to choose, ranging from a hearty Minestrone or Split-Pea Soup to a very light, yet flavorful Egg Drop Soup.

For warm weather enjoyment, we have two cold soups: Gazpacho and Chilled Garden Soup. Cream soups take little time to prepare and can help turn a small portion of leftovers into a satisfying dish.

Basic stock recipes are included for use in preparing your own Beef, Chicken and Vegetarian Broths. Make them when time is available and freeze them in small containers for future use. Adjust the vegetables and seasoning to your family's preferences. We want these recipes to serve as a starting point that you can build on.

Gazpacho

3 cups tomato juice
1 beef bouillon cube or
   1 teaspoon granules
3 tablespoons wine vinegar
1 teaspoon Worcestershire
   sauce
4 to 6 drops Tabasco sauce
1 teaspoon olive oil
1 large tomato, chopped

1 cucumber, chopped
1 small onion, chopped
2 celery stalks, chopped
1/2 green bell pepper,
   chopped
1 tablespoon chopped
   cilantro (Chinese parsley)
1 cup croutons

In a small saucepan, heat tomato juice to boiling; add bouillon and stir until dissolved. Remove from heat; add vinegar, Worcestershire sauce, Tabasco and oil. Cool. Pour into a large bowl or container with a cover. Add tomato, cucumber, onion, celery, green pepper and cilantro. Cover and chill several hours. Serve cold. Top with croutons. Additional chopped vegetables may be added if desired. Makes 6 servings.

♥ Each 1-cup serving contains:
   Saturated fat   Trace   Cholesterol   None

French Onion Soup

2 tablespoons olive oil
6 or 7 cups sliced onions
1 teaspoon sugar
2 quarts Beef Broth,
   page 159

1/2 cup white wine, if
   desired
6 slices French bread,
   toasted

Heat oil in a 4-quart pot; sauté onions in oil. Cover and cook over medium-low heat until tender. Add sugar and stir about 10 minutes until golden brown. Add stock. Cover and simmer until onions are soft, about 15 to 20 minutes. Add wine if desired. To serve, ladle soup into bowls; top each with a slice of toasted French bread. Makes 8 servings.

♥ Each 1-cup serving contains:
   Saturated fat   0.8 gram   Cholesterol   None

Leek & Potato Soup

2 leeks, chopped, include
    4 inches of green, or
    1 large onion, chopped
1 quart Chicken Broth,
    page 158, Vegetarian
    Broth, page 148

2 cups chopped raw
    potatoes
Non-fat plain yogurt
Parsley
Salt and pepper

In a 4-quart pot, combine leeks or onion, broth and potatoes. Bring to a boil; reduce heat, partially cover and simmer for 55 minutes. In a blender or food processor, purée potato mixture. Serve with a topping of non-fat yogurt. Garnish with sprigs of parsley. Season with salt and pepper to taste. Serve hot or cold. Makes 6 servings.

♥ Each 1-cup serving contains:
    Saturated fat   0.3 gram   Cholesterol   Trace

Split-Pea Soup

2 cups dried split peas
3 quarts water
6 bouillon cubes
1 garlic clove
1 large onion, chopped
4 carrots, sliced
4 celery stalks, sliced

2 bay leaves
1/2 teaspoon dried leaf
    thyme
Salt and coarse pepper
Imitation bacon bits, if
    desired

Rinse peas and place in a 4-quart pot. Add water, bouillon cubes, garlic, onion, carrots, celery, bay leaves and thyme. Bring to a boil; reduce heat. Cover and simmer 45 to 50 minutes until peas and vegetables are tender. If desired, remove bay leaves and purée mixture in a blender or food processor. Season with salt and pepper to taste. Garnish with bacon bits, if desired. Makes 8 servings.

♥ Each 1-cup serving contains:
    Saturated fat   Trace   Cholesterol   None

Carrot & Onion Soup

1-1/2 cups shredded
   carrots
1/2 cup chopped onions
1 quart fat-free broth
1/4 cup tomato paste or
   sauce

1 tablespoon uncooked
   rice
1/2 package Butter Buds®
1 cup frozen peas
Chives or parsley, chopped

Place all ingredients except peas and chives in a 4-quart pot and bring to a boil. Simmer uncovered about 35 minutes. Add peas. Garnish with chives or parsley. Makes 6 servings.

❤ Each 1-cup serving contains:
   Saturated fat   Trace   Cholesterol   None

Egg-Drop Soup

6 cups Chicken Broth,
   page 158
2 slices fresh ginger root,
   peeled
2 teaspoons cornstarch
1 tablespoon water
1 teaspoon soy sauce

2 green onions, chopped
1/3 cup frozen peas
1 teaspoon rice wine or
   sherry, if desired
1/8 cup egg substitute
1 egg white

Pour chicken broth into a medium saucepan, add ginger root and bring to a boil. Reduce heat and simmer 5 minutes. In a small bowl, blend cornstarch, water and soy sauce. Stir into broth; add green onions and peas. Continue cooking 3 to 4 minutes. Add wine. Remove ginger root and discard. In a small bowl, beat egg substitute and egg white. Pour in a stream into hot broth; stir lightly, forming threads. Serve at once. Makes 8 servings.

❤ Each 1-cup serving contains:
   Saturated fat   Trace   Cholesterol   None

Vegetarian Broth

2 onions, quartered
2 parsnips or turnips
3 or 4 medium carrots
4 inches celery tops,
   including leaves

2 bay leaves
2 quarts water
2 cups chopped,
   mixed fresh vegetables
4 to 5 sprigs fresh parsley

In a 4-quart pot, combine all ingredients. Simmer, covered until vegetables are tender. Strain mixture through cheese-cloth into a container. Discard vegetables and herbs. Use broth at once or refrigerate, tightly covered. Broth may be frozen for later use. Makes about 6 cups.

♥ 1 cup contains:
   Saturated fat   None   Cholesterol   None

Minestrone Soup

2 cups tomato juice
1 garlic clove
1 onion, chopped
1 zucchini, chopped
2 celery stalks, chopped
2 carrots, sliced
2 tablespoons chopped
   parsley
1 (10-1/2-oz.) can beef
   bouillon
4 cups water

1 teaspoon dried leaf
   oregano
1 teaspoon basil
1/2 cup shredded cabbage
1 cup chopped tomatoes
1/2 cup kidney beans,
   cooked, drained
1/2 cup garbanzo beans,
   cooked, drained
1 cup cooked pasta
Salt and pepper

In a 4-quart pot, combine tomato juice, garlic, onion, zucchini, celery, carrots, parsley, beef bouillon and water. Bring to a boil; reduce heat, partially cover and simmer until vegetables are tender. Add oregano, basil, cabbage, tomatoes, kidney beans and garbanzo beans. Continue cooking about 10 minutes. Add pasta, cook until heated. Serve hot. Makes 10 servings.

♥ Each 1-cup serving contains:
   Saturated fat   Trace   Cholesterol   None

Orange-Tomato Bisque

1 (10-1/2-oz.) can
  condensed tomato soup
1 (14-1/2-oz.) can stewed
  tomatoes, chopped
1/3 cup orange-juice
  concentrate (undiluted)
2 teaspoons sugar, if
  desired

2 teaspoons dried leaf
  tarragon
2 teaspoons basil leaves
1/2 teaspoon parsley leaves
2/3 cup skim milk
1 teaspoon orange extract

In a medium saucepan, combine all ingredients; stir to blend. Simmer about 10 minutes. Serve hot or chilled. Makes 4 servings.

❤ Each 1-cup serving contains:
  Saturated fat Trace   Cholesterol None

Spiced Tomato Soup

4 cups tomato juice
1 cup beef bouillon
2 tablespoons lemon juice
2 teaspoons Worcester-
  shire sauce

1/4 teaspoon celery salt
1/8 teaspoon ground
  cinnamon
1/8 teaspoon ground
  cloves

In a medium saucepan, combine all ingredients. Bring to a boil; reduce heat and simmer about 5 minutes. Makes 4 to 5 servings.

❤ Each serving contains:
  Saturated fat Trace   Cholesterol None

Chilled Garden Soup

1 carrot, chopped
1/2 cup chopped
   cauliflower
1 small onion, chopped
1 cup water
1 cup fresh or frozen peas
1/2 teaspoon salt
1 quart non-fat plain
   yogurt
3 tablespoons chopped
   fresh dill

1 tablespoon chopped
   mint leaves
2 tablespoons lemon juice
1 cucumber, peeled,
   seeded, chopped
Chives
4 to 6 radishes, sliced
Coarse pepper
Paprika

Place carrot, cauliflower, onion and water in a small saucepan. Bring to a boil; cook vegetables until tender. Add peas and salt; reduce heat and simmer about 3 minutes. Remove from heat and cool. Refrigerate about 30 minutes until vegetables are thoroughly chilled. Mix vegetables with yogurt, dill, mint, lemon juice and cucumber. Garnish with chives and sliced radishes, coarse pepper and paprika. Served chilled. Makes 6 servings.

❤ Each serving contains:
   Saturated fat   Trace   Cholesterol   None

Black-Bean Soup

2 cups dried black beans
Water
2 quarts Chicken broth,
    page 158, Vegetarian
    Broth, page 148, or
    water
2 onions, chopped
2 bay leaves

1 carrot, sliced
2 green bell peppers,
    chopped
2 celery stalks, chopped
Salt and pepper
Vinegar
2 cups cooked rice
4 chopped green onions

Rinse beans. In a large pot, combine beans and 2 quarts water. Boil 2 minutes. Remove from heat; cover. Set aside 1 to 1-1/2 hours. Drain and discard water. Add Chicken Broth, Vegetarian Stock or water, onions and bay leaves. Bring to a boil; reduce heat and simmer about 1 hour. Add carrot, bell peppers and celery; simmer about 45 minutes, until beans are tender. Season to taste with salt and pepper. To serve, ladle soup into bowls. Season with vinegar to taste, about 1 teaspoon per bowl. Add cooked rice and chopped green onions. Makes 2 quarts, about 8 servings.

♥ Each serving contains:
    Saturated fat   Trace   Cholesterol   None

Great Northern White-Bean Soup

3 cups great northern
    white beans
2 quarts water
1 onion, chopped
1 carrot, finely chopped
2 leeks, chopped
1 bay leaf
2 garlic cloves

1/2 cup chopped celery
    tops (including leaves)
6 beef bouillon cubes or 6
    teaspoons granules
1 pkg. Butter Buds,® if
    desired
Salt and pepper

Rinse beans; place in 4-quart pot. Add water, covering beans 3 to 4 inches. Bring to a boil. Boil 2 minutes. Cover and remove from heat. Let stand 1 to 2 hours. Drain beans, discarding soaking water. Return beans to pot. Cover with 2 quarts water; add onion, carrot, leeks, bay leaf, garlic, celery tops and bouillon. Bring to a boil, reduce heat and cover. Simmer until beans are tender, 1-1/2 to 2 hours. Add Butter Buds,® if desired. Simmer about 15 minutes. Season to taste with salt and pepper. Remove bay leaf. Makes 12 servings.

❤ Each 1-cup serving contains:
    Saturated fat   Trace   Cholesterol None

Navy-Bean Soup

2 cups dried navy beans
2 quarts water
1 small onion, chopped

1 bay leaf
1 garlic clove
Salt and pepper

Rinse navy beans; place in a 4-quart pot. Add water, covering beans 3 to 4 inches. Bring to a boil. Boil 2 minutes. Cover and remove from heat. Let stand 1 to 2 hours. Drain beans, discard soaking water. Return beans to pot. Cover with 2 quarts water; add onion, bay leaf and garlic. Bring to a boil, reduce heat and cover. Simmer until beans are tender, about 1-1/2 to 2 hours. Season to taste with salt and pepper. Remove bay leaf. Makes 8 servings.

❤ Each 1-cup serving contains:
    Saturated fat   Trace   Cholesterol None

Russian Borscht

1 (16-oz.) can sliced beets
1 (14-1/2-oz.) can stewed
   tomatoes
2 medium onions, sliced
1 tablespoon lemon juice
   or vinegar
1-1/2 cups Beef Broth,
   page 159
1 carrot, sliced

1 green bell pepper,
   chopped
2 celery stalks, sliced
3 cups shredded cabbage
2 teaspoons sugar, if
   desired.
1/2 teaspoon dillweed
Salt and pepper
Non-fat plain yogurt

In a 4-quart pot, combine beets, tomatoes, onions, lemon juice or vinegar, broth, carrot, green pepper, celery and cabbage. Bring to a boil. Cover, reduce heat and simmer 20 minutes or until vegetables are tender. Add sugar, if desired, dillweed, salt and pepper to taste. Serve hot or cold. Top each serving with 1 tablespoon non-fat yogurt. Makes 8 servings.

♥ Each 1-cup serving contains:
   Saturated fat   Trace   Cholesterol   None

Cauliflower-Curry Soup

1 medium cauliflower,
  chopped
1/2 onion, chopped
3 green onions, chopped
1 garlic clove
2 celery stalks, chopped
1/2 cup peas
3 cups Chicken Broth,
  page 158
2 teaspoons curry powder

1/4 teaspoon dried leaf
  thyme
1/4 teaspoon dried leaf
  basil
1/4 teaspoon dried leaf
  savory
1/4 teaspoon ground
  nutmeg
Salt and pepper

Place cauliflower in a medium saucepan; cover with water and cook until tender. Remove from heat and drain. Set aside. Spray a 2-quart saucepan with vegetable cooking spray. Sauté onions and garlic. Add celery, peas and broth. Bring to a boil; cover and simmer 15 minutes or until vegetables are tender. Add cauliflower, curry powder, thyme, basil, savory and nutmeg. If desired, pour 2 cups vegetable mixture into a blender or food processor. Blend until smooth; repeat with remaining mixture. Season with salt and pepper to taste. Makes 6 servings.

♥ Each 1-cup serving contains:
  Saturated fat   Trace   Cholesterol   None

Mixed-Bean Soup

1-lb. mixture of 3 to 15
   kinds of dried beans
2 quarts water
1 cup shredded, smoked
   turkey breast
1/2 large onion, chopped
2 carrots, sliced
1 (14-1/2-oz.) can tomatoes

Garlic powder
1 teaspoon dry mustard
1 teaspoon dried leaf
   marjoram
1 cup cooked pasta
Salt and lemon pepper
1 to 2 tablespoons lemon
   juice, if desired

Rinse beans; place in a 4-quart pot. Add water covering beans 3 to 4 inches. Bring to a boil. Boil 2 minutes. Cover and remove from heat. Let stand 1 to 2 hours. Drain beans, discarding soaking water. Return beans to pot. Cover with 2 quarts water; add smoked turkey and onion. Cook about 45 minutes. Add carrots and tomatoes. Simmer until vegetables are tender. Stir in garlic powder, mustard, marjoram and cooked pasta. Season with salt and lemon pepper to taste. If desired, add lemon juice. Makes 10 servings.

♥ Each 1-cup serving contains:
Saturated fat   Trace   Cholesterol   None

Curry-Corn Chowder

2 tablespoons Puritan® oil
1/2 onion, chopped
3 tablespoons chopped
  celery
2 tablespoons chopped
  red bell pepper
1 (12-oz.) can evaporated
  skimmed milk
1/4 cup water

1 (17-oz.) can creamed
  corn
1/2 cup raisins
1 teaspoon curry powder
1 medium apple, cored,
  chopped
Lemon pepper
Curry powder

In a 2-quart pan, heat oil and sauté onion. Add celery, red bell pepper, evaporated milk, water, corn, raisins and curry powder. Bring to a boil; reduce heat and simmer about 10 minutes, stirring occasionally. Add chopped apple and cook 5 minutes longer. Season to taste with lemon pepper and additional curry powder. Makes 6 cups.

❤ Each 1-cup serving contains:
  Saturated fat   0.4 gram   Cholesterol   None

Lentil-Tomato Soup

1-1/2 cups dried lentils
5 cups water
1/2 cup chopped onion
1 garlic clove, minced
1 tablespoon olive or
   Puritan® oil
2 teaspoons salt
1/8 teaspoon pepper
2 teaspoons sugar
1/4 teaspoon dried leaf
oregano
1/4 teaspoon dried leaf
   basil
1 tablespoon chopped
   fresh parsley
1 (16-oz.) can tomatoes,
   diced
3 tablespoons tomato paste
Parsley sprigs

Sort through lentils, discarding foreign material. Rinse under running water. In a large saucepan, combine lentils and 5 cups water. In a small skillet, sauté onions and garlic in oil until onion is tender but not browned. Add to lentils. Stir in salt, pepper, sugar, oregano, basil and parsley. Bring to a boil; reduce heat. Cover and simmer until lentils are tender, about 45 minutes. Add tomatoes, including juice, and tomato paste. Stir well. Simmer 15 minutes longer. Ladle into bowls. Garnish each bowl with a fresh parsley sprig. Makes 4 servings.

♥ Each serving contains:
  Saturated fat   Trace   Cholesterol   None

Chicken Broth

2-1/2 to 3 lbs. skinned
   chicken pieces
6 cups water
1 large onion, sliced
2 carrots
1 parsnip, if desired
1 celery stalk with leaves

2 bay leaves
4 to 5 whole black pepper
   corns
4 to 5 parsley sprigs
1/2 teaspoon dried sage
   leaves
Salt and pepper

Place chicken and water in a large pot. Add remaining ingredients. Bring to a boil. Reduce heat, partially cover and simmer about 2 hours. Remove vegetables and chicken. Refrigerate chicken for future use. Strain broth into another container; refrigerate for several hours. Remove and discard any fat from surface of broth. Adjust seasoning to taste before using. Makes 4 cups broth.

♥ Each 1-cup serving contains:
   Saturated fat   1 gram*   Cholesterol   10mg

* Amount of saturated fat varies considerably depending on how well the fat is trimmed away and how much fat is removed from the surface of the broth.

Beef Broth

3 to 4 lbs. meaty beef
  shank or soup bones
6 cups water
1 large onion, chopped
2 bay leaves
3 celery stalks with leaves

1 carrot
4 to 5 black peppercorns
3 to 4 parsley sprigs
Salt and pepper

Preheat oven to 350F (175C). Place soup bones in a shallow baking dish. Bake uncovered about 30 minutes, until browned. Place browned bones and water in a large pot. Bring to a boil. Reduce heat; simmer about 2 hours. Remove any foam that may form on the surface. Add remaining ingredients; simmer about 2 hours longer. Remove meat, bones and vegetables. Reserve meat for another use. Strain broth into another container; refrigerate several hours. Remove and discard any fat from surface of broth. Adjust seasoning to taste before using. Makes 4 cups broth.

❤ Each 1-cup serving contains:
  Saturated fat   1 gram*   Cholesterol   10mg

* Amount of saturated fat varies considerably depending on how well the fat is trimmed away and how much fat is removed from the surface of the broth.

Cream-of-Celery Soup

4 celery stalks, sliced
1 cup water
1/4 cup chopped onion
1/4 teaspoon dry mustard

White Sauce, page 297
3 tablespoons white wine,
   if desired
Salt and pepper

Combine celery, water and onion in a saucepan. Cook uncovered until celery and onion are tender. Add remaining ingredients. Stir until heated. Season to taste with salt and pepper. Makes 4 servings.

Variation

Omit celery and substitute 1 cup cooked vegetables, season as desired.

♥ Each serving contains:
   Saturated fat   0.3 gram   Cholesterol   Trace

Salads

Salads are almost limitless; turn your imagination loose.

Choose Fruit-Filled Pineapple for a satisfying light luncheon dish. Enjoy Mideast flavors in Couscous Salad, which can be either a meal in itself or a side dish. This recipe is an excellent way to add more grain and fiber to your diet. Marinated Medley is a fine accompaniment for either broiled chicken or fish.

Remember these tips: Salad greens should be rinsed, patted dry with paper towels and chilled before serving. Salad dressing clings to a dry surface better than one that is still wet. For added interest, cut ingredients into bite-size pieces of various shapes. A chilled plate helps keep chilled ingredients crisp. Finally, garnishing is that extra touch appreciated by all.

Fruit-Filled Pineapple

Juice of 1 lemon
1 tablespoon maraschino-
  cherry syrup
1 fresh pineapple
1/2 cup fresh or frozen
  strawberries
3 kiwis

3 oranges
1 apple
1/4 cup marshmallow
  creme
1/4 cup non-fat plain
  yogurt

In a small bowl, blend lemon juice and maraschino-cherry syrup. Cut pineapple in half. With a sharp knife, cut in 1/2 inch around edge of pineapple, leaving shell intact. Remove core and discard; cut remaining pineapple into bite-size pieces. In a large bowl, combine with fruit and lemon syrup. Refrigerate at least 1 hour. Fill pineapple shells with chilled fruit. Mix marshmallow creme and yogurt. Pour over fruit. Makes 4 servings.

♥ Each serving contains:
  Saturated fat   Trace   Cholesterol   None

Fruit Cocktail

1 cup sliced strawberries
1 cup melon pieces
2 peaches, sliced
1/2 cup blueberries
1 banana

1/2 cup cran-raspberry
  juice
1/4 cup club soda, lemon-
  lime soda or sparkling
  white grape juice

Mix all fruits except banana in a bowl. Cover and refrigerate 1 hour. When ready to serve, cut up banana and mix with fruit in bowl. Serve in individual bowls. Mix cran-raspberry juice and soda or sparkling grape juice. Pour juice mixture over each serving. Makes 6 servings.

♥ Each serving contains:
  Saturated fat   None   Cholesterol   None

Fruit-Salad Combo

Apples	Mangoes	Strawberries
Apricots	Melons	2 tablespoon
Bananas	Oranges	honey
Grapefruit	Peaches	1/2 cup non-fat
Grapes	Pears	plain yogurt
Guavas	Pineapples	
Kiwis	Raspberries	

Make a delicious fruit salad by using a combination of various fruits which may include some of those listed above. Cut fruit into interesting slices, pieces or sections. Allow 2 cups per person. Arrange using a variety of colors. When possible include strawberries, blueberries or kiwis as accent colors. If bananas are prepared before serving, sprinkle with lemon juice to avoid darkening. Stir honey into yogurt. Spoon over salad. Makes 1/2 cup or 2 to 3 servings.

❤ Each serving contains:
   Saturated fat   None   Cholesterol   None

Variation

Powdered orange or raspberry drink concentrate may be blended with non-fat plain yogurt to make a tasty dressing which may be mixed with the fruits or as a topping. Sweeten with honey, sugar or sweetener as desired.

❤ Each serving contains:
   Saturated fat   None   Cholesterol   None

Spinach Salad

1 bunch fresh spinach
1/4 red onion, sliced
1/4 pound fresh
    mushrooms, sliced
1 (6-oz.) can sliced water
    chestnuts, drained
2 to 3 radishes, sliced
1 cup frozen peas or pea
    pods, thawed

1 tablespoon Grape Nuts®
    cereal
Lemon or lime wedges
Poppy Seed Dressing,
    page 176, if desired
Salt and pepper

Wash spinach, remove stems; pat leaves dry with paper towels. Line 4 to 6 plates with spinach leaves. Add a layer of onion rings. Combine mushrooms, water chestnuts, radishes and green peas. Spoon mushroom mixture on top of spinach and onion rings. Sprinkle with cereal. Squeeze lemon or lime on each salad before serving. Or serve with Poppy Seed Dressing. Season with salt and pepper to taste. Makes 4 to 6 servings.

♥ Each serving contains:
    Saturated fat   None   Cholesterol   None

♥ With Poppy Seed Dressing:
    Saturated fat   Trace   Cholesterol   None

Seafood Salad

1/2 cup non-fat plain
　yogurt
1/4 cup chili sauce or
　Fresh Salsa, page 140
1 celery stalk, chopped
1 tablespoon lemon juice
1 teaspoon prepared
　horseradish
1 (12-oz.) pkg. frozen
　cooked shrimp, imitation
　crab, water-packed tuna
　or pink salmon

Lettuce or spinach leaves
1 (15-oz.) can asparagus
　spears, drained
2 medium tomatoes,
　chopped
Salt and lemon pepper

In a small bowl, blend non-fat yogurt with chili sauce or salsa. Add celery, lemon juice, horseradish and seafood. Line plates with lettuce or spinach leaves. Spoon seafood mixture on top. Garnish with asparagus spears and chopped tomatoes. Season to taste with salt and lemon pepper. Makes 4 servings.

♥ Each serving contains:

	Saturated fat	Cholesterol
Shrimp	0.3 gram	120mg
Crab	Trace	45mg
Tuna	0.3 gram	50mg
Salmon	0.5 gram	50mg

Cucumber Sticks

6 tablespoons non-fat
  plain yogurt
2 to 3 tablespoons minced
  green onion
2 teaspoons basil, mint or
  dried leaf tarragon

1 tablespoon lemon juice
3 cucumbers or zucchini,
  cut in 2-inch matchstick
  lengths
1 teaspoon paprika
Salt and pepper

In a small bowl, stir non-fat yogurt, green onions, basil, mint or tarragon and lemon juice until well blended. Combine with cucumber or zucchini sticks. Chill before serving. Sprinkle with paprika. Season to taste with salt and pepper. Makes 6 servings.

♥ Each serving contains:
  Saturated fat   None   Cholesterol   None

Cole Slaw

3 tablespoons vinegar
3 tablespoons orange juice
1/2 teaspoon pepper
3 tablespoons sugar
1 teaspoon caraway seeds

4 cups shredded red
  cabbage
1 apple, cored, sliced
1/2 cup raisins

In a cup, combine vinegar, orange juice, pepper, sugar and caraway seeds. In a salad bowl, mix cabbage, apple and raisins. Pour vinegar mixture over and toss to coat. Makes 6 servings.

♥ Each serving contains:
  Saturated fat   None   Cholesterol   None

Artichoke & Asparagus Salad

1 lb. fresh asparagus,
   cooked, or 1 (15-oz.) can
4 fresh artichoke hearts,
   cooked, or 1 (14-oz.) can
   plain artichoke hearts
   or 1 (9-oz.) pkg. frozen
   artichoke hearts
Lettuce leaves
1 large tomato, chopped
   or sliced
2 green onions, sliced
   or 1/2 red onion, sliced
   in rings
1/2 cup mushrooms, sliced
1/2 red or yellow bell
   pepper, sliced
4 tablespoons lemon juice
   or Italian Dressing,
   page 181
Salt and pepper
1 tablespoon sesame
   seeds, toasted

Cut asparagus and artichoke hearts into bite-size pieces. Chill 1 hour. Line plates with lettuce leaves. In a bowl, combine tomato, onions, mushrooms and bell pepper. Sprinkle with lemon juice or Italian Dressing; toss to coat. Season to taste with salt and pepper. Place on lettuce and top with toasted sesame seeds. Makes 4 servings.

♥ Each serving contains:
   With Italian Dressing:
   Saturated fat   1.2 grams   Cholesterol   None
   With lemon juice:
   Saturated fat   trace   Cholesterol   None

Russian Potato Salad

Lettuce or spinach leaves
1 (16-oz.) can cubed beets,
    drained
2 small potatoes, cooked,
    peeled, cubed
2 carrots, sliced, cooked
2 tomatoes, chopped
1 green onion, finely
    chopped

1/4 cup cut green beans,
    cooked
1 teaspoon lemon or lime
    juice
2 tablespoons non-fat
    plain yogurt
1/2 tablespoon beet horse-
    radish, if desired
Dillweed

Line salad bowl with lettuce or spinach leaves. In a large bowl, combine beets, potatoes, carrots, tomatoes, onion and green beans. In a cup, blend lemon or lime juice with yogurt and horseradish, if desired. Pour over vegetable mixture and carefully mix. Chill until ready to serve. Sprinkle top with dill weed. Makes 6 to 8 servings.

❤ Each serving contains:
    Saturated fat   Trace   Cholesterol   None

Black-Bean Salad

2 tablespoons wine vinegar
2 tablespoons olive oil
1 tablespoon chopped
    cilantro (Chinese parsley)
    or parsley
1 cup black beans, cooked,
    drained

3 green onions, chopped
1/2 green bell pepper,
    chopped
2 celery stalks, chopped
1/4 cup sliced green olives
3 tablespoons pimientos,
    chopped

In a salad bowl, mix together vinegar, oil and cilantro or parsley. Add remaining ingredients. Stir to combine. Chill before serving. Makes 4 servings.

❤ Each serving contains:
    Saturated fat   1 gram   Cholesterol   None

Marinated Medley

2 cups sliced yellow
  crookneck squash
1 cup fresh or frozen peas
1 leek or 1/2 onion,
  chopped

1/2 red bell pepper,
  chopped
6 tablespoons Italian
  Dressing, page 181

In a saucepan, cover squash with water and cook until tender-crisp, about 5 minutes. Add peas; cover and remove from heat. Thoroughly rinse leek, if using; trim off green end. Cut lengthwise in half, then into 1-inch pieces. Cook chopped leek or onion in a saucepan with water to cover, about 5 to 7 minutes. Drain squash, peas and leek or onion. Place in a salad bowl, add red bell pepper and Italian Dressing. Stir to coat all pieces. Cover and chill at least 1 hour before serving. Makes 6 servings.

❤ Each serving contains:
  Saturated fat   1.2 grams   Cholesterol   None

Vegetable Gelatin Salad

1 (3-oz.) pkg. lemon
  gelatin
1 cup boiling water
3/4 cup cold water
1-1/2 teaspoons vinegar
1 small green bell pepper,
  chopped

3/4 cup shredded carrots
3/4 cup fresh or frozen
  green peas
4 green onions, chopped
1 cup chopped ripe tomato
1 teaspoon chopped fresh
  parsley

Dissolve gelatin in hot water, add cold water and vinegar. Chill until slightly thickened. Fold in green pepper, carrots, peas, onions, tomato and parsley. Chill in 1 large or 6 small individual molds. Makes 6 servings.

❤ Each serving contains:
  Saturated fat   None   Cholesterol   None

Couscous Salad

2 teaspoons frozen orange-
   juice concentrate
1-1/2 cups water
4 teaspoons sugar
1 tablespoon diet soft
   margarine
1 cup couscous
1/2 cup peas, cooked
1 large tomato, chopped
1/2 cup mushrooms, sliced

1/2 cup currants or raisins
1 teaspoon chopped mint,
   if desired
1/4 teaspoon ground
   nutmeg
3 tablespoons lemon juice
3 tablespoons Puritan® oil
1 (11-oz.) can mandarin
   oranges, drained

In a saucepan, combine orange-juice concentrate, water, sugar and margarine. Bring to a boil. Stir in couscous; cover and remove from heat. Let stand 5 to 10 minutes. Turn into a salad bowl; fluff with a fork. Add peas, tomato, mushrooms and currants or raisins. Gently stir with a fork. In a cup combine mint, if desired, nutmeg, lemon juice and oil. Pour over couscous mixture and gently mix with a fork. Garnish with mandarin-orange segments. Serve either warm or chilled. Makes 6 servings.

♥ Each serving contains:
   Saturated fat   1 gram   Cholesterol   None

Pasta Salad

2 cups cooked ziti or
  spiral pasta
1 cup chopped broccoli,
  cooked
1 cucumber or 2 zucchini,
  sliced
1 small red bell pepper,
  chopped
1 medium carrot, peeled,
  sliced

1 fennel bulb, trimmed,
  sliced, or 2 celery stalks,
  sliced
1 (6-1/2-oz.) can water-
  packed tuna, drained
1/3 cup Italian Dressing,
  page 181
1 tablespoon capers

Combine pasta, broccoli, cucumber or zucchini, bell pepper, carrot, fennel or celery and tuna. Pour about 1/3 cup Italian Dressing over all. Toss to coat. Scatter capers on top. Chill before serving. Makes 6 servings.

Variation

Omit tuna, substitute 3 oz. chopped, skinned, cooked chicken breast.

❤ Each serving contains:

	Saturated fat	Cholesterol
Tuna	1.0 gram	50mg
Chicken	1.2 grams	70mg

Orange-Cucumber Salad

2 navel oranges or 2
  (11-oz.) cans mandarin
  oranges, drained
1 cup sliced red onion
1 cucumber, thinly sliced
2 tomatoes, sliced
1 tablespoon chopped
  fresh mint, cilantro
  (Chinese parsley) or
  parsley

1/4 cup vinegar
2 tablespoons sugar
1/4 cup Puritan® oil
1/4 cup water

With a sharp knife, remove peel and white membrane from fresh oranges. Cut oranges into thin slices. Place orange slices or segments, onion, cucumber and tomatoes in a large glass salad bowl. In a small container, stir mint, cilantro or parsley with vinegar, sugar, oil and water. Pour over orange and vegetable mixture. Cover and refrigerate 4 hours or longer. Makes 6 to 8 servings.

♥ Each serving contains:
  Saturated fat   1.2 grams   Cholesterol   None

Shrimp Salad

Lettuce or spinach leaves
1 papaya, peeled, sliced
1 (12-oz.) pkg. cooked
    shrimp
2 celery stalks, sliced

1 green onion, finely
    chopped
1 cup seedless green
    grapes
2 limes or lemons

Line plates with lettuce or spinach leaves. Place 1/4 of papaya slices on each plate. Add a mound of shrimp, top with celery and green onion. Place grapes on the side. Cut limes or lemons into wedges; place on plates. Squeeze lime or lemon juice over salad. Makes 4 servings.

♥ Each 3-oz. serving contains:
    Saturated fat   0.3 gram   Cholesterol   120mg

Hawaiian Rice Salad

2 cups cooked rice
1 cup seedless green
    grapes
1 peach, peeled, sliced
1/2 papaya, peeled,
    chopped
1 (11-oz.) can mandarin
    oranges, drained

1/2 cup Poppy-Seed
    Dressing, page 176, or
    Fruit Dressing, page 181
1 (20-oz.) can pineapple
    slices, drained
1/2 cup cherries
1 tablespoon chopped
    crystallized ginger

In a large salad bowl, combine rice, grapes, peach, papaya, oranges and dressing. Cover and refrigerate at least 2 hours. To serve, place 1 pineapple slice on each plate; top with a mound of rice-fruit mixture. Garnish with cherries and crystallized ginger. Makes 6 to 8 servings.

♥ Each serving contains:
    Saturated fat   Trace   Cholesterol   None

Summer Potato Salad

1 cup (1/2 lb.) fresh
   mushrooms, sliced
3 cups sliced, peeled,
   cooked potatoes
2 small zucchini, sliced
1/2 cup chopped celery
4 green onions, chopped

1/2 red or green bell
   pepper, chopped
1 fennel bulb, sliced, if
   desired
2 tablespoons capers
1/3 cup Italian Dressing,
   page 181

In a large salad bowl, combine all ingredients. Cover and refrigerate at least 4 hours before serving. Makes 6 servings.

❤ Each 1 cup serving contains:
   Saturated fat   1 gram   Cholesterol   None

Potato Salad

3 cups sliced, peeled,
   cooked potates
1/2 cup chopped dill,
   sweet or bread-and-
   butter pickles
2 teaspoons dried parsley
   leaves
1/4 cup chopped green
   onions

1 tablespoon prepared
   mustard
1/3 cup light mayonnaise
1/4 cup non-fat plain
   yogurt
2 or 3 radishes, sliced
1/4 cup chopped green
   bell pepper
Salt and pepper

Place potatoes in a large bowl. Add remaining ingredients; stir to combine. Serve either warm or cold. Makes 4 servings.

❤ Each serving contains:
   Saturated fat   0.7 gram   Cholesterol   Trace

Dressings, Relishes, Sauces & Vinegars

Our dressings are quick and easy to prepare. Keep several in the refrigerator at all times, ready for use without any fuss. Make your own vinegars. It's simple and can give that personal touch to a tossed green salad. If you enjoy sharing foods, make Tomato Relish or Fresh Cranberry Chutney for that special friend.

Poppy-Seed Dressing

2 tablespoons Dijon
  mustard
2 tablespoons olive oil
1/4 cup red-wine vinegar
1/2 cup orange juice
1/4 cup crushed pineapple,
  drained

1/3 cup honey
2 teaspoons poppy seeds
1/4 cup finely chopped red
  onion

In a blender, combine mustard, oil, vinegar, orange juice, pineapple and honey. Add poppy seeds and onion. Use at once or store in a container with a tight-fitting lid. Makes about 1-3/4 cups.

Variation

For use with Spinach Salad, page 164, omit orange juice and pineapple.

❤ Each 1-tablespoon serving contains:
  Saturated fat   Trace   Cholesterol   None

Spicy Salad Dressing

6 tablespoons non-fat
  plain yogurt
1 teaspoon minced fresh
  horseradish
1 teaspoon Dijon style
  mustard

1/4 teaspoon Worcester-
  shire sauce
2 teaspoons low-fat
  mayonnaise

In a small bowl, beat ingredients until smooth. Chill and serve. Refrigerate in a container with a tight-fitting lid. Makes about 1/2 cup.

❤ Each 1-tablespoon serving contains:
  Saturated fat   Trace   Cholesterol   Trace

Dill Sauce

1/4 cup non-fat cottage
   cheese
1 tablespoon diet low-fat
   mayonnaise
1 teaspoon lemon juice
1 to 2 tablespoons
   chopped fresh or dried
   dillweed

1 teaspoon Mrs. Dash®
   seasoning
1 tablespoon chopped
   pimiento
1/2 cup non-fat plain
   yogurt
Salt and pepper

In a blender or food processor, mix together cottage cheese, mayonnaise, lemon juice, dill and seasoning. Blend or process until smooth. Scoop mixture into a bowl; fold in pimiento and yogurt until thoroughly mixed. Season with salt and pepper to taste. Serve as a sauce for seafood or vegetable dip. Refrigerate in a container with a tight-fitting lid. Makes about 1-1/2 cups.

❤ Each 1-tablespoon serving contains:
   Saturated fat Trace   Cholesterol Trace

Creamy Herb Dressing

1/2 cup low-fat buttermilk
1/2 cup non-fat plain
   yogurt
1 teaspoon each dried leaf
   basil, oregano, dillweed,
   parsley

1 teaspoon dry or
   prepared mustard
1 tablespoon finely diced
   red onion
Salt and pepper

In a small bowl, combine buttermilk and yogurt. Stir until smooth. Add basil, oregano, dillweed, parsley, mustard and onion. Season with salt and pepper to taste. Chill several hours before serving. Refrigerate in a container with a tight-fitting lid. Makes about 1-3/4 cups.

❤ Each 1-tablespoon serving contains:
   Saturated fat Trace   Cholesterol Trace

Cocktail Sauce

1/2 cup bottled chili sauce
  or Fresh Salsa, page 140
1/3 cup catsup
1-1/2 teaspoons Worcestershire sauce

2 tablespoons prepared
  horseradish
2 tablespoons lemon juice
Tabasco sauce, if desired
Pepper

Mix ingredients and chill. For a sharper flavor add more Tabasco sauce or horseradish. Makes about 1 cup.

♥ Each serving contains:
  Saturated fat   None   Cholesterol   None

Sweet & Sour Sauce

3/4 cup vinegar
1/2 cup pineapple juice
1/2 cup water
1 tablespoon catsup

2 tablespoons soy sauce
1 tablespoon cornstarch
1/4 cup water
3/4 cup sugar

Combine vinegar, pineapple juice, 1/2 cup water, catsup and soy sauce. Dissolve cornstarch in 1/4 cup of water; stir in sugar. Add to pineapple-juice mixture. Stir over medium heat until sugar is completely dissolved and mixture is slightly thickened, 7 to 10 minutes. Serve on chicken or seafood, or use as a dip. Makes 3 cups.

♥ Each serving contains:
  Saturated fat   None   Cholesterol   None

Garlic-Herb Vinegar

5 garlic cloves
3/4 teaspoon peppercorns
2 or 3 sprigs fresh basil,
   tarragon, marjoram,
   oregano, rosemary or sage

2 cups red-wine or cider
   vinegar

Add garlic, peppercorns and herb sprigs to vinegar in a glass container. Cover tightly; place in a dark cool area for a minimum of 3 weeks. Longer aging increases flavor. Strain mixture into a glass container; discard garlic and peppercorns. Makes 2 cups.

♥ Each serving contains:
   Saturated fat   None   Cholesterol   None

Lemon Vinegar

1 lemon
2 cups white vinegar

1/4 teaspoon lemon
   pepper
Lemon juice

With a sharp knife, remove thin colored layer of lemon peel without any white membrane. Place peel in a glass container with vinegar, lemon pepper and juice from lemon. Cover tightly; place in a dark cool area for a minimum of 3 weeks. Longer aging increases the flavor. Strain mixture into a glass container; discard lemon peel. Makes 2 cups.

Variation
Omit lemon and lemon pepper; substitute 1 cup very ripe raspberries, strawberries, blackberries or fresh pineapple. Proceed as directed above.

♥ Each serving contains:
   Saturated fat   None   Cholesterol   None

Buttermilk Salad Dressing

1/2 small cucumber,
  seeded, chopped
1/4 cup low-fat buttermilk
1/4 cup Yogurt Cream
  Cheese, page 301
2 green onions or 2
  tablespoons chopped
  onion

1 parsley sprig or 1/2
  teaspoon parsley flakes
4 teaspoons lemon juice
1 teaspoon dillweed
1 teaspoon chives
1/2 teaspoon garlic powder
Salt and pepper

Place cucumber and buttermilk in a blender or food processor. Blend or process briefly, do not over blend. Pour into a small bowl; stir in remaining ingredients. Refrigerate in a container with a tight-fitting lid. Makes about 1 cup.

❤ Each serving contains:
Saturated fat Trace   Cholesterol Trace

Tomato-Cream Dressing

1/2 cup low-fat buttermilk
1 tomato, peeled, chopped
2 teaspoons tomato paste
1 green onion

Paprika
Chives
Salt and pepper

Combine buttermilk, tomato, tomato paste and onion in a blender or food processor. Blend or process to desired consistency. Season to taste with paprika, chives, salt and pepper. Refrigerate in container with a tight-fitting lid. Makes about 1 cup.

❤ Each serving contains:
Saturated fat Trace   Cholesterol Trace

Fruit Dressing

1 cup fruit juice	Sugar, as desired
1 teaspoon lemon juice	Lemon or orange peel, if
1 tablespoon cornstarch	desired

Combine all ingredients in a small saucepan. Stir over medium heat 7 to 10 minutes. Cook until mixture becomes clear and slightly thickened. Makes about 1 cup.

♥ Each serving contains:
Saturated fat   None   Cholesterol   None

Italian Dressing

2/3 cup olive oil	1 teaspoon chopped chives
1/3 cup wine vinegar	1/2 teaspoons paprika
1 teaspoon chopped parsley	1 garlic clove
1 teaspoon fresh chopped basil, or oregano	Salt and pepper

Combine all ingredients in a jar with a tight-fitting lid. Shake vigorously before using. Store in a covered container. Makes about 1 cup.

♥ Each 1-tablespoon serving contains:
Saturated fat   1.2 grams   Cholesterol   None

Relish

4 cups chopped tomatoes
2 cups chopped green bell
   peppers
1 red bell pepper, chopped
2 onions, chopped
1/4 cup shredded cabbage
1/4 teaspoon ground
   cloves
1/4 teaspoon ground
   allspice
1/4 teaspoon pepper
1/4 teaspoon mustard seed
1/8 teaspoon celery seed
1/8 teaspoon turmeric
1 cup sugar
3/4 cup cider vinegar

In a Dutch oven or heavy pot, combine all ingredients. Simmer about 2 hours. Chill before serving. Refrigerate in a container with tight-fitting lid. Makes about 6 cups.

❤ Each serving contains:
   Saturated fat   None   Cholesterol   None

Tomato Relish

4 cups chopped, peeled
   tomatoes
1 small onion, chopped
1/2 green bell pepper,
   chopped
1 mild green chili,
   chopped
1/4 teaspoon ground
   cloves
1/4 teaspoon ground
   allspice
1/4 teaspoon ground
   cinnamon
1-1/2 cups vinegar

Combine all ingredients in a large saucepan or Dutch oven. Cook over medium heat, stirring occasionally, about 40 minutes. Serve either hot or cold. Refrigerate in a container with a tight-fitting lid. This is especially good with beef or chicken. Makes about 6 cups.

❤ Each 1-cup serving contains:
   Saturated fat   None   Cholesterol   None

Corn-Raisin Relish

1 (17-oz.) can whole-
kernel corn, drained
1 cup raisins
1/4 cup chopped red bell
pepper
1/2 onion, chopped
1/4 cup chopped celery

1 cup brown sugar
1 cup cider vinegar
1/2 teaspoon turmeric
1 teaspoon dry mustard
1 (3- to 4-inch) cinnamon
stick

Combine all ingredients in a large saucepan. Cook over medium heat, stirring occasionally, about 20 minutes. Remove cinnamon stick. Serve either hot or cold. Refrigerate in a container with a tight-fitting lid. Makes about 4 cups.

❤ Each 1-cup serving contains:
Saturated fat   None   Cholesterol   None

Fresh Cranberry Chutney

4 cups fresh or frozen
cranberries
2 cups water
1 cup white sugar
2 cups brown sugar
1 onion, chopped
6 (4-inch) cinnamon sticks

1/2 cup currants or raisins
6 tablespoons chopped
crystallized ginger
1 cup cider vinegar
1/2 cup chopped dates
2 firm green apples,
peeled, cored, chopped

Combine all ingredients in a large saucepan. Cook over medium heat, stirring occasionally, about 25 minutes. Remove cinnamon sticks. Serve either hot or cold. Refrigerate in a container with a tight-fitting lid. Makes about 6 cups.

❤ Each serving contains:
Saturated fat   None   Cholesterol   None

Peach Chutney

5 or 6 large fresh peaches, peeled, or canned peaches, sliced
1/2 cup raisins
1/3 cup raspberry or cider vinegar
3/4 cup brown sugar
1 tablespoon ground ginger
2 green onions, chopped
1 teaspoon dry mustard
1 tablespoon grated orange peel
1/2 teaspoon red-pepper flakes
4 or 5 whole cloves
1 cinnamon stick
1/2 cup water

In a large heavy pot, combine all ingredients. Simmer uncovered 30 to 35 minutes, stirring often, until desired consistency. Serve at once or spoon into a container with a tight-fitting lid. May be stored in the refrigerator for several months. Makes about 2-1/2 cups.

Variation

Omit peaches and substitute any firm near-ripe fruit. Try apples, apricots, pears or a combination of fruits, both fresh and dried. For a milder chutney, omit pepper flakes and cloves.

♥ Each 1-cup serving contains:
Saturated fat   None   Cholesterol   None

Breads

Is anything more inviting than the aroma of fresh baked bread? That delightful aroma entices everyone into the kitchen immediately. You, too, can create this special atmosphere by baking any one of our breads.

We have a Classic French Bread, along with our Favorite White Bread. Like something different? Try Pinto Wheat Bread, hardy and flavorful. If time is a problem, our muffins can be made quickly.

In an effort to appeal to your tastes we offer Almond, Raisin, Applesauce, Zucchini and Old-Country Bran Muffins. Try them all and select your favorite. And pancakes make a wonderful light supper. Made with yogurt or cottage cheese, they are delightfully tender. Top with fresh fruit.

Almond-Bran Muffins

1/4 cup egg substitute
1/4 cup Puritan® oil
1 cup low-fat buttermilk
6 tablespoons brown sugar
3 tablespoons dark
   molasses
2 tablespoons honey
1/2 teaspoon ground
   cardamom

2-1/2 cups raisin-bran
   cereal
1 cup plus 2 tablespoons
   all-purpose flour
1/2 teaspoon baking soda
1-1/2 teaspoons baking
   powder
1/2 cup chopped almonds

Preheat oven to 400F (205C). Line muffin pan cups with paper baking cups or spray with vegetable cooking spray; set aside. In a large bowl, beat egg substitute until light. Stir in oil, buttermilk, brown sugar, molasses, honey and cardamom. Fold in cereal, flour, baking soda, baking powder and almonds. Spoon batter into prepared muffin cups. Bake 25 minutes or until a wooden pick inserted into center of a muffin comes out clean. Remove from pan; cool 5 minutes and serve. Makes 12 muffins.

❤ Each muffin contains:
   Saturated fat   0.7 gram   Cholesterol   None

Raisin-Oat Muffins

1-1/2 cups low-fat buttermilk	2 teaspoons ground cinnamon
1-1/2 cups rolled oats	1/2 cup egg substitute
1-1/2 cups all-purpose flour	1/2 cup brown sugar
	1/3 cup Puritan® oil
1 tablespoon baking powder	1 teaspoon maple flavoring
1/2 teaspoon baking soda	1 cup raisins

Preheat oven to 400F (205C). Line muffin pan cups with paper baking cups or spray with vegetable cooking spray; set aside. In a medium bowl, pour buttermilk over oats. In a small bowl, stir together flour, baking powder, baking soda and cinnamon; add mixture to soaked oats. In a small bowl, combine egg substitute, brown sugar, oil and maple flavoring. Pour into flour mixture; add raisins. Gently fold together until flour is moistened, batter will be lumpy. Spoon batter into prepared muffin cups. Bake 20 to 25 minutes or until a wooden pick inserted into center of a muffin comes out clean. Remove from pan; cool 5 minutes and serve. Makes 12 large muffins.

Variations

Cherry-Almond Muffins: Omit raisins, cinnamon and maple flavoring. Substitute 1 cup chopped cherries and 1 teaspoon almond extract.

Apricot-Orange Muffins: Omit raisins, cinnamon and maple flavoring. Substitute 1 cup chopped dried apricots, 1 tablespoon grated orange peel and 1 teaspoon vanilla extract.

Apple-Date Muffins: Omit raisins and maple flavoring. Substitute 2/3 cup chopped apple and 1/3 cup chopped dates. Reduce cinnamon to 1 teaspoon, add 1/2 teaspoon ground cardamom.

❤ Each muffin contains:
   Saturated fat   0.6 gram   Cholesterol   None

Applesauce-Bran Muffins

2 cups unprocessed bran
1 cup oat bran
1/2 cup egg substitute
3/4 cup unsweetened
    applesauce
1/2 cup brown sugar
3/4 cup chopped dried
    apricots or raisins

1/2 teaspoon almond
    extract
1 teaspoon ground
    cinnamon
3 tablespoons canola oil
1 tablespoon baking
    powder

Preheat oven to 425F (220C). Line muffin pan cups with paper baking cups or spray with vegetable cooking spray; set aside. In a large bowl, combine all ingredients. Gently fold together until dry ingredients are moistened, batter will be lumpy. Spoon batter into prepared muffin cups. Bake 17 to 20 minutes or until a wooden pick inserted into center of a muffin comes out clean. Remove from pan; cool 5 minutes and serve. Makes 12 large muffins.

♥ Each muffin contains:
    Saturated fat   Trace   Cholesterol   None

Zucchini Muffins

1/2 cup egg substitute
1/3 cup non-fat milk
1/3 cup Puritan® oil
1/2 cup grated zucchini
1-1/2 tablespoons unsweetened cocoa powder
1 cup all-purpose flour
1/2 cup sugar
1/2 teaspoon baking soda

1/2 teaspoon baking
powder
1 teaspoon ground
cinnamon
1/2 teaspoon ground
ginger
1/2 teaspoon chocolate
flavoring

Preheat oven to 375F (190C). Line muffin pan cups with paper baking cups or spray with vegetable cooking spray; set aside. In a large bowl, thoroughly mix egg substitute, milk, oil and zucchini. Add remaining ingredients. Gently fold together until dry ingredients are moistened, batter will be lumpy. Spoon batter into prepared muffin cups. Bake 15 to 18 minutes or until a wooden pick inserted into center of a muffin comes out clean. Remove from pan; cool 5 minutes and serve. Makes 12 large muffins.

♥ Each muffin contains:
Saturated fat   0.5 gram   Cholesterol   Trace

Old-Country Muffins

1-2/3 cups oat bran
1 cup whole-wheat flour
1 cup brown sugar
2 tablespoons unsweet-
ened cocoa powder
5 teaspoons baking
powder
1-1/2 teaspoons baking
soda
1/2 cup bran flakes cereal

1/4 cup honey
5 tablespoons dark
molasses
3 tablespoons mono-
unsaturated oil
1 cup low-fat buttermilk
1 teaspoon vanilla extract
2 egg whites, beaten
1-1/2 cups raisins

Preheat oven to 375F (190C). Line muffin-pan cups with
paper baking cups or spray with vegetable cooking spray;
set aside. In a large bowl, combine oat bran, flour, sugar,
cocoa powder, baking powder, baking soda and cereal. In
a small bowl, stir together honey, molasses, oil, buttermilk
and vanilla. Stir mixture into dry ingredients. Fold in beaten
egg whites and raisins. Spoon batter into prepared mufffin
cups. Bake 20 to 25 minutes, or until a wooden pick inserted
into center of a muffin comes out clean; cool 5 minutes and
serve. Makes 24 large muffins.

♥ Each muffin contains:
Saturated fat   Trace   Cholesterol   Trace

Whole-Wheat Pancakes

1 cup non-fat milk	1/4 cup melted diet soft
3/4 cup all-purpose flour	margarine
3/4 cup whole-wheat flour	1/2 teaspoon baking soda
3/4 cup egg substitute	1 tablespoon baking
1 tablespoon sugar	powder
1 tablespoon brown sugar	1/2 cup currants or raisins

Pour milk into a blender or food processor; add flours, thoroughly blend. Add egg substitute, sugars, melted margarine, baking soda and baking powder. Blend or process briefly, until batter is smooth. Spray a non-stick griddle with vegetable cooking spray. Preheat griddle. Pour about 1/4 cup batter for each pancake. When bubbles appear and edges look dry, turn and cook other side. Makes 16 (4-inch) pancakes or 4 servings. Serve with jam, maple syrup, honey or fruit syrup.

♥ Each 4-pancake serving contains:
   Saturated fat   0.3 gram   Cholesterol   None

Note: If margarine is used on pancakes, it increases the amount of saturated fat.

Quaker Oats® Pancakes

1 cup all-purpose flour
1/2 cup Quaker Oats,®
   quick or old-fashioned,
   uncooked
1 tablespoon baking
   powder

1 cup non-fat milk
1/4 cup egg substitute or
   2 egg whites, beaten
2 tablespoons Puritan® oil

Spray a non-stick griddle or electric fry pan with vegetable cooking spray. Preheat griddle. In a large bowl, combine flour, oats and baking powder. Add milk, egg substitute or beaten egg whites and oil. Pour about 1/4 cup batter for each pancake. When bubbles appear and edges look dry, turn and cook other side. Serve with syrup and fruit. Makes 12 pancakes.

❤ Each 3-pancake serving contains:
   Saturated fat   Trace   Cholesterol   None

(Courtesy of The Quaker Oats Company)

Blueberry Pancakes

2/3 cup non-fat cottage
  cheese
1/3 cup non-fat plain
  yogurt
1 tablespoon brown sugar
3/4 cup all-purpose flour
1/2 teaspoon baking soda

3/4 cup egg substitute
2 egg whites
3 tablespoons melted diet
  soft margarine
1/2 cup fresh or thawed
  frozen blueberries

Spray a non-stick griddle or electric fry pan with vegetable cooking spray. Preheat griddle. In a blender or food processor, combine cottage cheese, yogurt and brown sugar. Blend or process until smooth. Add flour, soda and egg substitute. Beat egg whites in a separate bowl. Pour mixture over beaten egg whites; fold together with melted margarine and blueberries. Pour about 1/4 cup batter for each pancake. When bubbles appear and edges look dry, turn and cook other side. Makes 12 pancakes.

❤ Each 3-pancake serving contains:
  Saturated fat   0.3 gram   Cholesterol   None

Orange-Yogurt Pancakes

2 egg whites
3/4 cup egg substitute
1 (8-oz.) container non-fat
   mandarin-orange yogurt

1 cup all-purpose flour
3/4 teaspoon baking soda
1 (11-oz.) can mandarin
   oranges

Spray a non-stick griddle or electric fry pan with vegetable cooking spray. Preheat griddle. In a mixer bowl, beat egg whites until soft peaks form. Add egg substitute and beat at low speed to blend. Continue beating and add yogurt, flour and baking soda. Pour about 1/4 cup batter for each pancake. When bubbles appear and edges look dry, turn and cook other side. Top pancakes with mandarin oranges. Makes 12 pancakes.

Variation

Substitute any other fruit flavor for orange yogurt. Top with the same fruit, fresh or canned.

❤ Each 3-pancake serving contains:
Saturated fat   Trace   Cholesterol   None

Cornmeal Pancakes

1 tablespoon lemon juice
or vinegar
1-1/4 cups non-fat milk
1/2 cup cornmeal
1/2 cup all-purpose flour
1/2 teaspoon baking soda

1 tablespoon baking
powder
1 tablespoon sugar, if
desired
1/2 cup egg substitute

Spray a non-stick griddle or electric fry pan with vegetable cooking spray. Preheat griddle. Add lemon juice or vinegar to milk; set aside for 5 minutes. In a mixing bowl, stir together cornmeal, flour, baking soda and baking powder. Add sugar, if desired. Add milk mixture and egg substitute, stir to blend. Pour about 1/4 cup batter for each pancake. When bubbles appear and edges look dry, turn and cook other side. Serve with syrup on fruit. Makes 12 pancakes.

❤ Each 3-pancake serving contains:
Saturated fat   Trace   Cholesterol   None

Classic French Bread

6 to 6-1/2 cups bread flour
  (divided)
1 (1/4-oz.) pkg. active dry
  yeast
1 teaspoon salt

1 teaspoon sugar, if
  desired
2-1/4 cups warm water
1 tablespoon water
Cornmeal

In a large mixer bowl, using a dough hook, combine 2 cups flour, yeast, salt and sugar. Gradually add water. Continue to mix 1-1/2 to 2 minutes; add an additional 2 cups flour. Mix until thoroughly blended. Beat in more flour, making a stiff and manageable dough. Turn out on a floured board; knead about 10 minutes. Dough should be smooth and elastic. Place dough in a large oiled bowl, turning dough to coat top. Place bowl in a draft-free area. Let dough rise until doubled, 1-1/2 to 2 hours. Punch dough down, cover and let rise again until doubled. Spray a baking sheet with vegetable cooking spray; sprinkle with cornmeal. Place dough on floured surface. Cover and let rest about 10 minutes. Divide dough in half. Pat or roll each piece into a 15 x 10-inch rectangle. Starting from the long side, roll dough up tightly; gently press loaf with each turn. Gently roll dough between hands to seal edges and taper ends. Place loaves seam-side down, on baking sheet. Brush with water. Cover and let rise about 1 hour. Heat oven to 450F (205C). With a sharp knife, make slashes on the top, about 2 inches apart and 1/4 inch deep. Brush with water. Bake in upper third of oven. Brush with water every 3 minutes during first 10 minutes of baking. Bake another 15 to 20 minutes, until bread is brown. Remove from oven; lightly brush with water, set on a rack and cool. Makes 2 loaves.

Variation

For a glazed crust, combine 1 egg white and 1 tablespoon water. Bake 10 minutes, brush with egg glaze; bake 10 more minutes, brush again. Continue baking 15 to 20 minutes.

♥ Each slice contains:
Saturated fat   Trace   Cholesterol   None

Light Oatmeal Bread

3 cups lukewarm water
2 (1/4-oz.) pkgs. or 2
    tablespoons active dry
    yeast
1/2 cup honey
1/4 cup Puritan® oil
3 cups whole-wheat flour

1 cup cracked wheat
3 to 5 cups all-purpose
    flour
1 cup oat bran
1 egg white
1 tablespoon water

In a large mixer bowl, combine water, yeast, honey, oil and whole-wheat flour. Let rise until double in bulk. Stir down. Beat at medium speed; add cracked wheat and about 2 cups all-purpose flour and oat bran. Mix thoroughly for about 10 minutes or by hand 12 to 15 minutes. Add some remaining flour and mix until dough pulls away from sides of bowl. Turn out dough onto a lightly floured board. Knead about 15 minutes. Place dough in a large greased bowl; turn dough to coat all sides. Cover with a dry cloth towel or plastic wrap. Place bowl in a warm draft-free area and let dough rise until double in bulk, 1-1/2 to 2 hours. Punch dough down. Form into loaves or rolls. Place in pans sprayed with vegetable cooking spray. Let rise again until doubled in bulk, 45 to 60 minutes. Preheat oven to 375F (190C). Combine egg white and water. Brush tops with egg mixture. Bake 30 to 40 minutes. Remove from pans, and cool. Makes 2 loaves (12 slices each.)

❤ Each large slice contains:
    Saturated fat   Trace   Cholesterol   None

Pinto Wheat Bread

1 cup pinto Bean Puree,
   see following page
1 cup lukewarm water
1 tablespoon honey
1 (1/4-oz.) pkg. active dry
   yeast

2 tablespoons Puritan® oil
1 teaspoon salt
2 cups whole-wheat flour
3/4 to 1-1/2 cups all-
   purpose flour

Prepare Bean Purée. In a large bowl, combine water and honey, stirring to mix completely. Dissolve yeast in honey-water mixture. Let stand until foamy. Stir in Bean Purée, oil and salt. Add whole-wheat flour. Mix well. Stir in all-purpose flour until dough is stiff. Turn out onto a lightly floured surface and knead until smooth and elastic. Return dough to greased bowl. Cover bowl with plastic wrap. Let rise in a warm place until doubled in bulk. Spray a 9 x 5-inch loaf pan or 8-inch round pan with vegetable cooking spray. Punch down dough and knead 3 or 4 times until easy to handle. Shape into a loaf and place in loaf pan or shape into a ball and place in round pan. Cover and let rise until doubled, about 45 minutes. Preheat oven to 350F (175C). Bake bread until golden brown, about 50 minutes. Immediately remove from pan. Cool on a rack. Store bread in an airtight plastic bag at room temperature or in the refrigerator. Makes 1 loaf (16 slices).

❤ Each slice contains:
   Saturated fat   Trace   Cholesterol   None

Bean Purée

1 cup dried beans; large
   lima, great northern,
   pinto, pink or red
Water for soaking

2-1/2 cups water
1 teaspoon salt
1 tablespoon Puritan® oil

Pick over beans. Place in a saucepan with water to cover by more than 2 inches. Bring to a boil. Boil 2 minutes. Remove from heat; cover. Set aside 1 hour. Drain. In a medium saucepan, combine drained beans, 2-1/2 cups water, salt and oil. Bring to a boil; reduce heat. Cover and simmer until beans are tender, 1 to 1-1/2 hours. Drain beans, reserving cooking liquid. Put about 1 cup beans at a time in blender or food processor with half reserved cooking liquid. Blend on medium speed until smooth, stopping blender occasionally to scrape down sides and stir purée up from bottom. Mixture should circulate slowly when it reaches proper consistency. Makes 2 cups purée.

♥ Each cup contains:
   Saturated fat   0.7 gram   Cholesterol   None

Onion-Caraway Bread

1/2 cup finely chopped
   onion
2 cups (16 oz.) large-curd
   non-fat cottage cheese,
   room temperature
1/4 cup sugar
3 tablespoons melted diet
   soft margarine
1 teaspoon salt

1/2 teaspoon baking soda
3-1/2 cups all-purpose
   flour
1/2 cup egg substitute
2 (1/4-oz.) pkgs. active dry
   yeast
1 cup quick or rolled oats
2 tablespoons caraway
   seeds

In a large mixer bowl, beat onion, cottage cheese, sugar, margarine, salt and baking soda until well combined. Stir in 2 cups flour, egg substitute and yeast; beat 2 minutes. Stir in oats, caraway seeds and remaining flour. Cover with a dry cloth towel or plastic wrap. Place bowl in a warm draft-free area and let dough rise until double in bulk; about 1 hour. Stir batter down. Spray 2 deep 1-1/2-quart casseroles or soufflé dishes with vegetable cooking spray. Place batter in prepared dishes. Brush with melted margarine. Let rise, un-covered in a draft-free area until doubled, about 45 minutes. Preheat oven to 350F (175C). Bake 35 to 40 minutes or until golden brown. Remove pans and cool. Makes 2 loaves (12 slices each).

❤ Each large slice contains:
   Saturated fat   Trace   Cholesterol   Trace

Golden Herbed Rolls

1 (1/4-oz.) pkg. active dry
   yeast
1/2 cup sugar
1 cup warm skim milk
3 tablespoons Puritan® oil
1/2 teaspoon salt, if desired
1 cup puréed, cooked
   yellow squash or
   pumpkin

1 tablespoon dried leaf
   oregano
1 tablespoon dill weed
1/4 teaspoon lemon
   pepper
5 cups all-purpose flour,
   divided

In a mixer bowl, sprinkle yeast and sugar into warm, not hot, milk and oil. Let stand about 5 minutes. Turn mixer to low; gradually add salt, squash, oregano, dill weed, lemon pepper and about 2 cups flour. Beat until well blended. Remove beaters and gradually beat in remaining flour by hand. Cover with a dry cloth towel or plastic wrap. Place bowl in a warm draft-free area and let dough rise until double in bulk, 1 to 1-1/2 hours. Turn dough out onto a floured board or pastry cloth. Knead gently about 2 minutes. Roll out dough to 1-inch thickness. Cut into rolls using 3-inch cutter. Place on baking sheet or 13 x 9-inch pan sprayed with vegetable cooking spray. Cover and let rise until doubled in bulk. Preheat oven to 400F (205C). Uncover rolls and bake 20 to 25 minutes until golden brown. Makes 12 large rolls.

❤ Each roll contains:
   Saturated fat   0.4 gram   Cholesterol Trace

Mixed-Fruit Bread

1 cup chopped dried figs
1 cup chopped dates
1 cup raisins
2 cups hot apple juice
2 teaspoons baking soda
1/2 cup egg substitute
1 egg white

1-1/2 cups sugar
4 tablespoons melted soft
   diet margarine
4 cups all-purpose flour
1/2 teaspoon ground
   allspice
1 teaspoon vanilla extract

In a large bowl, combine figs, dates and raisins with hot apple juice. Set aside for 10 minutes. In a mixer bowl, beat together egg substitute, egg white, sugar and margarine. Alternately add fruit mixture and flour, blending well after each addition. Add allspice and vanilla. Spray 2 (9 x 5-inch) baking pans with vegetable cooking spray. Spoon batter into prepared pans. Bake 35 to 40 minutes, until a wooden pick inserted into center of a loaf comes out clean. Remove from pans and cool. Makes 2 loaves (12 slices each).

❤ Each slice contains:
   Saturated fat   Trace   Cholesterol   None

Favorite White Bread

2 (1/4-oz.) pkgs. active dry
    yeast
3 tablespoons sugar
2-1/2 cups warm water
1 teaspoon salt

1/2 cup non-fat milk
    powder
5-1/2 to 6-1/2 cups all-
    purpose flour, divided
4 tablespoons Puritan® oil

In a large mixer bowl, preferably with a dough hook, dissolve yeast and sugar in water. Let stand until foamy. Mix in salt, milk powder and 3-1/2 cups flour. Mix until thoroughly blended. Add oil and gradually blend in enough remaining flour to make a soft dough. Continue to mix dough until smooth and elastic. Or turn out onto a floured surface and knead by hand about 10 minutes. Lightly spray a large bowl with vegetable cooking spray. Shape dough into a ball. Place dough in prepared bowl, turn to coat all sides. Cover with a cloth. Let rise in a warm draft-free area, 1 to 1-1/2 hours, until double in bulk. Coat 2 (8 x 4-inch) loaf pans with vegetable cooking spray. Punch down dough; divide in half. Shape loaves; place in prepared pans. Cover with a cloth and let rise again until doubled, about 1 hour. Preheat oven to 400F (205C). Bake 30 to 35 minutes until golden brown and loaves sound hollow when tapped. Remove from pans and cool. Makes 2 loaves (12 slices each).

❤ Each slice contains:
    Saturated fat Trace   Cholesterol None

Cornbread

1 cup corn meal
1/2 cup all-purpose flour
1/2 cup oat bran
3 tablespoons sugar
2 teaspoons baking
  powder

1 teaspoon baking soda
1/4 teaspoon salt
1/2 cup plain non-fat
  yogurt
3 egg whites, beaten

Preheat oven to 400F (205C). Spray a 9-inch pie pan with vegetable cooking spray; set aside. In a medium bowl, thoroughly combine corn meal, flour, oat bran, sugar, baking powder, baking soda and salt. Stir in yogurt. Fold in egg whites. Pour into prepared pan. Bake 20 to 25 minutes. Makes 8 servings.

❤ Each serving contains:
  Saturated fat Trace   Cholesterol Trace

Beans & Other Legumes

We are all relearning the simple truth that plain, wholesome foods are good for us. In this chapter we help you explore new recipes with a variety of grains, legumes and beans.

It is easy to work these into your diet, with just a little thought. For a change try Lentil-Tomato Pilaf or Chili Barley as a side dish with turkey or fish. Here's a great combination for entertaining: easy-to-prepare and delicious Jamaican Bean Pot served with a tossed salad, Classic French Bread, page 196, and Buttermilk Sherbet, page 277.

Brown rice has a distinct flavor that complements other foods. Brown Rice with Vegetables is a good example. Spanish Rice & Bean Pie gives a different look to basic ingredients. This is a taste-award winner.

Beans and rice are a vital part of cooking for the healthy heart.

Black-Eyed Peas

2 cups dried or 1 (16-oz.)
   pkg. frozen black-eyed
   peas
3 quarts water
1/2 small onion, chopped

1 garlic clove, chopped
1/2 teaspoon salt
Coarse pepper to taste

Presoak dried black-eyed peas; drain. In a large pot, place peas and remaining ingredients. Bring to a boil, reduce heat and simmer until tender, 1-1/2 to 2 hours. If using frozen peas, thawing is not necessary. Place all ingredients in a large pot. Bring to a boil, reduce heat and simmer until tender, 45 to 50 minutes.

♥ Each 1-cup serving contains:
  Saturated fat None   Cholesterol None

Dinner Wheat

4 cups cold water
1/2 cup whole-wheat
   berries
1/2 teaspoon salt

Soft diet margarine
Salt and pepper
Barbecue Sauce, page 248

In a heavy saucepan containing 4 cups cold water, slowly stir in whole-wheat berries and 1/2 teaspoon salt. Heat to full rolling boil; reduce heat. Simmer 30 minutes; turn off heat. Cover; set aside for 20 to 30 minutes. Drain excess water and serve. Season to taste with soft diet margarine, salt, pepper or Barbecue Sauce. Makes 6 servings.

♥ Each serving contains:
  Saturated fat Trace   Cholesterol None

Barbecued Beans

2 quarts water
2 cups dried navy beans
1 onion, diced
1 (6-oz.) can tomato
   sauce
1/4 cup sweet relish
1 tablespoon vinegar

1 teaspoon dry mustard
1 teaspoon ground pepper
2 tablespoons Worcester-
   shire sauce
5 tablespoons brown sugar
Salt and pepper

In a large pot, bring 2 quarts water to a boil. Rinse beans thoroughly, add to hot water. Boil 2 minutes. Turn off heat and let beans sit covered, 1 hour. Or soak beans in water overnight. Drain; add fresh water to beans. Bring to a boil, reduce heat and cook about 1 hour, until beans are soft and tender. Spray a small non-stick skillet with vegetable cooking spray. Sauté onion. Add remaining ingredients; cook about 5 minutes to blend. Drain liquid from beans. Add tomato mixture to beans. Season to taste with salt and pepper. Mix thoroughly. Preheat oven to 350F (175C). Pour beans into a 2-quart baking dish or bean pot and bake uncovered about 1 hour. Makes about 8 servings.

❤ Each 1-cup serving contains:
  Saturated fat Trace   Cholesterol None

Lentil-Tomato Pilaf

1 leek, sliced
1/4 cup chopped green
   bell pepper
1/4 cup chopped celery
2 garlic cloves, chopped
1 cup lentils
3 cups Chicken Broth,
   page 158
1 cup chopped stewed or
   fresh tomatoes

1/3 cup raisins
1 tablespoon chopped
   mint leaves
1 tablespoon chopped
   parsley
1/8 teaspoon ground
   nutmeg
1/8 teaspoon ground
   cloves

In a medium saucepan or Dutch oven, place leek, bell pepper, celery, garlic, lentils, chicken broth and tomatoes. Bring to a boil, reduce heat. Cover and simmer 20 to 25 minutes. Add raisins, mint, parsley, nutmeg and cloves. Stir to blend and cook 10 minutes longer. Makes 6 servings.

♥ Each serving contains:
   Saturated fat   Trace   Cholesterol   None

Brown Rice with Vegetables

1 tablespoon olive or
   Puritan® oil
1 onion, chopped
3 carrots, sliced
3 celery stalks, sliced
1 cup brown rice
2 cups Chicken Broth,
   page 158

1 tablespoon chopped
   parsley
1/2 cup fresh mushrooms,
   sliced
Salt and pepper

In a 2-quart pan or Dutch oven, heat oil. Sauté onion, carrots and celery. Add rice and stir to coat. Add chicken broth and parsley. Cover and cook over low heat about 40 minutes. Add mushrooms and continue cooking about 5 minutes. Season with salt and pepper to taste. Makes 6 servings.

♥ Each serving contains:
   Saturated fat   0.3 gram   Cholesterol   None

Brown Rice in Tomato Sauce

2 tablespoons olive or
   Puritan® oil
2 medium onions,
   chopped
2 garlic cloves
1 cup brown rice
1 cup water

2 cups tomato juice
1/2 teaspoon pepper
1 cup sliced mushrooms
1 teaspoon fresh parsley
1 cup peas
Salt and pepper
Tabasco sauce

Heat oil in a Dutch oven or heavy pot. Sauté onions and garlic. Add rice and stir to coat. Pour in water, tomato juice and pepper. Bring to a boil; cover and reduce heat to a simmer. Continue cooking 40 to 45 minutes. Add mushrooms, parsley and peas; cook about 10 minutes more. Season with salt, pepper and Tabasco sauce to taste. Makes 6 to 8 servings.

♥ Each serving contains:
   Saturated fat   0.3 gram   Cholesterol   None

Wild Rice Stir-Fry

1/2 (10-oz.) can beef
   consommé
1 tablespoon Puritan® oil
2 teaspoons grated fresh
   ginger or 1/4 teaspoon
   ground ginger
1 medium onion, sliced
1/2 cup fresh or canned
   sliced mushrooms,
   drained

1 (8-oz.) can water chestnuts, drained
1/2 cup Chinese pea pods
3 teaspoons chopped
   pimiento
2 cups cooked wild rice
1/2 cup fresh bean
   sprouts
Soy sauce

Chill consommé. Remove fat that rises to top. Heat oil in a wok or large skillet. Add ginger and onion, stir-fry about 1 minute. Add remaining ingredients, stirring after each addition. Continue stirring until liquid is absorbed. Serve at once. Season with soy sauce to taste. Makes 4 servings.

❤ Each serving contains:
   Saturated fat   0.3 gram   Cholesterol   None

Baked Beans with Smoked Turkey

4 cups dried navy beans	1 teaspoon dry mustard
2 quarts water	1/2 teaspoon salt
1 medium onion,	1 tablespoon Worcester-
chopped	shire sauce
1 cup brown sugar	8 ounces shredded,
1/2 cup chili sauce	smoked turkey breast

Pick through beans. Rinse in sieve under running water. In a large pot, combine beans, 2 quarts water and onion. Bring to a boil; reduce heat. Cover and simmer until beans are tender, about 1-1/2 to 2 hours. Add hot water as needed to keep beans covered while cooking. Drain water; combine beans and onion with brown sugar, chili sauce, mustard, salt, Worchestershire sauce and turkey. Pour mixture into a baking dish or bean pot. Preheat oven to 350F (190C). Bake about 30 minutes. Makes 8 servings.

❤ Each 1-cup serving contains:
Saturated fat   0.6 gram   Cholesterol   15mg

Chili Barley

1/2 cup barley
1-1/2 cups fat-free broth
1 green onion, chopped
1/2 (4-oz.) can chopped
   green chilies, drained
1/2 cup ricotta cheese
1/2 cup non-fat plain
   yogurt
1/2 teaspoon dried leaf
   oregano

1/2 teaspoon dried leaf
   basil
1 tablespoon
   chopped fresh parsley
1 tablespoon chopped
   pimiento
1/2 cup fresh frozen or
   fresh green peas
Salt and pepper

Combine barley and broth in a large pot. Bring to a boil; reduce heat. Cover and simmer 45 to 50 minutes. Stir in onion, chilies, cheese, yogurt, oregano, basil, parsley, pimiento and peas. Season with salt and pepper to taste. Spray a 2-quart casserole or baking dish with vegetable cooking spray. Spoon barley mixture into casserole. Bake in a 350F (175C) oven about 35 minutes. Serve at once. Makes 4 servings.

Variation

To make a complete meal, add 1 cup (5 oz.) chopped, skinned, cooked turkey or chicken breasts and 1 cup chopped broccoli. After baking 30 minutes, top casserole with 2 thinly sliced tomatoes. Makes 6 servings.

♥ Each serving contains:
  Saturated fat   Trace   Cholesterol   None
♥ With chicken:
  Saturated fat   0.4 gram   Cholesterol   19mg

Easy Bean Bake

1 (15-oz.) can pinto
   beans, drained
1 (15-oz.) can kidney
   beans, drained
1 (15-oz.) can garbanzo
   beans, drained
1 (8-oz.) can tomato
   sauce
1/2 cup chopped onion
2 teaspoons Italian herbs
2 teaspoons chopped
   fresh parsley

1 teaspoon garlic powder
1 fennel bulb, sliced or
   2 celery stalks, sliced
1 green bell pepper,
   chopped
1 red or yellow bell
   pepper, chopped
2 medium tomatoes,
   chopped
3 tablespoons grated
   Parmesan cheese

In a large bowl, combine all beans, tomato sauce, onion, Italian herbs, parsley, garlic powder, fennel or celery and bell peppers. Spray a 13 x 9-inch baking dish with vegetable cooking spray. Pour in bean mixture. Top with chopped tomato. Bake in a 350F (175C) oven 35 to 40 minutes. To serve, sprinkle with Parmesan cheese. Makes 8 servings.

❤ Each serving contains:
   Saturated fat   Trace   Cholesterol   None

Jamaican Bean Pot

1 lb. dried black beans	1-1/2 teaspoons salt
10 cups water	1/4 cup dark molasses
1/2 cup chopped onion	1/4 cup packed brown
1 garlic clove, minced	sugar
1/2 cup sliced celery	1/4 cup dark Jamaican
1/2 cup sliced carrot	rum
2 tablespoons olive or	1 teaspoon dry mustard
Puritan® oil	Pinch of dried leaf thyme
1 bay leaf	

Rinse beans in sieve under running water. In a large pot, combine beans and 10 cups water. In a skillet, sauté onion, garlic, celery and carrot in oil until onion softens. Add vegetables, bay leaf and salt to beans. Bring to a boil; reduce heat. Cover and simmer until beans are almost tender, 1-1/2 to 2 hours. Add hot water as needed to keep beans just covered while cooking. Drain beans, reserving liquid. Discard bay leaf. Preheat oven to 300F (150C). In a small bowl, combine molasses, brown sugar, rum, dry mustard and thyme; mix well. Put beans in a 2-1/2-quart bean pot or casserole with cover. Pour molasses mixture over beans; stir. Add enough reserved cooking liquid to just cover beans, about 1-1/2 cups. Cover and bake 2 hours. Uncover; bake 30 minutes longer or until beans are tender. Serve bubbling hot. Makes 8 (1/2-cup) servings.

❤ Each serving contains:
    Saturated fat   0.4 gram   Cholesterol   None

Spanish Rice & Bean Pie

1 cup dried pinto, red or
    pink beans
Water for soaking
2-1/2 cups water
1 garlic clove, minced
1/3 cup chopped onion
2 teaspoons imitation
    bacon bits
1/2 teaspoon salt
1/8 teaspoon pepper
1 cup water
1 chicken bouillon cube
1/2 cup uncooked rice
1/2 cup chopped onion

1/2 cup chopped green
    bell pepper
1 tablespoon olive or
    Puritan® oil
2 tablespoons chopped
    pimiento
2 tablespoons egg
    substitute
1 cup non-fat cottage
    cheese
1/2 cup (2 oz.) shredded
    imitation low-fat
    Cheddar cheese

Place beans in a saucepan with water to cover by more than 2 inches. Bring to a boil. Boil 2 minutes. Remove from heat; cover. Set aside 1 hour. Drain. In a saucepan, combine beans, 2-1/2 cups water, garlic, 1/3 cup onion, bacon bits, salt and pepper. Bring to a boil; reduce heat. Cover; simmer until beans are tender, 1 to 1-1/2 hours. In a small saucepan, bring 1 cup water and bouillon cube to a boil. Stir to dissolve bouillon. Add rice. Reduce heat to lowest setting. Cover and simmer 20 minutes. Preheat oven to 325F (165C). In a small skillet, sauté 1/2 cup onion and 1/2 cup green pepper in oil until onion is limp. Stir in pimiento. Add onion mixture and egg substitute to cooked rice; mix well. Spray a 9-inch pie pan with vegetable cooking spray. Press rice mixture into pie pan to form a crust. Spread cottage cheese over rice crust. Pour beans over cottage cheese. Bake 20 minutes. Sprinkle top with Cheddar cheese; bake another 20 minutes. Remove from oven; let stand 10 minutes before cutting into wedges. Serve with a spatula. Makes 6 servings.

❤ Each serving contains:
    Saturated fat   1 gram   Cholesterol   15mg

Vegetables

We are so fortunate to live in a time when wonderful vegetables are available year round.

Vegetables can be served in a variety of ways: baked, steamed, stir-fried, stewed and, of course, raw. As a side dish or the basis of a main dish, vegetables offer nutrition, fiber, color, texture and—most of all—flavor. Some of the recipes are super simple, such as Baked Hubbard Squash or Garden Medley. For special occasions, fix Spinach Souffle or Pineapple Yams.

Stuffed Tomatoes

4 tomatoes
4 green onions, chopped
4 tablespoons crushed
　corn flakes
1/4 bunch fresh spinach,
　washed, chopped
1/2 teaspoon dried leaf
　basil

1 tablespoon parsley
1 tablespoon crushed corn
　flakes
1 tablespoon grated
　Parmesan cheese
Salt and pepper

Preheat oven to 375F (190C). Slice tops off tomatoes. Scoop out pulp and place tomato shells in a baking dish. Chop tomato pulp. In a small bowl, combine chopped tomato with green onions, 4 tablespoons corn flakes, spinach, basil and parsley. Fill tomato shells with mixture. Sprinkle tops with additional crushed corn flakes, Parmesan cheese and salt and pepper to taste. Bake about 15 minutes. Makes 4 servings.

Variation

Omit corn flakes and spinach; substitute 1/4 cup sliced celery, 2 slices of bread, cubed and 2 tablespoons chopped green bell pepper.

♥ Each serving contains:
　Saturated fat　Trace　　　Cholesterol　Trace

Broiled Tomatoes

1/2 cup non-fat plain
  yogurt
1/4 cup shredded-wheat
  crumbs
1 teaspoon each chives,
  parsley and dill

1/2 teaspoon garlic powder
1/2 teaspoon dry mustard
Salt and pepper
2 teaspoons capers, if
  desired
4 tomatoes

Preheat broiler. In a small bowl, mix non-fat yogurt with shredded-wheat crumbs, chives, parsley, dill, garlic powder, mustard, salt and pepper to taste and capers, if desired. Cut tomatoes into 1/2-inch slices; place on a broiler pan or baking sheet. Spread mixture evenly on tomato slices. Broil until topping begins to brown. Remove from oven and serve at once. Makes 4 to 6 servings.

❤ Each serving contains:
  Saturated fat None   Cholesterol None

Quick Crispy Vegetables

2 cups chopped vegetables
  such as asparagus,
  broccoli, carrots,
  cauliflower, green beans,
  spinach

1/4 cup water
1 pkg. Butter Buds®
Soy sauce

Vegetables should be cut into bite-size pieces for quick and even cooking. Combine water and Butter Buds® in a wok or large fry pan. Add vegetables. Stir-fry 3 to 5 minutes until tender-crisp. More dense vegetables like carrots and broccoli may require longer cooking. Serve at once. Season with soy sauce to taste. Makes 4 servings.

❤ Each serving contains:
  Saturated fat None   Cholesterol None

Honey-Glazed Carrots

2 cups mini carrots	1/4 teaspoon ground
3 tablespoons water	cinnamon
2 tablespoons honey	1/4 teaspoon ground
1 tablespoon soft diet	nutmeg
margarine	2 tablespoons orange juice

In a saucepan, cook carrots with water to cover about 15 minutes. Drain water. Return carrots to heat. Add remaining ingredients; stir until honey mixture is hot and all carrots are well coated. Makes 4 servings.

♥ Each serving contains:
Saturated fat   0.2 gram   Cholesterol   None

Baked-Zucchini Casserole

4 zucchini, trimmed, sliced	1/2 teaspoon garlic powder
3 tomatoes	1 teaspoon dried leaf
1 (12-oz.) can whole-	oregano
kernel corn, drained	1 teaspoon dried leaf
3 chopped green onions	basil
1/4 cup bread crumbs	Salt and lemon pepper

Preheat oven to 350F (175C). Spray a 2-quart casserole with vegetable cooking spray. Alternate layers of zucchini, tomatoes, corn and green onions. Repeat. Cover and bake 20 minutes. Mix together bread crumbs, garlic powder, oregano and basil. Sprinkle on top. Bake uncovered 10 to 12 minutes. Season to taste with salt and lemon pepper. Makes 6 servings.

♥ Each serving contains:
Saturated fat   Trace   Cholesterol   None

Corn Fritters

1 cup all-purpose flour
3/4 teaspoon baking
   powder
1/2 cup egg substitute
1/4 cup non-fat milk
1 pkg. Butter Buds®

1-1/2 cups creamed corn,
   drained
1/2 teaspoon sugar
1 to 2 teaspoons Puritan®
   oil

In a medium bowl, stir flour and baking powder together. Add remaining ingredients; stir well to blend. Spray a non-stick skillet with vegetable cooking spray. For each fritter, drop 2 spoonfuls mixture, adding oil to skillet if needed. Makes 4 to 6 servings. Turn once to brown, both sides.

♥ Each serving contains:
   Saturated fat   Trace   Cholesterol   None

Parsnip Casserole

2 cups (2 to 3) parsnips,
   cooked, puréed
1/2 teaspoon salt
1 pkg. Butter Buds®
3 small green onions,
   finely chopped

1/4 cup egg substitute
1/2 cup chopped peanuts
1 green bell pepper,
   cut in rings
1/3 cup corn-flake crumbs
Pepper

Preheat oven to 350F (175C). Spray a 1-quart baking dish with vegetable cooking spray; set aside. In a bowl, combine parsnips, salt, Butter Buds,® green onions and egg substitute. Fold in 1/4 cup peanuts. Pour into prepared baking dish. Place pepper rings on top. Combine corn flakes and remaining peanuts, sprinkle over pepper rings. Bake about 25 minutes. Serve at once. Season with pepper to taste. Makes 6 servings.

♥ Each serving contains:
   Saturated fat   0.8 gram   Cholesterol   None

Steamed Greens

Juice of 1 lemon
1/2 cup non-fat plain
  yogurt

1 lb. swiss chard, mustard
  greens or spinach
Lemon pepper

Stir lemon juice into yogurt. Bring water to a boil in steamer or large saucepan. Place chard, mustard greens or spinach in vegetable steamer. Cover and cook 3 to 4 minutes until leaves soften, but still retain their bright color. Top with lemon yogurt and lemon pepper. Serve at once.

❤ Each serving contains:
  Saturated fat   None   Cholesterol   None

Creamed Green Beans

1 lb. fresh green beans
2 green onions, chopped
1 pkg. Butter Buds, if
  desired
3/4 cup Chicken Broth,
  page 158
1 teaspoon caraway seeds
2 tablespoons all-purpose
  flour

4 tablespoons non-fat
  plain yogurt
1/2 teaspoon sugar
2 tablespoons vinegar
1 tablespoon chopped
  pimiento
Chopped parsley

Rinse beans; cut or break into 2-inch pieces. In a saucepan, simmer green beans, onions, Butter Buds,® if desired, chicken broth and caraway seeds about 20 minutes. Mix flour, yogurt and sugar together. Add to beans, cook stirring constantly for several minutes, until thickened. Stir in vinegar and pimiento; sprinkle with parsley. Serve at once. Makes 6 servings.

❤ Each serving contains:
  Saturated fat   Trace   Cholesterol   None

Baked Hubbard Squash

1 lb. hubbard or banana
    squash, peeled
Water

3 tablespoons melted, soft
    diet margarine
1/3 cup light-brown sugar
Ground nutmeg

Preheat oven to 400F (205C). Cut squash into serving-size pieces. Place in baking dish cut-side up; add water until 1/4-inch deep. Cover and bake about 30 minutes, until tender when pierced with a fork. Drizzle margarine over pieces. Sprinkle brown sugar and nutmeg to taste on top. Return to oven for 5 minutes or until sugar is melted. Makes 6 servings.

❤ Each serving contains:
    Saturated fat   0.5 gram   Cholesterol None

Celery Casserole

4 cups diagonally sliced
    celery
1 (10-oz.) pkg. frozen
    boiling onions, thawed
1 pkg. Butter Buds®
3 tablespoons all-purpose
    flour

1-3/4 cups Chicken Broth,
    page 158
1/2 cup frozen peas,
    thawed
1/4 cup chopped peanuts
2 tablespoons imitation
    bacon bits

Preheat oven to 350F (175C). Spray a shallow baking dish with vegetable cooking spray. In a large saucepan, combine celery and boiling onions with 1-1/2 cups water. Cover and cook until vegetables are tender. Drain water; set vegetables aside. In a small saucepan blend Butter Buds,® flour and chicken broth. Cook, stirring constantly until thickened; add peas to mixture. Combine with celery and onions. Pour into prepared baking dish. Top with chopped peanuts and bacon bits. Bake about 20 minutes. Makes 6 servings.

❤ Each serving contains:
    Saturated fat   0.7 gram   Cholesterol Trace

Spinach Soufflé

1 (10-oz.) pkg. frozen
chopped spinach,
thawed
3 tablespoons soft diet
margarine
3 tablespoons all-purpose
flour
1 cup non-fat milk
1/2 cup egg substitute

1 tablespoon chopped
green onions
1/4 teaspoon grated
nutmeg
Salt and pepper
5 egg whites
1/4 teaspoon cream of
tartar

Preheat oven to 400F (205C). Place thawed spinach in a strainer to drain. In a saucepan melt margarine; stir in flour. Add milk and cook, stirring constantly, until thickened. Remove from heat. Beat in egg substitute. Add drained spinach, green onions, nutmeg, salt and pepper to taste. In a large mixer bowl, beat egg whites and cream of tartar until very stiff. Carefully fold spinach mixture into egg whites. Spray a 6-cup soufflé dish or deep casserole with vegetable cooking spray. Pour spinach mixture into prepared dish. Bake about 35 minutes, until golden brown. Serve at once. Makes 4 servings.

Variation

Omit spinach and substitute 1 cup chopped cooked vegetable. Try asparagus, broccoli, carrots or squash.

♥ Each serving contains:
Saturated fat   0.8 gram   Cholesterol   None

Garden Medley

1 tablespoon olive oil	1 yellow bell pepper, sliced
1 garlic clove, crushed	4 large tomatoes, cut in
1 large onion, sliced	eighths
1 green bell pepper, sliced	Dillweed

In a large skillet, heat oil. Sauté garlic and onion for about 2 minutes. Add bell peppers and tomatoes. Continue stirring and cooking another 4 to 5 minutes, until peppers are tender-crisp. Sprinkle with dillweed. Serve at once. Makes 6 servings.

❤ Each serving contains:

Saturated fat   Trace   Cholesterol   None

Pineapple Yams

1 (8-oz.) can pineapple slices, drained	1/2 cup orange juice
1 (20-oz.) can yams, sliced, drained	1/2 cup pineapple-orange preserves
1/3 cup raisins	2 teaspoons rum flavoring

Preheat oven to 350F (175C). Spray a shallow baking dish with vegetable cooking spray. Arrange alternate slices of pineapple and yams in prepared baking dish. In a small saucepan, combine raisins, orange juice and pineapple-orange preserves. Stir over low heat about 5 minutes. Remove from heat, add rum flavoring. Pour mixture over pineapple and yams. Bake uncovered about 25 minutes, until heated. Serve either hot or cold. Makes 6 servings.

❤ Each serving contains:

Saturated fat   Trace   Cholesterol   None

Marinated Broccoli

2 lbs. fresh or 2 (10-oz.)
  pkgs. frozen broccoli
  spears
1 (8-oz.) can water chestnuts, drained

2 tablespoons chopped
  pimiento
6 tablespoons Italian
  Dressing, page 181

Trim ends and peel stems of fresh broccoli. Cook with water to cover 10 to 12 minutes, until tender-crisp. If using frozen, cook according to package directions, drain. Combine broccoli, water chestnuts and pimiento in a shallow bowl. Pour Italian Dressing over broccoli mixture. Cover and refrigerate at least 1 hour. Stir twice while chilling. Makes 6 servings.

♥ 1 tablespoon of dressing contains:
   Saturated fat   1.2 grams   Cholesterol   None

Hash Browns with Onions

2 teaspoons olive oil
1 teaspoon soft diet
  margarine
1/2 teaspoon paprika
1/2 teaspoon garlic salt

1/4 teaspoon pepper
1 small onion, chopped
1/2 green bell pepper,
  chopped
4 cooked, grated potatoes

Spray a large, non-stick skillet with vegetable cooking spray. Add oil and margarine, stir in paprika, garlic salt and pepper. Add onion and bell pepper; cook about 1 minute. Add potatoes, stir to blend. Cover and reduce heat. Cook 2 to 3 minutes, until crisp and brown on the underneath side. Carefully turn and brown other side. Serve at once. Makes 6 servings.

♥ Each serving contains:
   Saturated fat   Trace   Cholesterol   Trace

Mushroom & Tomato Surprise

2 teaspoons water
2 teaspoons beef or
  chicken bouillon granules
4 teaspoons Worcester-
  shire sauce
1 teaspoon dried leaf
  thyme

1 teaspoon ground celery
  seed
1 lb. mushrooms, sliced
4 English muffins or plain
  bagels, cut in half
Prepared mustard
8 tomato slices

In a skillet, combine water, bouillon granules, Worcestershire sauce, thyme and celery seed. Stir to blend. Add mushrooms; stir and cook until mushrooms are tender, 4 to 5 minutes. Do not overcook. Spread each muffin or bagel with mustard. Place a tomato slice on each; spoon mushroom topping over tomato. Serve as a brunch or light entree. Makes 4 servings.

♥ Each serving contains:
  Saturated fat   Trace   Cholesterol   None

Whipped Potatoes

6 potatoes, peeled
1/4 cup non-fat milk
1/2 teaspoon salt

1 pkg. Butter Buds®
1/2 cup hot potato water

Steam or boil potatoes until tender. Reserve 1/2 cup potato water. In a mixer bowl, combine potatoes, milk, salt and Butter Buds.® Beat until smooth. Slowly beat in potato water until desired consistency is reached. Serve at once. Makes 6 servings.

♥ Each serving contains:
  Saturated fat   Trace   Cholesterol   Trace

Fish

Short on time and long on appetite? Fish or seafood is the answer for you.

Ease of preparation and short cooking time make fish or seafood an ideal choice. And don't overlook the benefits of omega-3 oils gained by eating these foods. What a great combination—good and good for you.

Enjoy the Easy Seafood Platter if you are in the mood for something cold. Or there's the opposite side, with Hot Crab Salad or Baked Orange Roughy. Tender Scallops in Wine tastes so great no one will suspect it was prepared in minutes. If you are a salmon lover, several recipes will satisfy your tastes.

When purchasing tuna remember: Use water-packed tuna. If it is not available, place oil-packed tuna in a strainer and rinse with water. Drain well before using. This helps to eliminate the excess oil.

Blackened Fish

Cajun Pepper Mix, below
6-oz. fillets orange roughy
   or Icelandic cod
1 to 2 teaspoons olive or
   Puritan® oil

Lemon or lime slices or
   Barbecue Sauce,
   page 248

Shake Cajun Pepper Mix on both sides of fillets. Preheat an iron skillet; add oil and carefully place fillets in hot oiled skillet. Cook uncovered about 2 to 3 minutes. Turn fillets over and continue cooking 3 to 4 minutes more until fish is flaky. Serve immediately with lemon or lime slices or Barbecue Sauce. Makes 1 serving.

❤ Each 6 oz. fillet contains:

	Saturated fat	Cholesterol
Orange Roughy	0.5 gram	30mg
Cod	0.6 gram	100mg

Cajun Pepper Mix

2 tablespoons paprika
2 teaspoons salt
4 teaspoons cayenne
   pepper
2 teaspoons coarse black
   pepper
1/2 teaspoon white pepper
1/2 teaspoon crushed red-
   chili-pepper flakes

1/4 teaspoon onion
   powder
1/4 teaspoon garlic powder
1 teaspoon crushed dried
   chives
1 teaspoon dried leaf basil

In a small bowl, thoroughly blend all ingredients together. For a finer mix, place ingredients in a blender or food processor and process briefly. Store unused mix in a shaker or small container with a tight-fitting lid. Makes about 1/3 cup.

❤ Each serving contains:
Saturated fat None   Cholesterol None

Classic Broiled Salmon

1 (6-oz.) salmon steak,	1 lemon or lime
skin removed	Chopped fresh parsley
Coarse pepper	or dill

Sprinkle coarse pepper on salmon steak. Preheat broiler or grill; lightly spray broiler pan or grill with vegetable cooking spray. Place salmon on prepared surface and cook 4 inches from heat 7 to 10 minutes. Turn salmon and continue cooking 5 to 7 minutes until fish flakes easily. Cooking time may vary depending on thickness of salmon steak. Remove from heat. Squeeze on fresh lemon or lime juice, sprinkle with chopped parsley or dill and serve immediately. Makes 1 serving.

♥ Each 6-oz. serving without skin contains:

	Saturated fat	Cholesterol
Sockeye	2.4 grams	120mg
Pink	1.0 gram	90mg
Coho	2.0 grams	70mg

Salmon Casserole

1/4 cup chopped onion
1 (8-oz.) can salmon,
    without oil, drained
1/2 cup diced celery
1/2 cup red or green bell
    pepper
2 teaspoons dry mustard
1 tablespoon marjoram or
    parsley leaves

4 cups soft French-bread
    crumbs
2 tablespoons diet low-fat
    mayonnaise
1-1/2 cups non-fat milk
1 tablespoon grated
    Parmesan cheese
Paprika

Preheat oven to 350F (175C). Spray a 2-quart casserole with vegetable cooking spray. In a large bowl, combine onion, salmon, celery, bell pepper, mustard, marjoram or parsley and bread crumbs. Stir mayonnaise into milk; pour over mixture and thoroughly combine. Spoon mixture into prepared casserole. Bake about 35 minutes. Makes 4 servings.

❤ Each serving contains:

	Saturated fat	Cholesterol
Sockeye	1.7 grams	40mg
Pink	1.2 grams	30mg

Linguini with Clam Sauce

1 tablespoon olive oil
1 medium onion, diced
1 garlic clove, diced
1 (8-oz.) can minced clams
  or oysters
1/4 cup white wine or cider
1/2 teaspoon pepper

Juice of 1 lemon
2 tablespoons chopped
  pimiento
1/4 pound linguini or
  spaghetti
1/4 cup chopped fresh
  parsley, basil or oregano

Heat oil in a medium skillet; sauté onion and garlic. Stir while cooking about 2 to 3 minutes. Add juice from clams or oysters and wine or cider. Continue cooking over medium heat until the total volume is reduced to almost half. This will take about 15 minutes. Add clams or oysters, pepper and lemon juice. Cover, reduce heat and simmer 5 minutes; add chopped pimiento. Cook pasta according to package directions. Drain; return pasta to skillet. Pour clam mixture and parsley into pasta and cook about 5 to 8 minutes more. Or combine clam mixture and pasta in a 1-1/2-quart casserole and bake at 350F (175C) 15 minutes. Makes 4 servings.

❤ Each serving contains:

	Saturated fat	Cholesterol
Clams	0.6 gram	36mg
Oysters	1.0 gram	60mg

Easy Seafood Platter

6 oz. smoked or baked salmon, sliced	1 orange, segmented
6 oz. cooked shrimp	1 banana, sliced
Lettuce leaves	1 tablespoon lemon juice
6 pineapple spears	2 teaspoons sesame seeds

Arrange chilled salmon slices and shrimp on a lettuce-lined plate. Make an attractive arrangement of pineapple spears, orange segments and banana slices. Drizzle lemon juice over bananas; sprinkle with sesame seeds. Makes 2 servings.

Variation

Substitute any fresh fruit. Try apples, apricots, grapes, papaya or peaches. Or omit fruit and substitute celery sticks, chilled cooked peas and carrots, sliced radishes and sweet red onion rings. Top with capers.

♥ Each 3-oz. serving contains:

	Saturated fat	Cholesterol
Sockeye	1.2 grams	85mg
Pink	0.5 gram	45mg
Coho	1.0 gram	35mg
Shrimp	0.3 gram	120mg

Tuna Salad

1/2 (6-oz.) can water-
   packed tuna, drained
1 cup shredded cabbage
1 carrot, grated
1 green onion, chopped
2 tomatoes, chopped
1 teaspoon diet low-fat
   mayonnaise

2 tablespoons non-fat
   plain yogurt
1 tablespoon lemon juice
Lemon pepper
Salt and pepper
Mrs. Dash® (mild), if
   desired

In a medium bowl, combine tuna, cabbage, carrot, green onion and tomatoes. In a small bowl or cup, blend mayonnaise with yogurt; add lemon juice, lemon pepper, salt and pepper to taste and Mrs. Dash,® if desired. Stir mayonnaise mixture into tuna, thoroughly combine. Chill. Makes 4 servings.

❤ Each serving contains:
   Saturated fat   Trace   Cholesterol   12mg

Hot Crab Salad

12 oz. precooked frozen
    crab or imitation crab
1 cup bottled chili or
    seafood sauce
1 teaspoon minced fresh
    ginger root
1/3 cup brown sugar
1 tablespoon vinegar
1 teaspoon prepared
    horseradish

1/2 lb. pasta, fettuccine or
    spaghetti, broken into
    2-inch pieces
2 tablespoons olive oil
1 carrot, julienned
1 small zucchini, julienned
1/2 red or green bell
    pepper, julienned
1 tomato, chopped
1 green onion, chopped
Salt and pepper

Thaw seafood and cut into bite-size pieces. In a small saucepan, combine chili sauce, ginger root, brown sugar, vinegar and horseradish; simmer over low heat about 10 minutes. Set aside. Pour chili sauce over thawed crab pieces and marinate at least 1 hour. Cook pasta according to package instructions, drain and set aside. Heat oil in a large skillet; sauté carrot, zucchini and pepper. Add tomatoes, green onions and cooked pasta. Lightly toss together, cover and set aside. Preheat broiler, spray rack with vegetable cooking spray. Place crab pieces on prepared rack and broil 5 minutes; turn and brush pieces with additional sauce; broil 3 minutes more. Combine warm pasta mixture and broiled crab. Season to taste with salt and pepper. Makes 4 servings.

❤ Each serving contains:
    Saturated fat   1.0 gram   Cholesterol   45mg

Poached Salmon

1 cup chopped onions	2 tablespoons lemon juice
2 celery stalks with leaves	1 cup white wine, if
2 carrots	desired
1 bunch parsley	1/2 or 1 whole salmon
2 bay leaves	Lemon wedges
2 quarts water	

In a fish poacher or roasting pan, combine onions, celery, carrots, parsley, bay leaves and water. Bring to a boil, reduce the heat and simmer uncovered 20 minutes. Remove vegetables and add lemon juice and wine, if desired. Rinse fish and pat dry with paper towels. Place fish on a rack so it is covered by liquid. If the fish is large, add hot water to cover. Bring liquid to a simmer; cover and reduce heat so water quivers, but does not bubble. Cook about 45 minutes or just until the fish flakes easily with a fork. Another method is to bring the liquid to a boil and immediately turn off heat. Cover and let stand until liquid is cold. Serve immediately or chilled. Top with freshly squeezed lemon juice.

♥ Each 3-oz. serving contains

	Saturated fat	Cholesterol
Sockeye	1.2 grams	60mg
Pink	0.5 gram	45mg
Coho	1.0 gram	35mg

Salmon Loaf

1 (6-oz.) can salmon or
water-packed tuna
1-1/2 cups fresh French-
bread cubes
1 cup non-fat milk
1/2 cup egg substitute
3 tablespoons lemon juice
or vinegar
1 pkg. Butter Buds®
1/2 teaspoon paprika
1/2 teaspoon dry mustard
1/2 onion, chopped
1/4 teaspoon coarse
pepper

2 tablespoons chopped
chives
1/4 cup sliced fresh
mushrooms
1 tablespoon chopped
pimiento
1/2 cup non-fat plain
yogurt
2 tablespoons lemon juice
2 teaspoons dried leaf
tarragon

Preheat oven to 350F (175C). Drain salmon or tuna; place
in a mixing bowl and flake. Add the remaining ingredients
except yogurt, lemon juice and tarragon; thoroughly combine. Spray a 9 x 5-in. loaf pan with vegetable cooking spray.
Turn fish mixture into prepared pan and smooth top. Bake
in preheated oven 30 to 35 minutes. In a small bowl, blend
yogurt, lemon juice and tarragon. Serve loaf from pan or
place on a serving dish. Top with yogurt mixture. Makes 4
servings.

♥ Each serving contains:

	Saturated fat	Cholesterol
Sockeye	0.7 gram	30mg
Pink	0.4 gram	23mg
Tuna	0.3 gram	25mg

Baked Orange Roughy

2 teaspoons soft diet
  margarine
2 (6-oz.) orange-roughy
  fillets
3 tablespoons lemon juice
1/4 cup orange juice
1 orange, thinly sliced
2 teaspoons grated orange
  peel

1 teaspoon chopped
  cilantro (Chinese parsley)
  or parsley
1/2 teaspoon dried leaf
  thyme
Salt and pepper

Spread margarine in non-stick baking dish, add fillets. In a cup, combine lemon and orange juices with orange peel. Pour juice over fillets. Top with layer of orange slices and sprinkle with chopped cilantro or parsley and thyme. Bake uncovered at 375F (190C) about 10 minutes until fish flakes with a fork. Season to taste with salt and pepper. Makes 2 servings.

❤ Each 6-oz. fillet contains:
  Saturated fat   0.5 gram   Cholesterol   30mg

Stuffed Fish Fillets

3 tablespoons non-fat
   plain yogurt
1 tablespoon non-fat milk
3 slices fresh French-
   bread cubes
2 tablespoons wine
   vinegar or lemon juice
2 tablespoons finely
   chopped onion
2 tablespoons finely
   chopped green bell pepper

2 tablespoons sliced
   pimiento-stuffed olives
2 (6-oz.) fillets orange
   roughy, cod or sole
Salt and coarse pepper
Paprika
Dillweed

Preheat oven to 350F (175C). Spray an 8-inch round baking dish with vegetable cooking spray. In a small bowl, combine yogurt, milk, bread cubes, wine vinegar or lemon juice, onion, bell pepper and olives; mix well. Sprinkle both sides of fillets with salt, pepper and paprika. Place 1 fillet in prepared dish. Spread stuffing evenly over fillet; place second fillet on top of stuffing like a sandwich. Cut in half; sprinkle tops with paprika and dillweed. Bake 20 to 25 minutes. Makes 2 servings.

♥ Each 6-oz. serving contains:

	Saturated fat	Cholesterol
Orange Roughy	0.5 gram	30mg
Cod	0.3 gram	100mg
Sole	0.6 gram	120mg

Barbecue Shrimp

1 tablespoon olive or
   Puritan® oil
1/2 onion, chopped
2 tablespoons vinegar
2 tablespoons brown sugar
1 cup catsup
2 tablespoons dry mustard

1/2 teaspoon garlic powder
5 to 6 drops Tabasco sauce
2 tablespoons dried leaf
   oregano
24 large raw shrimp,
   peeled, deveined
1 lime or lemon

In a small saucepan, heat oil; sauté onion briefly. Add vinegar, brown sugar, catsup, mustard, garlic powder, Tabasco sauce and oregano. Stir to combine; cook over low heat about 5 minutes. Set aside to cool. Place shrimp in a bowl; pour cooled sauce over. Turn shrimp, coating well with sauce. Cover tightly and refrigerate at least 4 hours or overnight. Preheat broiler or grill. Thread shrimp on skewers. Broil 3 to 4 minutes on each side. To serve, squeeze fresh lime or lemon juice over shrimp. Makes 6 servings.

♥ Each serving contains:
   Saturated fat   1.4 grams   Cholesterol   140mg

Scallops in Wine

1 tablespoon olive oil
1/3 cup chopped onions
1-1/2 tablespoons minced
    shallots or green onions
1-1/2 lbs. scallops, washed,
    sliced
1/2 cup all-purpose flour
1 tablespoon soft diet
    margarine
1 tablespoon olive oil

1 garlic clove, crushed
3/4 cup dry white wine
1/2 cup vermouth
1 bay leaf
4 tomatoes, chopped
1 teaspoon dried leaf
    oregano
1 teaspoon chopped
    parsley
Salt and pepper

In a skillet, heat oil and sauté onions and shallots. Toss scallops with flour to coat. Shake off excess flour. Add scallops to onions. Stir quickly 2 to 3 minutes to combine. In another skillet, heat margarine, olive oil and garlic. Add wine, vermouth, bay leaf, tomatoes, oregano and parsley. Cook about 2 minutes; add scallops. Stir to combine and cook about 4 to 5 minutes. Season to taste with salt and pepper. Serve at once. Makes 6 servings.

♥ Each serving contains:
    Saturated fat   0.8 gram   Cholesterol   40mg

Salmon Soufflé

1 (6-oz.) can salmon, drained or 1 cup cooked salmon, tuna or red snapper
3 tablespoons all-purpose flour
1 pkg. Butter Buds®
1 cup non-fat milk
1/2 cup egg substitute

1/2 teaspoon dry mustard
1 teaspoon dried leaf tarragon
1/4 finely chopped celery
5 egg whites
1/2 teaspoon cream of tartar
1/2 teaspoon chopped fresh parsley

Preheat oven to 400F (205C). Spray a 6-cup soufflé dish or deep baking dish with vegetable cooking spray. Remove all skin and bones from fish. Flake fish in a saucepan. Combine flour, Butter Buds® and milk. Stirring constantly, cook until thickened. Remove from heat. Beat in egg substitute, mustard, tarragon and celery. Add fish. In a large mixer bowl, beat egg whites and cream of tartar until stiff. Gently fold in fish mixture. Pour into prepared dish. Bake 35 to 40 minutes. Makes 4 servings.

♥ Each serving contains:

	Saturated fat	Cholesterol
Sockeye	0.7 gram	30mg
Pink	0.3 gram	23mg

Tuna Casserole

1 (7-oz.) can water-pack
   tuna, drained
2 green onions, chopped
1/4 cup chopped pimiento-
   stuffed olives
1/4 cup chopped green
   bell pepper
1/4 cup chopped celery

White Sauce, page 297
1/2 teaspoon prepared
   mustard
1/4 cup white wine, if
   desired
2 cups cooked pasta
Salt and pepper

Preheat oven to 350F (175C). Spray a 2-quart baking dish with vegetable cooking spray. In a medium bowl, mix all ingredients. Pour into prepared baking dish. Cover and bake about 20 minutes. Uncover; bake 10 minutes longer. Makes 6 servings.

♥ Each serving contains:
   Saturated fat   0.3 grams   Cholesterol   20mg

Poultry & Meats

Years ago we ate chicken on Sunday. Now that we know the health benefits of eating poultry, we are encouraged to eat it three or four times a week.

White meat is preferred over dark because it contains less fat. And be sure to remove skin and all visible fat when preparing any poultry dish. White meat tends to dry out if overcooked, so we suggest shorter than usual cooking times. Chicken and turkey can easily be substituted for other meats in many recipes.

Enjoy beef in smaller amounts and purchase *select lean* beef which has a lower proportion of fat. Two rabbit dishes are included because rabbit is readily available and similar to poultry in fat content. It, too, is a good source of protein.

We also include fruits and vegetables with many poultry and meat recipes to give added fiber as well as flavor. Some of the combinations may be new to you. Try Cranberry Chicken or Holiday Turkey Rolls. Perhaps Brunswick Stew or Chili Mac Casserole will be your choice.

Personalize the recipes as you choose.

Savory Crepes

3/4 cup egg substitute
2 egg whites
2 cups non-fat milk
1-1/2 cups all-purpose
  flour

1/2 teaspoon salt
1/2 teaspoon white pepper

In a mixer bowl, beat egg substitute and egg whites. Add milk and flour alternately; continue beating until smooth. Add salt and pepper. Batter can rest for an hour before making crepes. Use either a non-stick crepe pan or a skillet sprayed with vegetable cooking spray. Heat pan; add about 1/4 cup batter. Quickly tilt pan to evenly spread batter. When batter surface appears dry and begins to bubble, turn crepe. Repeat with remaining batter. Fill cooked crepes; either roll or fold as desired. Makes 12 crepes.

❤ Each crepe contains:

Saturated fat Trace   Cholesterol Trace

Chicken Florentine Crepes

1 recipe Savory Crepes,
   page 244
1 tablespoon Puritan® oil
1/4 cup chopped onion
1/4 cup chopped celery
1/2 cup sliced mushrooms
2 tablespoons all-purpose
   flour
1 cup Chicken Broth,
   page 158

2 cups (10 oz.) cooked
   chicken breast, cubed
1/2 cup chopped spinach,
   cooked, drained
1 teaspoon sweet paprika
1 teaspoon poultry
   seasoning
1/4 cup non-fat plain
   yogurt
Dillweed

Prepare crepes. Heat oil in a skillet; sauté onion, celery and mushrooms. Mix flour with chicken broth and stir into onion mixture. Continue stirring; cook 3 to 4 minutes until thickened and smooth. Add chicken, well-drained spinach, paprika and poultry seasoning. Cook until chicken is heated. Place 2 to 3 tablespoons filling on center of crepe. Roll up and place seam side down. Top with dollop of yogurt; sprinkle with dillweed. Bake in 350F (175C) oven for 15 minutes. Serve at once. Makes 12 crepes.

♥ Each crepe contains:
   Saturated fat   0.4 gram   Cholesterol   20mg

Turkey & Wild-Rice Crepes

1 recipe Savory Crepes,
   page 244
1 tablespoon olive or
   Puritan® oil
2 tablespoons chopped
   onion
1 teaspoon dried leaf
   tarragon
1/4 cup all-purpose flour
1 cup non-fat milk
1/2 cup Chicken Broth,
   page 158
1/2 cup vermouth or dry

white wine
2 tablespoons chopped
   pimiento
1/4 cup raisins
1-1/2 cups (7-1/2-oz.)
   cooked turkey breast,
   cubed
1/2 cup cooked carrots,
   sliced
2/3 cup cooked wild rice
   or long-grain and wild
   rice
1 cup whole cranberry

Prepare crepes. Heat oil in a skillet; sauté onions. Add tarragon. Mix flour with milk and broth; stir into onion mixture. Continue stirring; cook 3 to 4 minutes until thickened and smooth. Add vermouth or wine, pimiento, raisins, turkey, carrots and rice. Cook until all ingredients are heated. Spray a 13 x 14-inch baking dish with vegetable cooking spray. Place 2 to 3 tablespoons filling on center of crepe. Roll up and place seam side down. Place in prepared baking dish. Spoon cranberry sauce over filled crepes. Bake in oven at 350F (175C), about 15 minutes until heated. Serve at once. Makes 12 crepes.

❤ Each crepe contains:
   Saturated fat   0.4 gram   Cholesterol   13mg

Lemon-Broiled Chicken Breasts

Chicken or turkey breasts,
  boned, skinned
Lemon juice
Lemon pepper

Fresh spinach leaves
Lemon or lime wedges
Salt and pepper

Remove all visible fat from breasts; cut into fillets. Sprinkle with lemon juice and lemon pepper. Broil about 10 minutes, turning often, until meat is no longer pink. Serve on a spinach-lined platter. Season with additional fresh lemon juice or lime juice. Season with salt and pepper to taste.

❤ Each 3-oz. serving contains:
  Saturated fat 1 gram   Cholesterol 70mg

Barbecue Chicken

Chicken breasts or sliced
  turkey breasts, skinned
  and boned
Lemon juice

Barbecue Sauce, page 248

Place chicken or turkey in a single layer in a baking dish. Brush with lemon juice. Pour 1 cup Barbecue Sauce over all; turn to coat both sides. Cover and let stand at least 1 hour. Place chicken or turkey on grill; cook about 10 minutes, brushing with additional sauce as needed. Turn pieces often; continue grilling until meat is no longer pink when cut.

❤ Each 3-oz. serving contains:
  Saturated fat 1 gram   Cholesterol 70mg

Barbecue Sauce

1 onion, chopped
1 (6-oz.) can tomato sauce
1/4 cup sweet relish
1 tablespoon vinegar

1 teaspoon pepper
2 tablespoons
   Worcestershire sauce
5 tablespoons brown sugar

Sauté onion in a small non-stick coated skillet or sauce-pan. Add tomato sauce, relish, vinegar, pepper, Worchester-shire sauce and brown sugar. Cook over low heat about 5 to 7 minutes. Makes about 1-3/4 cups.

❤ Each serving contains:
   Saturated fat   None   Cholesterol   None

Baked Orange-Chicken Breasts

4 chicken breasts, skinned
   boned
1/2 cup corn-flake crumbs
1-1/2 teaspoons paprika
1/2 teaspoon grated
   orange peel
2 teaspoons dried leaf
   mint or basil

1/4 cup egg substitute
2 tablespoons soy sauce
1 teaspoon water
1 pkg. Butter Buds®
1/3 cup orange-juice
   concentrate, thawed

Remove all visible fat from chicken breasts. Combine crumbs, paprika, orange peel and mint or basil in a pie plate or small paper bag. In another pie plate, blend egg substi-tute, soy sauce, water, Butter Buds and orange-juice con-centrate. Spray a baking sheet with vegetable cooking spray. Preheat oven to 375F (190C). Dip each chicken piece into egg mixture and then into crumb mixture. Place coated pieces on prepared baking pan. Bake 30 to 40 minutes. Makes 4 servings.

❤ Each 3-oz. serving of chicken contains:
   Saturated fat   1 gram   Cholesterol   70mg

Chicken & Grape Casserole

2 cups toasted French-
  bread crumbs
1/2 teaspoon dried leaf
  basil
1/2 teaspoon dried leaf
  oregano
1/2 teaspoon garlic powder
2 cups (10 oz.) cooked,
  skinned, diced chicken
  breast
2 cups thinly sliced celery

1 cup fresh green grapes
  or 1 (8-oz.) can green
  grapes, drained
2 green onions chopped
4 tablespoons diet low-fat
  mayonnaise
6 tablespoons non-fat
  plain yogurt
1 tablespoon lemon juice
1 tablespoon grated
  Parmesan cheese
Salt and pepper

Preheat oven to 350F (175C). Mix bread crumbs with basil, oregano and garlic powder. In a large bowl, combine chicken, celery, grapes, green onions and 1 cup crumb mixture. In a cup or small bowl, blend mayonnaise, yogurt and lemon juice. Spread mayonnaise mixture in a baking dish. Arrange 1 layer of chicken mixture on top. Sprinkle remaining crumbs over mixture. Top with Parmesan cheese. Season with salt and pepper to taste. Bake uncovered 20 to 25 minutes. Serve immediately. Makes 4 servings.

❤ Each serving contains:
  Saturated fat   2 grams   Cholesterol   52mg

Cranberry Chicken

2 tablespoons honey
2 tablespoons orange juice
1 teaspoon grated orange peel
1/2 teaspoon ground allspice

1 (16-oz.) can whole cranberry sauce
4 chicken breasts, boned, skinned

Preheat oven to 375F (190C). Mix honey, orange juice, orange peel, allspice and cranberry sauce in a small bowl. Remove all visible fat from chicken breasts. Pour 1/2 of mixture over chicken breasts. Bake 15 minutes. Turn chicken pieces; pour on remaining sauce. Continue baking another 30 to 35 minutes.

♥ Each 3-oz. chicken serving contains:
Saturated fat   1 gram   Cholesterol   70mg

Hearty Chicken & Rice Casserole

1 recipe Brown Rice with Vegetables, page 209
2 cups (10 oz.) cooked, skinned, chopped chicken breast

1/2 cup peas
2 tablespoons chopped pimiento
1/2 cup Chicken Broth, page 158

Preheat oven to 350F (175C). Spray a 2-1/2-quart baking dish with vegetable cooking spray; set aside. Prepare Brown Rice with Vegetables mixture; combine with chicken, peas. pimiento and broth. Spoon into prepared baking dish. Bake about 15 minutes, until heated through. Makes 8 servings.

♥ Each serving contains:
Saturated fat   0.4 gram   Cholesterol   26mg

Chicken Stir-Fry

2 tablespoons Puritan® oil
1 teaspoon grated ginger
    root or 1/2 teaspoon
    ground ginger
2 chicken breasts, skinned,
    boned, cut into 1/2-inch
    strips
2 green bell peppers, sliced
4 green onions including
    tops, cut in 1-1/2-inch
    lengths

1 zucchini, cut in 1-1/2-
    inch lengths
1 (6-oz.) can water
    chestnuts, drained
2 medium tomatoes, cut in
    eighths
2 teaspoons cornstarch
1 teaspoon sugar
3 tablespoons soy sauce
1/4 teaspoon five-spice
    powder

Preheat a wok or large fry pan. Add oil and ginger; add chicken pieces. Stir-fry chicken until white. Remove chicken, cover and set aside. Add bell peppers, green onions and zucchini. Stir-fry until vegetables are tender crisp. Return chicken to wok; add drained chestnuts and tomatoes. Gently stir to combine. In a cup or small bowl, blend cornstarch, sugar, soy sauce and five-spice powder. Pour mixture over chicken and vegetables. Stir-fry, turning to coat all ingredients until sauce thickens. Serve at once. Makes 4 servings.

Variation

Add 1 cup walnuts and 1/4 cup sliced mushrooms with the vegetables.

❤ Each serving contains:
    Saturated fat   1.5 grams   Cholesterol   100mg
❤ With walnuts:
    Saturated fat   2.0 grams   Cholesterol   100mg

Chicken-Almond Casserole

1/3 cup minced onions
1-1/4 cups non-fat milk
1/2 teaspoon salt
1/4 teaspoon pepper
1 pkg. Butter Buds®
1/4 cup all-purpose flour
4 cups (20-oz.) cooked
　chicken breast, cubed

1/2 pound fresh
　mushrooms, sliced
1 cup blanched sliced
　almonds
1 (10-1/2-oz.) pkg. frozen
　chopped broccoli,
　thawed

In a non-stick fry pan sprayed with vegetable cooking spray, sauté onions. In a small saucepan, combine milk, salt, pepper, Butter Buds® and flour. Stir to blend; cook, stirring, over medium heat until sauce thickens; add sautéed onions. Preheat oven to 350F (175C). Spray a 2-quart baking dish with vegetable cooking spray. Place chicken cubes, mushrooms, almonds and chopped broccoli in baking dish. Pour sauce over chicken mixture; stir to combine. Bake uncovered 30 minutes. Makes 6 servings.

❤ Each serving contains:
　Saturated fat　2.2 grams　　Cholesterol　70mg

Chicken à la King

2 teaspoons Puritan® oil
1 cup sliced mushrooms
1/2 cup diced green bell
  pepper
1/2 cup all-purpose flour
2 cups non-fat milk
1 cup Chicken Broth,
  page 158

2 cups (10 oz.) cooked,
  skinned, cubed chicken
  breast
1 (4-oz.) jar chopped
  pimiento
Salt and pepper
Toast, rice or pasta

Heat oil in a large non-stick skillet or saucepan. Cook and stir mushrooms and green bell peppers 5 minutes. Blend in the flour. Cook over low heat; stir until mixture is bubbly. Remove from heat and stir in the milk and broth. Heat to boiling, stirring constantly. Add chicken and pimiento. Season with salt and pepper to taste. Serve hot over toast, cooked rice or pasta. Makes 4 servings.

❤ Each serving contains:
  Saturated fat   1 gram   Cholesterol   52mg

Enchiladas

2 teaspoons olive or
  Puritan® oil
1/2 cup chopped onions
1/2 cup cooked pinto
  beans, drained
2 cups (10 oz.) cubed
  cooked, skinned,
  chicken breast
1/2 cup chopped green
  chilies
1 teaspoon dried leaf
  oregano

1 large tomato, chopped
1/4 teaspoon chili powder
1/4 teaspoon ground
  cumin
1 (12-oz.) can tomato
  sauce
12 corn tortillas
1 cup salsa
3/4 cup (3 oz.) grated
  low-fat mozzarella
  cheese

Heat oil in a saucepan, add onions and cook until softened. Stir in pinto beans, chicken, chilies, oregano and tomato. Heat mixture and set aside. In a small skillet, blend chili powder and cumin with tomato sauce; simmer 2 minutes. Remove from heat. Dip each tortilla in tomato sauce; set aside on a plate. Fill each tortilla with 3 tablespoons chicken mixture in a 13 x 9-inch baking dish. Roll and place seam side down. Pour about 1 cup salsa over filled enchiladas. Sprinkle with cheese. Bake in a 350F (175C) oven about 20 minutes. Makes 12 enchiladas.

♥ Each enchilada contains:
  Saturated fat   1.2 grams   Cholesterol   21mg

Teriyaki Chicken

1 tablespoon fresh grated
    ginger or 1 teaspoon
    ground ginger
4 green onions, chopped
1/4 cup soy sauce
3 tablespoons sugar

1/4 cup rice wine or dry
    sherry
1 garlic clove, crushed
6 chicken breasts, skinned,
    cubed
Sesame seeds

In a bowl, combine ginger, green onions, soy sauce, sugar, rice wine or sherry and garlic. Add chicken cubes; turn to coat all pieces. Cover and refrigerate at least 2 hours. Occasionally turn chicken. Thread chicken cubes on 6 skewers. Brush with additional soy mixture, as needed. Broil 4 to 5 minutes, turning frequently. Brush with soy mixture again and sprinkle with sesame seeds. Broil 3 to 4 minutes longer. Serve at once. Makes 6 servings.

♥ Each 4-oz. serving contains:
    Saturated fat   1.2 grams   Cholesterol   70mg

Tomato-Curry Chicken

1 tablespoon olive or
   Puritan® oil
4 cups (20 oz.) boned,
   skinned, cubed chicken
   breasts
1/2 onion, chopped
1/4 cup chopped celery
1 teaspoon curry powder
1/2 teaspoon chili powder
1 tablespoon all-purpose
   flour

1 tablespoon tomato paste
1 cup Chicken Broth, page
   158
1/2 cup dry white wine or
   water
1 apple, peeled, chopped
1 tomato, chopped
2 cups cooked rice
1/2 cup non-fat plain
   yogurt
Ground cinnamon

Heat oil in a heavy skillet. Add chicken, onion and celery. Stir-fry about 2 minutes. Stir in curry and chili powders. In a cup, blend flour, tomato paste and chicken broth. Add to chicken with white wine or water. Cover, reduce heat and simmer, stirring occasionally, about 20 minutes. Add apple and tomato; continue cooking another 7 to 10 minutes. To serve, spoon chicken curry over hot rice. Top with a dollop of yogurt. Sprinkle cinnamon to taste on top. Makes 6 servings.

❤ Each serving contains:
   Saturated fat   1.2 grams   Cholesterol   70mg

Cajun Chicken Bake

4 (4-oz.) chicken breasts,   Cajun Pepper Mix, page
  boned, skinned   228
1 (8-oz.) can tomato sauce
1 (4-oz.) can sliced
  mushrooms, drained

Preheat oven to 350F (175C). Spray a baking dish or pie pan with vegetable cooking spray; set aside. Place chicken breasts in prepared dish. Combine tomato sauce and mushrooms. Spoon over chicken. Sprinkle with Cajun Pepper Mix to taste. Bake uncovered 40 to 45 minutes. Makes 4 servings.

❤ Each serving contains:
  Saturated fat   1.2 grams   Cholesterol 100mg

Holiday Turkey Rolls

1/2 cup chopped dried figs
1/4 cup chopped dried
   apples
1/4 cup apple juice
1 lb. sliced, skinned, raw
   turkey breast
Salt and pepper
1 cup soft bread crumbs
2 green onions, chopped
1 tablespoon chopped
   celery

1/2 teaspoon poultry
   seasoning
1/2 teaspoon chopped
   parsley
1 tablespoon Puritan® oil
1 tablespoon diet soft
   margarine
1/2 cup Chicken Broth,
   page 158
Sauce, see next page

In a bowl, combine figs and apple juice; set aside. Remove all visible fat from turkey. With a meat mallet or cleaver, flatten turkey slices to about 1/4 inch thickness. Lightly sprinkle turkey slices with salt and pepper. Add bread crumbs, onions, celery, poultry seasoning and parsley to soaked fruits. Stir to blend. Spoon 2 to 3 tablespoons mixture on each turkey slice. Roll and secure with string or 3 wooden picks. Heat oil and margarine in a heavy skillet. Add turkey rolls; cook about 5 to 6 minutes, carefully turning rolls to cook all sides. Add broth. Cover; reduce heat and cook, turning rolls occasionally, about 25 minutes. Remove rolls, place on a warm serving dish. Remove string or wooden picks. Cover to keep warm. Prepare sauce. Pour sauce over turkey rolls. Serve at once. Makes 4 servings.

Holiday Turkey Rolls, continued

Sauce

1 tablespoon cornstarch
1/2 cup apple juice
1/3 cup apple liqueur or
   dry white wine

1/3 cup currants or raisins
1/3 cup peeled, chopped
   apple

In a cup, dissolve cornstarch into apple juice. Stir cornstarch mixture, apple liqueur or wine, currants or raisins and apple into liquid in skillet. Continue cooking and stirring until thickened.

♥ Each serving contains:
   Saturated fat   1.6 grams   Cholesterol   100mg

Chicken & Shrimp Oriental

3/4 lb. chicken breast, boned, skinned

1/2 lb. raw shrimp, shelled, deveined

3 tablespoons Puritan® oil

3 green onions, cut in 1-inch lengths

1 tablespoon chopped fresh ginger

1/2 cup sliced bamboo shoots

1/2 cup pea pods or 1/2 cup peas

1/2 cup sliced mushrooms

1/4 cup sliced blanched almonds

Marinade

1 egg white

1 teaspoon grated fresh ginger

1 teaspoon cornstarch

Seasoning Sauce

4 tablespoons soy sauce

2 tablespoons sugar

2 tablespoons rice wine or dry sherry

1 tablespoon cornstarch

Slice chicken into 1/2-inch strips. Cut each shrimp into thirds. Blend Marinade ingredients in a bowl. Add chicken and shrimp to marinade, mix to coat. Set aside for 20 minutes. Heat wok or large fry pan, add oil, green onions and ginger. Stir and add shrimp and chicken pieces. Stir-fry about 1 minute. Remove from wok. Add bamboo shoots, pea pods or peas and mushrooms. Stir-fry 1 to 2 minutes. In a small bowl, combine Seasoning Sauce ingredients and add to wok. Bring to a boil. Add chicken, shrimp and almonds; continue to stir-fry about 1 minute. Serve at once. Makes 6 servings.

❤ Each serving contains:

Saturated fat   1 gram   Cholesterol   100mg

Golden Turkey Curry

1 tablespoon olive or
Puritan® oil
1 onion, chopped
1/2 green bell pepper,
chopped
1 garlic clove, crushed
3 tablespoons all-purpose
flour
1 cup Chicken Broth,
page 158
1/4 teaspoon ground
cinnamon
1/4 teaspoon ground
cloves
2 teaspoons curry powder
1 tablespoon chopped
crystallized ginger
1/4 cup raisins
2 cups (10 oz.) cubed,
skinned turkey
breast
Hot cooked rice
1/4 cup chopped peanuts
1/4 cup imitation bacon
bits
Peach Chutney, page 184

In a saucepan, heat oil; add onion, bell pepper and garlic. Stir in flour and chicken broth. Simmer 5 minutes, stirring constantly. Add cinnamon, cloves, curry powder,
ginger, raisins and turkey. Cook about 15 minutes, stirring
occasionally. Mound hot cooked rice on a serving platter.
Spoon turkey curry over rice. Top with chopped peanuts
and bacon bits. Serve with Peach Chutney. Makes 6 servings.

❤ Each serving contains:
Saturated fat   2 grams   Cholesterol   35mg

Oven-Baked Chicken

1 cup non-fat plain yogurt
1/2 teaspoon ground
    cumin
2 teaspoons chopped
    chives
6 (4-1/2-oz.) boned,
    skinned chicken breasts

1-1/2 cups shredded-wheat
    crumbs
1/2 cup oat bran
1 teaspoon parsley
1 teaspoon dried leaf
    marjoram
1 teaspoon paprika

Blend yogurt with cumin and chives. Pour into a flat baking dish. Place chicken breasts in yogurt, turning to coat. Cover and refrigerate 24 hours, turning chicken several times. Preheat oven to 375F (190C). Combine shredded wheat, oat bran, parsley, marjoram and paprika. Dip chicken breasts into crumb mixture, turning and pressing to coat. Spray a baking sheet with vegetable cooking spray. Place chicken on prepared baking sheet. Bake 35 minutes. Makes 6 servings.

❤ Each serving contains:
    Saturated fat   1.5 grams   Cholesterol   100mg

Brunswick Stew

3 (4-1/2-oz.) boned,
  skinned chicken breasts
4 cups water
1 large onion, sliced
2 chicken bouillon cubes
1/8 teaspoon cayenne
  pepper
2 teaspoons Worcester-
  shire sauce
1/4 teaspoon dried leaf
  thyme
1/2 teaspoon dried leaf
  oregano

2 medium potatoes,
  peeled, diced
1 (10-oz.) pkg. frozen baby
  lima beans
1 (16-oz.) can diced
  tomatoes, undrained
1 (10-oz.) pkg. frozen
  whole-kernel corn
1 teaspoon salt
2 slices white bread

Remove visible fat from chicken breasts. Cut breasts in half. In a 4-quart pot, combine chicken, water, onion, bouillon, cayenne pepper, Worcestershire sauce, thyme and oregano. Bring to a boil; reduce heat. Cover and simmer until chicken is tender, about 20 minutes. Remove chicken; set aside. Add potatoes and lima beans to broth in pot. Cover and simmer until potatoes are tender, about 20 minutes. Add tomatoes with juice, corn, salt and chicken pieces. Cover and simmer 10 minutes longer. Break bread into bite-size pieces. Add to stew; stir constantly until stew has thickened. For each serving, put a piece of chicken in a large soup bowl. Surround with stew. Makes 6 (1-1/2-cup) servings.

❤ Each serving contains:
  Saturated fat   0.9 gram   Cholesterol   52mg

Rabbit Stew

1 rabbit, cut up or 1 pkg.
   frozen rabbit, thawed
1/4 cup vinegar or lemon
   juice
2 tablespoons olive or
   Puritan® oil
1 (10-oz.) pkg. frozen
   boiling onions

2 carrots, sliced
1/2 cup white wine
1/2 cup tomato juice
4 whole cloves
Peel of 1 orange
Salt and pepper
Hot cooked pasta or
   brown rice

Sprinkle rabbit with vinegar or lemon. Heat oil in a Dutch oven or heavy saucepan. Brown rabbit in oil. Add remaining ingredients except pasta or rice. Cover, reduce heat; cook until rabbit is tender, 30 to 40 minutes. Remove cloves. Season with salt and pepper to taste. Serve with hot cooked pasta or brown rice. Makes 4 servings.

❤ Each 3-oz. serving contains:
   Saturated fat   1.6 grams   Cholesterol   54mg

Rabbit Italian Style

2 tablespoons olive oil
1 rabbit, cut up or 1 pkg.
    frozen rabbit, thawed
1 onion, sliced
2 garlic cloves
1 green bell pepper, sliced
1/2 cup sliced celery
1 (14-1/2-oz.) can
    tomatoes, including
    juice
2 tablespoons tomato paste

1 tablespoon dried leaf
    basil
1 tablespoon oregano
1 cup sliced mushrooms
1 tablespoon capers
1/2 cup red wine or
    Chicken Broth,
    page 158
Salt and pepper
Hot cooked pasta

Heat oil in a Dutch oven or heavy saucepan. Brown rabbit in oil. Add remaining ingredients. Cover, reduce heat; cook until rabbit is tender, 30 to 40 minutes. Season with salt and pepper to taste. Serve with hot cooked pasta. Makes 4 servings.

❤ Each 3-oz. serving contains:
    Saturated fat   1.6 grams   Cholesterol   54mg

Chili Mac Casserole

2 teaspoons olive or
  Puritan® oil
3/4 lb. select extra-lean
  ground beef
1 onion, chopped
2 garlic cloves, crushed
1 green bell pepper,
  chopped
2 celery stalks, sliced
1 (8-oz.) can tomato sauce
1 (16-oz.) can whole
  tomatoes, or 4 fresh
  tomatoes, chopped

1 teaspoon dried leaf
  oregano
1/2 teaspoon Italian
  seasoning
1 (16-oz.) can kidney
  beans, drained
1-1/2 cups cooked
  macaroni
Salt and pepper

In a large non-stick fry pan, heat oil. Add beef and stir to brown; add onion, garlic, pepper and celery. Cook about 3 minutes, stirring often. Add tomato sauce, tomatoes, including juice, oregano and Italian seasoning. Cover, reduce heat and cook about 20 minutes. Add beans and macaroni. Cook 4 to 5 minutes until heated through. Season to taste with salt and pepper. Makes 6 servings.

♥ Each serving contains:
  Saturated fat   3.0 grams   Cholesterol   33mg

Beef with Peppers & Tomato

3/4 lb. select flank or
   round steak
2 tablespoons Puritan® oil
1 teaspoon chopped
   ginger root
2 garlic cloves
1/2 onion, sliced

1 green bell pepper, sliced
2 tomatoes, cut in eighths
1/2 cup Beef Broth, page
   159
1 teaspoon cornstarch
1 tablespoon soy sauce

Marinade

1 teaspoon sugar
1 teaspoon cornstarch
2 tablespoons soy sauce
1 tablespoon rice wine or
   vinegar

1 green onion, chopped
1 teaspoon chopped
   ginger root or 1/4
   teaspoon ground ginger

Chill or partially freeze steak for easier slicing. Remove all visible fat. Slice chilled steak into 1/2 x 2-inch strips. In a bowl, combine all ingredients for marinade. Add steak strips; stir to combine. Let stand at least 15 minutes. Heat oil in a wok or large non-stick fry pan. Add ginger and garlic; sauté until golden. Add steak strips, stir-fry until lightly browned. Remove and set aside. Add onion and bell peppers; stir-fry about 2 minutes. Add tomatoes and steak; continue stirring. Combine broth, cornstarch and soy sauce. Pour over beef mixture. Quickly stir-fry about 1 minute to coat all ingredients. Serve at once. Makes 4 servings.

❤ Each serving contains:
   Saturated fat   4.5 grams   Cholesterol   50mg

Veal Stew

1 lb. veal stew meat	4 potatoes, peeled, cubed
2 tablespoons all-purpose flour	1-1/2 cups fresh or frozen green beans
1 tablespoon olive or Puritan® oil	1 tablespoon all-purpose flour
1 to 2 tablespoons sweet paprika	1/2 cup non-fat plain yogurt
1 onion, chopped	Dillweed
5 carrots, sliced	
1-1/2 cups Chicken Broth, page 158	

Trim all visible fat from stew meat; cut into bite-size pieces. Toss with 2 tablespoons flour to coat. In a Dutch oven or heavy pot, heat oil. Add meat; stir to brown all sides evenly. Add paprika, onion, carrots and broth. Cover and simmer about 45 minutes. Add potatoes and green beans. Continue cooking until vegetables are tender. Stir 1 tablespoon flour into yogurt. Remove meat and vegetables to a serving bowl and cover. Stir yogurt mixture into remaining stew liquid. Heat, stirring, until blended. Pour over meat and vegetables, sprinkle with dillweed. Serve at once. Makes 6 servings.

❤ Each serving contains:
  Saturated fat   2.6 grams   Cholesterol   100mg

Oven Meatballs

1/2 cup rolled or quick
   oatmeal
1/2 cup soft bread crumbs
1/2 lb. select extra-lean
   ground beef
1/4 cup egg substitute
1/4 cup non-fat milk
1/4 teaspoon ground
   nutmeg
1/2 teaspoon celery seed

1/2 teaspoon chopped
   parsley
1 tablespoon Worcester-
   shire sauce
2 green onions, chopped
2 tablespoons chopped
   mushrooms
Salt and pepper
Red-currant or raspberry
   jelly

Preheat oven to 400F (205C). In a bowl, combine all ingredients except jelly. Shape into 12 (2-inch) balls. Place on an ungreased baking sheet. Bake 15 to 20 minutes, until browned. Heat red-currant or raspberry jelly. Place meatballs in a serving dish. Either pour jelly over meatballs or serve separately. Makes 4 servings.

❤ Each serving contains:
  Saturated fat   2.7 grams   Cholesterol   33mg

Fruited Meatloaf

18 dried or canned
  apricot halves
1 cup hot water
1/2 lb. skinned turkey
  breast, ground
1/2 lb. fat-free round steak,
  ground
1 cup rolled oats
1/4 cup egg substitute or
  2 egg whites

3 tablespoons tomato paste
1 celery stalk, chopped
1 medium onion, chopped
1 tablespoon chopped
  fresh parsley
1/2 teaspoon Fine Herbes
Salt and pepper
8 pitted prunes

Preheat oven to 350F (175C). Spray a 9 x 5-inch pan with vegetable cooking spray. Place dried apricots in a small bowl. Cover with 1 cup hot water. If using canned apricots, drain; set aside. In a large bowl, thoroughly combine turkey, steak, oats, egg substitute or egg whites, tomato paste, celery, onion, parsley and herbs. Season with salt and pepper to taste. Pat mixture into prepared pan. Drain apricots. Press prunes in a single row down center of meat loaf. Press apricots cut side-down on either side of prunes. Cover with foil and bake 30 minutes. Uncover and continue baking another 25 to 30 minutes. Let stand about 10 minutes before slicing. Makes 8 servings.

❤ Each serving contains:
  Saturated fat   1.7 grams   Cholesterol   40mg

Desserts

Even with fat and cholesterol counts in mind, we offer a great group of desserts. Crepes can be filled with any number of fillings that are tasty, yet contain little or no fat. Frozen desserts seem to be the most popular, so don't feel denied. Our suggestions are delicious.

Along with homemade sorbet or sherbet, serve one of our cookies. Homey Bread Pudding becomes a special treat when topped with one of the fruit sauces. Chilled Melon Soup is a delightful way to end a summer meal. Or create your own yogurt combination. Start with plain non-fat yogurt, add applesauce, cinnamon and nutmeg, and you have the choice of eating it as is or freezing it for later.

Dessert Crepes

3/4 cup egg substitute   2 tablespoons sugar
1-1/2 cups non-fat milk   1 teaspoon vanilla extract
1 cup all-purpose flour

In a small bowl, beat egg substitute until frothy; continue beating while adding non-fat milk. Gradually add flour, sugar and vanilla. Use either a non-stick crepe pan or a skillet sprayed with vegetable cooking spray. Heat pan; add about 1/4 cup batter. Quickly tilt pan to evenly spread batter. When batter surface appears dry and begins to bubble, turn crepe. Repeat with remaining batter. Use any of the fillings below, and either roll or fold as desired. Makes about 20 (8-inch) crepes.

Fillings

Spread cooked crepes with your favorite berries. Fold, roll or stack and top with jam or additional fruit. Dust with powdered sugar.

Fruit Crepes: Combine 1-1/2 cups cooked apples, apricots or peaches with 1/3 cup raisins or currants and 1/2 teaspoon pumpkin pie spice.

Cheese Crepes: Combine 1 cup non-fat cottage cheese with 2 tablespoons sugar and 1 teaspoon vanilla.

♥ Each plain crepe contains:
  Saturated fat   0.2 gram   Cholesterol Trace

Raspberry Sorbet

1/3 cup sugar
2 teaspoons lemon
   peel
1 cup water

3 cups fresh or frozen
   raspberries
1 orange, peeled,
   sectioned

In a small saucepan combine sugar, lemon peel and water. Bring to a boil; simmer until sugar is dissolved. Set aside to cool. Combine lemon syrup, raspberries and orange in a blender or food processor. Blend until smooth; pour into an ice-cream maker and freeze according to manufacturer's instructions. If you do not have an ice-cream maker, pour mixture into a freezer container, cover surface with plastic wrap. Freeze until firm. Remove, break into chunks. Beat in a mixer or food processor until fluffy, but not thawed. Spoon back into freezer container, cover with plastic wrap, return to freezer until firm. Makes about 1 quart.

Variations

For a smoother sorbet, substitute 1 (10-oz.) can frozen raspberry-juice concentrate and 1 cup strained orange juice.

Strawberry Gelatin: Dissolve 1 (3-oz.) pkg. strawberry gelatin in 1-1/2 cups boiling water; add 3 ice cubes. Stir until ice is melted. Pour into blender or food processor with 2 cups strawberries. Blend until smooth. Proceed according to instructions above.

❤ Each serving contains:
Saturated fat   None   Cholesterol   None

Fresh Fruit Ice

1-1/2 cups water   2-1/2 cups fresh fruit purée
1 cup sugar
2 teaspoons lemon or lime
   juice

In a saucepan, heat water and sugar until dissolved. Remove from heat; add juice. Combine with puréed fruit, pour into an ice-cream maker and freeze according to manufacturer's instructions. If you do not have an ice-cream maker, pour mixture into a freezer container, cover surface with plastic wrap. Freeze until firm. Remove, break into chunks. Beat in a mixer or food processor until fluffy, but not thawed. Spoon back into freezer container, cover with plastic wrap, return to freezer until firm. Makes about 1 quart.

Variation

Substitute fruit juice for the purée, or combine half fruit and half juice.

❤ Each serving contains:
   Saturated fat   None   Cholesterol   None

Frozen-Pineapple Whip

1 tablespoon lemon juice
2 tablespoons orange juice
2 cups water
3/4 cup light corn syrup

1 (8-oz.) can unsweetened
 crushed pineapple with
 juice
3 egg whites, stiffly beaten

In a bowl, combine lemon juice, orange juice, water and light corn syrup. Stir to blend; add pineapple with juices. Fold in beaten egg whites. Spoon into an ice-cream maker and freeze according to manufacturer's instructions. If you do not have an ice-cream maker, pour mixture into a freezer container, cover surface with plastic wrap. Freeze until firm. Remove, break into chunks. Beat in a mixer or food processor until fluffy, but not thawed. Spoon back into freezer container, cover with plastic wrap, return to freezer until firm. Makes about 1 quart.

Variation

Omit pineapple and substitute an equal amount of other canned or partially thawed, frozen fruits.

♥ Each serving contains:
Saturated fat   None   Cholesterol   None

Frozen Yogurt

2 cups non-fat plain yogurt   1 banana
1/4 cup light corn syrup   1 (10-oz.) pkg. frozen
1/4 cup egg substitute   berries or fruit

Combine all ingredients in blender or food processor. Pour into a freezer container. For individual servings, pour into 8 (4-oz.) paper cups. Cover and freeze until firm. For a smoother texture, break into pieces and place in a mixer bowl, blender or food processor. Blend until fluffy. Makes 1 quart.

Variation

Omit corn syrup, banana and fruit. Increase egg substitute to 1 cup, add 3/4 cup sugar, 1/3 cup lemon juice and 1 (12-oz.) can frozen juice concentrate.

Peach Melba: Omit egg substitute and banana. Substitute 1-1/2 cups puréed peaches and use frozen raspberries.

❤ Each serving contains:
  Saturated fat   Trace   Cholesterol   Trace

Buttermilk Sherbet

1/4 cup egg substitute
2 egg whites
2-1/2 cups chopped
   peaches

1-1/4 cups sugar
2 cups low-fat buttermilk
1/2 teaspoon almond
   extract

In a small bowl, beat egg substitute and egg whites until thickened and frothy; set aside. Combine peaches and sugar in a blender or food processor. Blend until sugar is dissolved and mixture smooth. Add buttermilk and almond extract. Combine with beaten egg mixture. Spoon into an ice-cream maker and freeze according to manufacturer's instructions. If you do not have an ice-cream maker, pour mixture into a freezer container, cover surface with plastic wrap. Freeze until firm. Remove, break into chunks. Beat in a mixer or food processor until fluffy, but not thawed. Spoon back into freezer container, cover with plastic wrap, return to freezer until firm. Makes about 2 quarts or 8 servings.

Pineapple: Omit peaches and almond extract. Substitute 1 (8-oz.) can unsweetened pineapple chunks, reduce sugar to 1/2 cup.

Blackberry: Omit peaches and almond extract. Substitute 1 (10-oz.) pkg. frozen blackberries, reduce sugar to 1/2 cup. Add 1 teaspoon grated lemon peel and 1 teaspoon vanilla.

Kiwi: Omit peaches and almond extract. Substitute 5 ripe peeled kiwi. Add 1 tablespoon lemon juice and 2 teaspoons orange extract.

Apricot-Rum: Omit peaches and almond extract. Substitute apricots and reduce sugar to 3/4 cup. Add 2 tablespoons rum flavoring.

❤ Each serving contains:
   Saturated fat   0.4 gram   Cholesterol   Trace

Apricot Cookies

2 cups rolled or quick
   oats
1 cup oat bran
1/2 cup brown sugar
1/2 cup granulated sugar
1/2 teaspoon baking
   powder
1 tablespoon Puritan® oil

1/4 cup non-fat milk
1/2 cup egg substitute
1 cup unsweetened
   applesauce
2 teaspoons vanilla extract
1-1/2 cups or 1 (6-oz.)
   pkg. chopped dried
   apricots

Glaze

1 cup powdered sugar
2 tablespoons lemon juice

1 teaspoon grated lemon
   peel

Preheat oven to 375F (190C). Spray a 9 x 13-inch baking pan with vegetable cooking spray; set aside. In a large bowl, combine oats, bran, sugars and baking powder; stir to blend. In a separate bowl, combine oil, milk, egg substitute, applesauce, vanilla and apricots. Stir together. Pour into oat mixture. Thoroughly mix together. Pour into prepared pan. Bake 25 to 30 minutes. Combine ingredients for Glaze; spread on warm cookies. Cut into 2 x 2-inch bars. Let cool completely before serving. Makes 24 cookies.

❤ 1 cookie contains:
   Saturated fat   Trace   Cholesterol None

Lace Cookies

3 tablespoons all-purpose flour
2 teaspoons unsweetened cocoa powder
1/2 cup oats, rolled or quick cooking
2 tablespoons Puritan® oil
2 tablespoons soft diet margarine
1/4 cup light-brown sugar
2 tablespoons light corn syrup
1/2 teaspoon vanilla extract

Preheat oven to 375F (190C). Line 2 cookie sheets with foil. In a small bowl, stir together flour, cocoa and oats. In a saucepan, heat together oil, margarine, sugar and corn syrup. Stir over medium heat until mixture is well blended. Remove from heat; add vanilla. Pour oat mixture into hot mixture. Quickly stir to blend. Drop by half-teaspoonfuls on to prepared cookie sheets. Place 3 inches apart. Bake about 8 minutes. Cool about 5 minutes. Carefully remove cookies. Makes 20 cookies.

❤ 1 cookie contains:
Saturated fat   Trace   Cholesterol   None

Apple Oatmeal Cookies

2 cups rolled oats
1/2 cup all-purpose flour
1/2 cup brown sugar
1/2 cup granulated sugar
1 teaspoon ground
   cinnamon
1/4 teaspoon nutmeg
1/2 teaspoon baking
   powder

1 tablespoon Puritan® oil
1/4 cup non-fat milk
2 egg whites, beaten
1/2 teaspoon almond or
   vanilla extract
1 cup finely chopped
   apple

Preheat oven to 350F (175C). Spray a cookie sheet with vegetable cooking spray. In a large mixing bowl, combine oats, flour, sugars, cinnamon, nutmeg and baking powder. Stir oil into milk. Fold milk, beaten egg whites and almond extract into oat mixture. Add apple. Stir to combine all ingredients. Drop by tablespoonfuls on prepared cookie sheets about 2 inches apart. Bake 10 to 12 minutes. Makes about 20 cookies.

❤ 1 cookie contains:
   Saturated fat   Trace   Cholesterol   None

Delicious Oatmeal Cookies

1-1/2 cups quick or instant
    oats
1/2 cup oat bran
1/2 cup all-purpose flour
2 tablespoons unsweet-
    ened cocoa powder
1 teaspoon baking soda
1 cup brown sugar

2 tablespoons peanut
    butter
1/3 cup non-fat milk
1 teaspoon vanilla extract
1 cup finely chopped
    apples
1/2 cup chopped dates

Preheat oven to 375F (190C). Spray cookie sheets with vegetable cooking spray. In a large mixer bowl, combine oats, oat bran, flour, cocoa powder, baking soda and sugar. In a cup, combine peanut butter, milk and vanilla. Stir into dry mixture; thoroughly combine. Add apples and dates. Batter will be stiff. Drop by tablespoonfuls onto prepared cookie sheets. Bake 15 to 17 minutes. Makes 48 cookies.

❤ 1 cookie contains:
    Saturated fat   Trace   Cholesterol   None

Bread Pudding

1/2 cup egg substitute	1/4 teaspoon nutmeg
1/4 cup non-fat plain	1/2 cup brown sugar
yogurt	3 cups bread cubes
2 cups non-fat milk	1/3 cup raisins
1 teaspoon vanilla extract	
3/4 teaspoon ground	
cinnamon	

Meringue

4 egg whites	1/2 teaspoon vanilla extract
1/2 cup sugar	

Preheat oven to 325F (165C). Spray a 2-quart baking dish with vegetable cooking spray. In a mixer bowl, beat egg substitute; blend in yogurt and milk. Add vanilla, cinnamon, nutmeg and sugar. Add bread and raisins, stir to completely coat bread cubes. Pour into prepared baking dish. Place a shallow pan on lowest oven rack. Pour in about 1-inch water. Place baking dish on rack above. Bake 45 minutes. To make Meringue, beat egg whites until foamy, continue beating and slowly add sugar and vanilla. Beat until mixture forms stiff peaks. Remove pan with water. Spread meringue over bread pudding and return to oven. Bake 12 to 15 minutes, until meringue is golden brown. Serve warm. Makes about 8 servings.

Variation

Omit meringue and top with Apricot-Orange Sauce, page 287, or Raisin-Rum Sauce, page 288.

Date Bread Pudding: Omit raisins and substitute 1 chopped banana and 1/3 cup chopped dates.

❤ Each serving contains:
   Saturated fat   Trace   Cholesterol None

Meringue

3/4 cup sugar	1/2 teaspoon cream of
2 teaspoons cornstarch	tartar
4 egg whites	1/2 teaspoon vanilla extract

Blend sugar and cornstarch. In a large bowl, whip egg whites and cream of tartar until soft peaks form. Continue whipping gradually adding sugar and cornstarch. Mixture should be very stiff.

Pie Shell

Spray a 9-inch pie plate with vegetable cooking spray. Spread meringue evenly on bottom and sides. Bake at 300F (165C) for an hour. Turn off heat; prop oven door open about 1 inch. Meringue crust should be left in oven until cool. Fill with fresh sliced fruit. Makes 1 pie shell.

Cookies

Spray a cookie sheet with vegetable cooking spray. Fill a piping bag with meringue. Pipe circular mounds about 2 inches apart. Or spoon a mound of mixture for each cookie. Bake as above. Makes about 48 cookies.

Almond Meringue Cookies: Fold in 1/2 cup finely chopped almonds to whipped meringue. Omit vanilla, substitute 1/2 teaspoon almond extract.

Currant or Date: Fold in 1/2 cup currants and 1/4 cup chopped dates. Omit vanilla, substitute 1 teaspoon orange flavoring.

Mocha: Blend 3 tablespoons decaffeinated coffee granules with sugar and cornstarch. Omit vanilla, add 1/2 teaspoon chocolate flavoring.

♥ Each 1/6 pie shell serving contains:
   Saturated fat   None   Cholesterol   None
♥ 1 cookie contains:
   Saturated fat   None   Cholesterol   None
♥ 1 cookie with almonds contains:
   Saturated fat   0.5 gram   Cholesterol   None

Yogurt Creme

3 egg whites
1 tablespoon sugar
1/2 teaspoon almond or
   vanilla extract

1 recipe Yogurt Cream
   Cheese, page 301
Sliced fruit or berries

Line a small cheese mold, sieve or loosely woven basket with 3 layers of dampened cheesecloth. In a mixer bowl, beat egg whites and sugar until stiff. Fold in almond or vanilla extract. Gently combine with Yogurt Cream Cheese. Spoon mixture into mold. Cover and refrigerate at least 4 hours. Unmold and serve with sliced fresh fruit. Makes 6 servings.

❤ Each serving contains:
   Saturated fat   Trace   Cholesterol   None

Cantaloupe Pie Supreme

1 single crust Basic Pastry,
    page 289
1/2 cup apricot preserves
1 tablespoon brandy
    flavoring, if desired
2 teaspoons sugar or
    sweetener

1/2 cup Yogurt Cream
    Cheese, page 301
1 to 2 ripe cantaloupes,
    cut in half, lengthwise,
    peeled, sliced
Powdered sugar
3/4 cup blueberries

Prepare and bake pie shell. Heat apricot preserves in a small saucepan. Remove from heat and stir in brandy flavoring, if desired. Brush over pie shell; set aside. Stir sugar or sweetener into Yogurt Cream. Spread mixture on bottom of coated pie shell. Arrange cantaloupe slices in a pinwheel design, starting from center. Overlap pieces on second layer. If melon is not sweet, sprinkle with powdered sugar. Cover with plastic wrap and refrigerate until serving. Top with blueberries when serving. Makes 6 servings.

❤ Each serving contains:
    Saturated fat   1 gram   Cholesterol   None

Old-English Oatmeal Pie

1 single crust Basic Pastry,
   page 289
1/2 cup sugar
3/4 cup rolled oats
2 tablespoons
   unsweetened cocoa
   powder
1/2 cup chopped dates
1/2 cup raisins

1/4 cup melted soft diet
   margarine
3/4 cup light corn syrup
1/2 cup egg substitute
1 teaspoon chocolate
   flavoring, if desired
1 egg white, beaten
Low-fat peach- or orange-
   flavored yogurt, if desired

Preheat oven to 375F (190C). Make single crust for 9-inch pie. In a large bowl, combine sugar, oats, cocoa powder, dates and raisins. In a 2-cup measure stir together melted margarine, corn syrup, egg substitute and chocolate flavoring, if desired. Combine with sugar-oat mixture. Fold in beaten egg white. Pour into unbaked pie shell. Bake 35 to 40 minutes. Serve with a dollop of peach or orange yogurt, if desired. Makes 8 servings.

❤ Each serving contains:
   Saturated fat   1.2 grams   Cholesterol   Trace

Chilled Melon Soup

1 large cantaloupe or
   crenshaw melon,
   peeled, chopped
1 peach, peeled, pitted

1 cup non-fat plain yogurt
1 cup low-fat peach yogurt
Grated nutmeg

Purée melon and peach in a blender or food processor. Pour into a large bowl; whisk in plain and peach yogurt. Chill before serving. Sprinkle with grated nutmeg. Makes 4 servings.

❤ Each 1-cup serving contains:
   Saturated fat   Trace   Cholesterol   None

Fruit Compote

1/2 cup pitted prunes
1/4 cup raisins
1 cup apple juice
1 cinnamon stick
1/3 cup honey, if desired
1 teaspoon grated lemon
   peel
1 cup each sliced apricots,
   apples, pears

1 cup red or green
   seedless grapes
1 (11-oz.) can mandarin
   oranges, drained
1 banana, sliced
1/2 cup rum, if desired
1 cup non-fat plain
   yogurt

In a medium saucepan, heat together prunes, raisins, apple juice, cinnamon stick, honey, if desired, and lemon peel. Simmer about 15 minutes, until prunes are plump. Set aside; remove cinnamon stick. This can be made ahead and reheated. To serve, heat dried-fruit mixture. Add remaining fruits and rum, if desired. Heat and flame rum before serving. To serve, top fruit with yogurt; spoon juice over all. Makes 10 servings.

❤ Each serving contains:
   Saturated fat   Trace   Cholesterol None

Apricot-Orange Sauce

1 tablespoon cornstarch
1 cup apricot nectar
1/2 cup dried chopped
   apricots
1 (11-oz.) can mandarin
   oranges, drained

2 tablespoons orange
   marmalade
2 teaspoons rum or rum
   flavoring, if desired

In a small saucepan, stir cornstarch into apricot nectar. Stir over medium heat until mixture begins to thicken. Add apricots, oranges and marmalade. Heat and add rum or rum flavoring, if desired. Serve at once. Makes about 2 cups.

❤ Each serving contains:
   Saturated fat   None   Cholesterol None

Lemon Sauce

2 tablespoons cornstarch
1/2 cup sugar
1/4 cup lemon juice

1-1/2 cups orange juice
2 teaspoons grated lemon
 peel

In a small saucepan, stir cornstarch and sugar into juices. Add lemon peel. Stir over medium heat until mixture begins to thicken. Remove from heat. Serve at once. Makes about 1-3/4 cups.

❤ Each serving contains:
 Saturated fat   None   Cholesterol   None

Raisin-Rum Sauce

2 tablespoons cornstarch
2 tablespoons sugar
1-1/2 cups cider or apple
 juice

3/4 cup raisins
2 tablespoons rum or rum
 flavoring

In a small saucepan, stir cornstarch and sugar into cider or apple juice. Add raisins. Stir over medium heat until mixture begins to thicken. Remove from heat; stir in rum or rum flavoring. Serve at once. Makes about 2 cups.

❤ Each serving contains:
 Saturated fat   None   Cholesterol   None

Basic Pastry

Single Crust

1-1/2 cups all-purpose flour	1 teaspoon vinegar
1/4 teaspoon salt	2 to 3 tablespoons ice water
6 tablespoons Puritan® oil	

In a small bowl, stir flour and salt. Combine oil, vinegar and water. Add to flour and quickly stir until mixture forms a ball. Place dough between 2 sheets of waxed paper. Roll dough into a 9- to 10-inch circle. Remove top paper. Place dough in pie plate; remove other paper. Fold overhanging edges under evenly; crimp with fork or fingers to make a raised edge. Chill 15 minutes before baking. Bake unfilled pie shell in 475F (245C) oven 8 to 10 minutes. Bake filled pie according to recipes.

♥ Each 1/6-pie serving contains:
   Saturated fat   1 gram   Cholesterol   None

Double Crust

Prepare as above, doubling ingredients.

♥ Each 1/6-pie serving contains:
   Saturated fat   2 grams   Cholesterol   None

Rhubarb Crisp

1/2 cup sugar
2 tablespoons cornstarch
1 cup cranberry juice
1/2 cup sugar
1/3 cup honey
1/2 teaspoon ground
 cinnamon
1/2 teaspoon ground
 allspice
2 tablespoons lemon juice

1 teaspoon vanilla extract
1 cup toasted rolled oats,
 see below
1 cup oat-raisin cereal
 flakes
2-1/2 cups chopped fresh
 or 1 (16-oz.)
 pkg. frozen rhubarb,
 blackberries or cherries

Preheat oven to 350F (175C). Spray a 9-inch square pan with vegetable cooking spray. In a small saucepan, stir sugar and cornstarch into cranberry juice. Stir over medium heat until mixture begins to thicken. Remove from heat. Set aside.

In a small saucepan, heat together sugar, honey, cinnamon, allspice and lemon juice. Cook, stirring, until sugar is dissolved. Remove from heat and add vanilla. Pour over oats and cereal; stir to mix. Spoon 1/2 oat mixture into prepared baking dish. Evenly distribute fruit over crumb mixture. Pour juice mixture over fruit; sprinkle remaining crumbs over all. Bake 25 to 30 minutes, until golden brown. Serve warm. Makes 9 servings.

To toast oats

Preheat oven to 350F (175C). Line a cookie sheet with foil. Spread oats on cookie sheet, bake about 10 minutes, stirring 2 or 3 times. Remove when oats are golden brown. Use at once, or store in a covered container for later use.

Variations

Omit rhubarb and cranberry juice, substitute apples, peaches, apricots, or pears and apple or orange juice. Try plums with grape juice; cherries and/or berries with cran-raspberry or cherry juice. Experiment with flavors, use almond, brandy, maple, mint or rum.

❤ Each serving contains:
Saturated fat   Trace   Cholesterol   None

Cottage Pudding

2 cups non-fat cottage
  cheese
1/2 cup sugar
2 tablespoons orange
  marmalade
3 tablespoons all-purpose
  flour

6 egg whites
1 teaspoon orange peel
1 teaspoon vanilla extract
2 (11-oz.) cans mandarin
  oranges, drained

Preheat oven to 350F (175C). Spray a 9-inch square pan with vegetable cooking spray; set aside. In a blender or food processor, combine cottage cheese, sugar, orange marmalade and flour. Blend until smooth. In a large bowl, beat egg whites until stiff. Fold in orange peel and vanilla. Fold cheese mixture into egg-whites. Spoon 1/2 mixture into prepared pan. Layer 1 can drained orange slices on mixture. Reserve remaining oranges. Top with remaining egg-white mixture. Bake 40 to 45 minutes, until top is lightly browned. Cool. Serve topped with reserved orange slices. Makes 9 servings.

Variations

Lemon-raisin: Omit orange marmalade, orange peel and vanilla. Substitute 1 tablespoon lemon juice, 1 teaspoon lemon peel and add 1/2 cup raisins.

Apricot-almond: Omit oranges, orange marmalade and peel. Substitute apricots and 1/2 teaspoon almond extract.

❤ Each serving contains:
  Saturated fat Trace   Cholesterol None

Mocha-Prune Cake

1 cup pitted prunes, chopped	1 teaspoon baking soda
1 cup coffee or apple juice	3 tablespoons mono-unsaturated oil
2/3 cup sugar	1 teaspoon chocolate or
1/4 cup oat bran	vanilla extract
1-1/4 cups all-purpose flour	3 egg whites, stiffly beaten
	Powdered sugar
3 tablespoons unsweet-ened cocoa powder	Cocoa Frosting, page 293

Preheat oven to 350F (175C). Spray a 9-inch square baking pan with vegetable cooking spray; set aside. Place prunes in a small bowl, add coffee or apple juice; set aside. In a medium bowl, stir together, sugar, oat bran, flour, cocoa powder and baking soda. Stir in oil, chocolate or vanilla extract and prunes with coffee or apple juice. Fold in beaten egg whites. Pour into prepared pan. Bake 30 to 35 minutes, until a wooden pick inserted in center comes out clean. Cool. Serve dusted with powdered sugar or frost with Cocoa Frosting. Makes 9 servings.

♥ Each serving contains:
    Saturated fat   0.4 gram   Cholesterol   None

Cocoa Frosting

3 tablespoons Yogurt
  Cream Cheese, page 301
1-1/2 teaspoons unsweet-
  ened cocoa powder
1/2 teaspoon vanilla extract

2 to 2-1/2 cups powdered
  sugar
1/2 teaspoon non-fat milk,
  if needed

In a small bowl, stir all ingredients together. If needed, add milk to make desired consistency. Makes about 3/4 cup. Frosts one (9-inch) cake or 12 cupcakes.

❤ Each serving contains:
  Saturated fat   Trace   Cholesterol   None

Whipped-Fruit Topping

3/4 cup plain non-fat
  yogurt
1/4 cup mashed fruit,
  canned or fresh, such
  as apricots, peaches,
  plums or berries

2/3 cup marshmallow
  creme
2 egg whites, stiffly beaten
1 cup chopped fruit

Place yogurt in a strainer; drain about 1 hour. In a small bowl, combine drained yogurt, fruit and marshmallow creme. Fold in egg whites. To serve, spoon chopped fruit over whipped mixture. Serve as a pudding or topping over angel food cake. Makes 6 servings.

❤ Each serving contains:
  Saturated fat   Trace   Cholesterol   None

Strawberry Cheesecake

1 cup crushed corn flakes
3 tablespoons brown sugar
2 (1/4-oz.) pkg. unflavored
  gelatin
1/4 cup water
1 cup sugar
1/2 cup non-fat milk
1/2 cup egg substitute or
  4 egg whites

2-1/2 cups non-fat cottage
  cheese
1/3 cup orange juice
1 teaspoon vanilla extract
3 egg whites, beaten
2 cups (1 pt.) strawberries

Spray a 9-inch spring-form pan with vegetable cooking spray; set aside. Combine corn flakes and brown sugar; sprinkle on bottom of prepared pan. Set aside. In a medium saucepan, combine gelatin and water; let stand 5 minutes. Stir in sugar, milk and egg substitute or egg whites. Cook, stirring constantly, over low heat 5 to 7 minutes. Gelatin should be completely dissolved and mixture slightly thickened. Remove from heat. In a mixer bowl, beat cottage cheese until smooth. Continue beating and slowly add orange juice and vanilla; slowly pour in gelatin mixture. Fold in beaten egg whites. Batter will be thin. Spoon about half of mixture into pan. Place 1 layer of sliced strawberries over mixture. Cover with remaining batter. Cover with plastic wrap and refrigerate at least 6 hours. Serve topped with remaining strawberries. Makes 12 servings.

❤ Each serving contains:
  Saturated fat Trace   Cholesterol None

Miscellaneous

We always seem to end up with recipes we want to include, but have a difficult time placing them. Thus the Miscellaneous chapter.

These recipes are not lessened in any way by being put here. The sandwiches we've included show possiblities on which you can expand. Drinks can be tailored to your personal choice. Try simple or complex combinations. Remember, the choice is yours.

Basic White Sauce

1 tablespoon monoun-
    saturated oil
2 tablespoons all-purpose
    flour
1 cup non-fat milk or fat-
    free broth

1/2 teaspoon onion
    powder
Salt and pepper

In a small saucepan, blend together oil and flour. Slowly stir in milk or broth. Combine until smooth. Add onion powder. Heat, stirring, over medium heat until thickened. Season to taste with salt and pepper. Makes about 1 cup.

♥ Each 1/4-cup serving contains:
    Saturated fat   0.3 gram   Cholesterol   None

Pita-Pocket Sandwich Bar

Pita bread, regular or
    whole-wheat
Turkey- or chicken-breast
    slices
Turkey ham slices
Assorted lettuces
Alfalfa sprouts
Bean sprouts
Lentil sprouts

Sliced tomatoes
Pickles
Garbanzo beans
Radishes
Cucumber slices
Shredded cabbage
Pea pods or peas
Non-fat plain yogurt

Serve fresh pita bread with an assortment of fillings and condiments. Invite everyone to create their own combinations.

♥ Each 3-oz. serving of turkey or chicken contains:
    Saturated fat   1.0 gram   Cholesterol   70mg
♥ Each 3-oz. serving of turkey ham contains
    Saturated fat   1.4 grams   Cholesterol   90mg

Oriental Pocket Sandwiches

1 cup mung bean sprouts
1 tablespoon olive or
    Puritan® oil
1 (3-oz.) boned, skinned
    chicken breast, cut in
    strips
1 celery stalk, diced
1/2 cup chopped onion
1 cup fresh or frozen snow
    peas, cut in thirds
1/3 cup sliced water
    chestnuts
1/2 teaspoon salt
2 tablespoons Chicken
    Broth, page 158

1 tablespoon white wine
    or additional Chicken
    Broth
2 teaspoons soy sauce
1/4 teaspoon sugar
1/8 teaspoon ground
    ginger
1 teaspoon cornstarch
1 tablespoon cold water
4 pita-bread rounds
2 tablespoons sliced
    almonds

Rinse bean sprouts in cold water. Drain on paper towels. Heat oil in a wok or large heavy skillet over high heat. Add chicken, celery and onion. Stir until chicken begins to turn white. Add snow peas, water chestnuts and salt. Stir in chicken broth, wine or additional chicken broth, soy sauce, sugar and ginger. Cover and simmer 5 minutes. Stir in bean sprouts. In a small bowl, combine cornstarch and cold water. Stir into chicken mixture. Stir constantly over medium heat until liquid thickens and boils. Cut each pita bread round in half and carefully separate side of bread to make pocket. Spoon chicken mixture into pockets. Sprinkle filling with almonds. Makes 4 servings.

♥ Each serving contains:
    Saturated fat   1 gram   Cholesterol   30mg

Reuben Sandwich

Prepared mustard
2 slices rye bread
1/3 cup drained sauerkraut
2 teaspoons grated
    Parmesan cheese

2 (1-oz.) slices smoked
    turkey ham
Salt and pepper

Spread prepared mustard on both pieces of rye bread. On 1 slice, layer half of sauerkraut, half of Parmesan cheese, smoked turkey ham, remaining sauerkraut and cheese. Season with salt and pepper to taste. Top with remaining bread. Spray a non-stick skillet with vegetable cooking spray. Heat and place sandwich in skillet, cook about 1 minute per side. Makes 1 sandwich.

❤ Each sandwich contains:
    Saturated fat 2 grams   Cholesterol 90mg

Fram Burger

3/4 lb. select extra-lean
    ground beef
2 tablespoons Worcester-
    shire sauce
1/2 teaspoon celery salt
1/2 teaspoon dry mustard

Hamburger buns
Onion slices, if desired
Tomato slices
Lettuce
Salt and pepper

In a medium bowl, combine beef, Worcestershire sauce, celery salt and mustard. Thoroughly mix together. Shape into 4 patties. Broil as desired. Serve on hamburger buns, topped with onions, if desired, tomato and lettuce. Season to taste with salt and pepper. Makes 4 burgers.

Variation

The fat content can be reduced almost by half by using equal parts soybean meat substitute and beef.

❤ Each serving contains:
    Saturated fat 4.5 grams   Cholesterol 50mg

Scandinavian Open-Face Sandwich

Prepared mustard
4 slices dark rye, pumper-
   nickel or crispbread
4 small lettuce leaves

1 tomato, thinly sliced
1 (3.75-oz.) can sardines,
   drained
1 tablespoon capers

Spread mustard on bread. Layer lettuce, tomato slices and sardines on each slice. Sprinkle with capers. Makes 4 open-face sandwiches

♥ Each sandwich contains:
   Saturated fat   2 grams   Cholesterol   130mg

Smoked-Salmon Open-Face Sandwich

3 tablespoons non-fat plain
   yogurt
6 slices dark rye, pumper-
   nickel or crispbread
Dill weed

6 thin slices smoked
   salmon
12 thin cucumber slices
Yellow or red bell-pepper
   strips

Spread yogurt evenly on bread. Sprinkle with dillweed. Top with salmon, cucumber and bell pepper. Makes 6 open-face sandwiches.

♥ Each serving contains:
   Saturated fat   1 gram   Cholesterol   16mg

Sour-Cream Substitute

1/2 cup non-fat plain
  yogurt
1/2 cup non-fat cottage
  cheese

2 teaspoons lemon juice

Place ingredients in blender or food processor. Blend until smooth. Refrigerate in container with a tight-fitting lid. Use for recipes calling for sour cream. Makes about 1 cup.

❤ 1 tablespoon contains:
  Saturated fat Trace   Cholesterol Trace

Yogurt Cream Cheese

2 cups non-fat plain yogurt

Line a sieve or colander with 3 layers of cheesecloth or paper towels. Place sieve in a bowl or pan to drain. Add yogurt. Cover; refrigerate at least 8 hours or overnight. Discard liquid. Use as cream cheese. If desired, add herbs, spices or fruit. Makes about 1 cup.

❤ Each 1-oz. serving contains:
  Saturated fat Trace   Cholesterol Trace

Note: Do not use fruit-flavored or gelatin-added yogurt.

Tropical Blend

2 cups pineapple-orange
   juice
2 bananas, cut in 1-inch
   cubes, frozen

1 cup non-fat milk
1 egg white

Combine ingredients in a blender or food processor. Blend until well combined and frothy. Pour into glasses. Makes 4 servings.

❤ Each serving contains:
   Saturated fat   Trace   Cholesterol   None

Yogurt Fruit Shake

2 cups non-fat plain yogurt
2 cups raspberries,
   strawberries, peaches
   or apricots

4 tablespoons orange or
   other fruit juice
Sugar

Combine yogurt, fruit and juice in a blender and process until well blended and frothy. Sweeten to taste. Pour into glasses. Makes 4 servings.

❤ Each serving contains:
   Saturated fat   Trace   Cholesterol   None

Icy Orange Cooler

3 oranges, peeled,
  sectioned
1/4 cup cold water

1/2 cup sugar
1 cup non-fat plain yogurt
6 ice cubes

Combine orange sections, water, sugar, yogurt and ice cubes in a blender or food processor. Blend mixture until ice is finely chopped and mixture is frothy. Pour into glasses. Makes 2 servings.

Variations

Orange Freeze: Omit yogurt, add more ice cubes until desired consistency is reached.

Omit oranges and substitute 1 cup fresh or frozen berries, grapefruit, pineapple, peaches or your favorite fruit.

❤ Each serving contains:
  Saturated fat Trace   Cholesterol None

Substitutions & Hints

Recipe Substitutions

Bacon	Imitation bacon bits
Bread crumbs, 1 cup	3/4 cup cereal, crackers or rolled oats
Bread crumbs, 1/4 cup	1 slice bread
Butter	Soft diet margarine
Butter, 1 tablespoon	2 teaspoons preferred or monounsaturated oil
Butter, Shortening or Lard, 1 cup	2/3 cup preferred or monounsaturated oil
Buttermilk, 1 cup	1 cup non-fat milk, plus 2 tbs. lemon juice or vinegar
Cake flour, 1 cup	7/8 cup all-purpose flour, plus 2 tablespoons cornstarch
Chocolate, 1 oz.	1/4 cup cocoa, plus 2 teaspoons oil
Cornstarch, 1 tablespoon	2 tablespoons flour or 4 teaspoons tapioca
Cream Cheese	Yogurt cream cheese
Egg, 1	2 egg whites or 1/4 cup egg substitute
Fresh herbs, 1 tablespoon	Dried herbs, 1 teaspoon
Garlic clove, 1	1/8 teaspoon garlic powder
Ground beef	Turkey breast, skinned and ground

Honey, 1 cup	1-1/4 cups sugar, plus 1/4 cup water
Lemon juice, 1 teaspoon	1/2 teaspoon vinegar
Mustard, 1 tsp. prepared	1/2 teaspoon dry
Onion, 1 medium	1-1/2 tablespoons dehydrated onion flakes
Sugar, 1 cup	3/4 cup honey
Sour cream	Plain non-fat yogurt
Whole milk	Non-fat milk or 1 can evaporated skim milk, plus 1 can water

Hints for better eating

- Use oat bran or oatmeal for breading poultry or fish.
- Use oats as an ingredient for baked goods.
- Substitute 1/3 oat bran for all-purpose flour in baked goods.
- Use 1/2 oat bran and 1/2 all-purpose flour to thicken sauces, stews and soups.
- Add 1/2 cup rolled oats to 1 lb. meat in meatloaf.
- Toast oats about 15 minutes in 325F (160C) oven, sprinkle over fruit.
- Leave peel on fruits and vegetables.
- Substitute brown rice for white.
- Do not strain fruit juices.
- Use USDA Select grade beef.
- Limit beef dishes to 3 to 4 meals per week.
- Do not salt food while cooking, season when served.
- Use a nonstick vegetable cooking spray.
- Use butter substitutes wherever possible.
- Store fresh fish on a layer of ice in a refrigerator dish.
- Use more seasonings in cold foods.
- Eat at least 2 whole fruits per day.
- Continue to read labels for fat and cholesterol content. Some that state "No Cholesterol" may contain considerable amounts of saturated fat.

Bibliography

Anderson, J.W. et al. "High-carbohydrate, High-fiber Diet: Is It Practical and Effective in Treating Hyperlipidemia?" *Postgraduate Medicine* vol. 82 (4) (1987), 40-55.

Blankenhorn, D.M. et al. "Beneficial Effects of Combined Colestipol-niacin Therapy on Coronary Atherosclerosis and Coronary Venous Bypass Grafts." *Journal of the American Medical Association* vol. 257 (1987), 3233-3240.

Boffey, Philip M. "For the First Time, Cut in Cholesterol Is Shown to Deter Artery Clogging." *The New York Times* (June 19, 1987), A-1.

Bonanome, A. et al. "Effect of Dietary Stearic Acid on Plasma Cholesterol and Lipoprotein Levels." *New England Journal of Medicine* vol. 318 (19) (1988), 1244-1248.

Castelli, W.P. "The Triglyceride Issue: A View from Framingham." *American Heart Journal* vol. 112 (1986), 432-327.

Castelli, W.P. "Cholesterol and Lipids in the Risk of Coronary Artery Disease: The Framingham Heart Study." *Canadian Journal of Cardiology* (Supplement A) (July 1988), 5A-10A.

Castelli, W.P. et al. "Incidence of Coronary Heart Disease and Lipoprotein Cholesterol Levels: The Framingham Study." *Journal of the American Medical Association* vol. 256 (20) (1986), 2835-2838.

Castelli, W.P. and G. Griffin. "A Simple Strategy to Limit Saturated Fat after Cholesterol Screening. *Postgraduate Medicine* vol. 84 (September 1, 1988) 44-56.

Cholesterol Awareness Survey. National Heart, Lung and Blood Institute. Boston, Mass.: 1983.

Cholesterol Awareness Survey. National Heart, Lung and Blood Institute. Boston, Mass.: 1986.

"Consensus Conference: Lowering Blood Cholesterol to Prevent Heart Disease." *Journal of the American Medical Association* vol. 253 (14) (1985), 2080.

Dawber, T.R. et al. "An Approach to Longitudinal Studies in a Community: The Framingham Study." *Annals of the New York Academy of Science* vol. 107 (1963), 539-556.

Frick, M.H. et al. "Helsinki Heart Study: Primary Prevention Trial with Gemfibrozil in Middle-aged Men with Dyslipidemia." *New England Journal of Medicine* vol. 317 (1987), 1237-1245.

Grundy, S.M. "Lessons from the Helsinki Heart Study." *Postgraduate Medicine* vol. 84 (1) (1988), 217-231.

Hjermann, I. et al. "Effect of Diet and Smoking Intervention on the Incidence of Coronary Heart Disease." Report from the Oslo Study Group of a Randomized Trial in Healthy Men. *Lancet* vol. 2 (1981), 1303-1310.

Keys, A. *Seven Countries: A Multivariate Analysis of Death and Coronary Artery Disease.* Cambridge, Mass.: Harvard University Press, 1980.

Lipid Research Clinics Program. "The Lipid Research Clinics Coronary Primary Prevention Trial Results: I. Reduction in the Incidence of Coronary Artery Disease." *Journal of the American Medical Association* vol. 251 (1984), 351-364.

Lipid Research Clinics Program. "The Lipid Research Clinics Coronary Primary Prevention Trial Results: II. The Relationship of Reduction in Incidence of Coronary Heart Disease to Cholesterol Lowering." *Journal of the American Medical Association* vol. 251 (1984), 365-374.

Malinow, M.R. et al. "Regression of Atherosclerotic Lesions." *Arteriosclerosis* vol. 4 (1984), 292-295.

Report of the National Cholesterol Education Program Expert Panel on Detection, Evaluation and Treatment of High Blood Cholesterol in Adults. *Archives of Internal Medicine* vol. 148 (1) (1988), 36-69.

Rinzler, S.H. "Primary Prevention of Coronary Heart Disease by Diet." *Bulletin of the New York Academy of Medicine* vol. 44 (1968), 936-949.

Rose, B. et al. "United Kingdom Heart Disease Prevention Project: Incidence and Mortality Results." *Lancet* vol. 1 (1983), 1062-1065.

Stone, N.J. et al. "Role of Diet in Controlling Blood Cholesterol." *Postgraduate Medicine* vol. 83 (8), (June 1988), 229-242.

U.S. Department of Agriculture. *Nutritive Value of Foods.* Home and Garden Bulletin No. 72. Washington, D.C.: 1985.

U.S. Department of Health and Human Services. *Planning a Diet for a Healthy Heart.* HHS Publication No. (FDA) 87-2220. Rockville, M.D.: 1988.

Index

...more quotes & endorsements

"This book helps me cook great meals and desserts for my doctor husband—a heart patient who loves to eat. The recipes are easy to prepare with many options, hints, and substitutions I never thought of."

Lee Ann Brune
Zanesville, Ohio

"Having had bypass surgery twice, I'm determined not to let my coronary arteries plug up again. That's why I wanted the best guide there is for us to follow—and this is it."

Dominic B. Brune, MD
Zanesville, Ohio

"*Good Fat Bad Fat*...is my choice because of its easy-to-understand, relatively simple text."

Marian Burros
The New York Times

"It isn't often one finds a book as helpful and easy to understand as *Good Fat Bad Fat*. Everyone who eats should follow its plan."

Ralph J. Dunnigan, MD
Bismark, North Dakota

"Patient-friendly. The diet advice is easy to follow and the concept of cholesterol/HDL ratio easy to understand."

David Scott, MD
Park Nicollet Heart Center

"After following the plan in *Good Fat Bad Fat* for 6 weeks, my cholesterol dropped from 225 to 176 and my cholesterol/HDL ratio from a worrisome 5.4 to a safe 4.4. This book may add years to my life."

David M. Brown
Plymouth, Minnesota

...more quotes & endorsements

"An enjoyable and readable book which can change and prolong your life. Two medical experts present the facts about the key killer in our diet and under the same cover share many healthy, mouth-watering recipes."

J. L. Montgomery, MD, President
Scott & White Clinic

"Drs. Griffin and Castelli have written a sensible, easy-to-follow guide which helps dispel some of the myths of the traditional American diet, and lays a framework for the healthy dietary habits of future generations."

Peter A. Stack, MD
Dallas, Texas

"*Good Fat Bad Fat* contains great information and wonderful recipes. I highly recommend it."

Robert Matthies, MD
Spokane, Washington

"This marvelous book has helped my wife adapt her recipes so they don't contain so much fat. I enthusiastically recommend it to my patients."

Franz H. Messerli, MD, FACC, FACP
Ochsner Clinic

"The most readable of the bunch, this paperback combines appealing recipes with persuasive arguments for changing your eating and cooking habits for a lifetime."

San Jose Mercury News

"I recommend this book to everyone who wants to keep members of their family from getting coronary artery disease."

Yas Takagi, MD
Fairfax, Virginia